RALM

1/3/2006

Technicians of Ecstasy

"Joseph Beuys I," by Nam June Paik
Computer generated airbrush and acrylic paint on canvas
121.9 x 104.1 cm
Hood Museum of Art, Dartmouth College, Hanover, NH;
purchased through the Miriam and
Sidney Stoneman Acquisition Fund

Technicians of Ecstasy

Shamanism and the Modern Artist

Mark Levy

BRAMBLE ❖ BOOKS
Connecticut

For information write to:

Bramble Books, PO Box 209, Norfolk, Connecticut 06058

Library of Congress Cataloging-in-Publication Data

Levy, Mark, 1946-
    Technicians of ecstasy : Shamanism and the modern artist / Mark Levy.
        p.   cm.
    Includes bibliographical references and index.
    ISBN 0-9626184-4-6
    1. Art, Modern—20th century—Themes, motives. 2. Art, Shamanistic. 3. Artists—
Psychology. I. Title.
N6490.L457   1993
700' . 1'9—dc20   93-14704
                                          CIP

First Printing 1993
3 5 7 9 10 8 6 4 2

Printed in the United States of America

The paper used in this publication meets the minimum requirements
of American National Standard for Information Sciences—
Permanence of Paper for Printed Library Materials,
ANSI Z39.48-1984.

Acknowledgements

This book owes its existence to the support, encouragement and advice of many people.

I would like to give special thanks to my wife Jamie Brunson for her many insights during the writing of this book, Michael Harner for introducing me to the practice of shamanism, and Ruth-Inge Heinze for her patience, stamina, and acute observations as editor of *Technicians of Ecstasy*. Without her help this book would not have materialized.

I am also grateful to the artists who opened themselves to my questions and lend this book authenticity with their answers: Mary Beth Edelson, Alex Grey, Sha Sha Higby, Ann McCoy, Rachel Rosenthal, Carolee Schneemann, and Arthur Tress.

Mark Levy
Oakland, California

The Author

Mark Levy, Ph.D., is Professor of Art History at California State University at Hayward. He has also taught at Kenyon College, the University of Nevada at Reno, and the San Francisco Art Institute. In addition to his scholarly work as an art historian, he is a prominent San Francisco Bay Area art critic who has published numerous articles and reviews in many of the leading magazines in California and the country. Twelve years ago he was introduced to shamanic techniques by anthropologist Michael Harner. His book *Technicians of Ecstasy: Shamanism and the Modern Artist* combines his ongoing experience of shamanic practices with his knowledge of art.

Foreword

Mark Levy is an art historian and art critic who is presently teaching at the California State University in Hayward. He has been practicing shamanic techniques, such as seeing, for many years and has also been reporting on his experiences regularly at the annual International Conference on the Study of Shamanism and Alternate Modes of Healing at the St. Sabina Center, San Rafael, California.

Mark Levy wrote this book to introduce his readers to a different way of looking at the underlying motivations and attitudes of artists because, during his explorations, he discovered that some artists do not only create new forms of expression but are also involved in activities which closely resemble those of shamans. Some artists do, indeed, see, dream, and perform like shamans.

Everyone of us have conceptions about artists. We have seen art work displayed and, perhaps, met some of the creators. We may even have tried to express ourselves, using one or another medium of art. Our opinions about art may differ considerably, according to taste and personal preference, but everyone of us has the capacity to respond to objects of art. We may be deeply touched and stimulated or we are provoked and repulsed or we are left unimpressed.

What do we know about shamans?

In earlier times, world travelers and missionaries and, only fairly recently, anthropologists have begun to report on "strange customs" in "foreign countries." The practitioners and all those who participated in these customs did not seem to fit into the framework of recognized world views and religions and were, therefore, treated as anomalies, i.e., exceptions "from the rule."

When we ask ourselves who has established these rules, we find that rules are obviously proclaimed by those in power, in other words, by those who may use religion to legitimize their rule, whether they are government officials, religious leaders or leading scientists. Naturally, leaders cannot tolerate any deviation from the rule because this would be challenging their position of power. Over time, this situation has led to serious misconceptions and misuse of the word "shaman."

It was anthropologists and psychologists who finally noticed that shamans continue to emerge, even in highly industrialized societies. It was quite a discovery to admit that shamans practice not only in the jungle or in distant, isolated villages but on the twenty-sixth floor of high-rise buildings in cities like Singapore, Hong Kong, and New York. Further research revealed that shamans emerge whenever certain needs remain unanswered. That means, where shamanic traditions seem to have died out, individuals would emerge who prove to be able to fulfill these needs, whether in a village or an urban setting. The fulfillment of personal needs always was ahead of scientific requirements and old feedback loops would finish another turn.

Tracing a Thai custom through time, I found twenty years ago that

> Concepts seem to move in a circular fashion—local beliefs are reinterpreted and codified by the elite and then, in a more elaborate form, superimposed on the original beliefs. So, on the one hand, local beliefs gain legitimacy through acceptance by the elite, and, on the other hand, normative religions are kept alive by local practices (Heinze, 1982:xx-xii)

During my over thirty years of fieldwork in Asia, Europe and the New World, I constantly had to face the problem of having to explain the survival of local beliefs and customs in the framework of a nation-state as well as in the framework of world religions. I was also asked to offer some explanations for the surprising emergence of apparently new images and ideas.

I am talking here not only about the persistence of local practices, I am talking about the sources for innovations which become available when a need arises. Innovative, provocative, inspiring thoughts do arise with one or two spiritually advanced individuals. These individuals shift attention and overcome stereotypes. These individuals bring problems to the surface so that they can be dealt with, and they translate ineffable messages of the sacred into secular language. Such individuals are considered to be "shamans" all over the world. ("Shaman" is used here in a generic sense, because "shamans" are called by different names in different countries, e.g., *angakok* by the Eskimo, *babalawo* by the Yoruba, *sangoma* by the Zulu, *houdan* by the Haitian, *kahuna* by the Hawaiian, *bakia* by the Garhwali, *ma khi* by the Thai, *bomoh* by the Malaysian, *tang-ki* by the Chinese, and *mudang* by the Korean, etc.)

Furthermore, in my work, I had to come to terms with the different definitions of the word "shaman." Shamans can be medicine men or women, diviners, magicians, mystics, prophets, geomancers, etc.; today we call some of them "channels." However, not all medicine men or women, diviners, geomancers, etc., can be called shamans because they do not enter alternate states of consciousness.

Therefore, my first criterion for calling an individual a shaman is that s/he can access alternating states of consciousness at will. It is important to recognize the qualities of each state. That means, we have to refine our perceptions to become aware of the differences between certain trances and what we have accepted in our consensus reality as the ordinary state of being. States may progress in the direction of mind expansion and increased control; in other words, shamans may go on "magical flights" into other realms of consciousness to access otherwise unavailable information or they may descend, with decreasing control, toward either the state of complete dissociation over which individuals have no control at all (formerly called "possession," now diagnosed as Multiple Personality Disorder) or controlled dissociation which is used by shamans and mediums to access the depth of their own sub-conscious mind. Some cultures still speak of inviting a spirit into a medium's body so that divining and healing will be performed by a higher spiritual force.

We can now say,

> The major difference between channels, mystics, prophets and shamans is that the former may be able to convey the encounter with the "Divine" while shamans facilitate its manifestations in the Here and Now and actively participate in the dynamic relationships between the explicate and the implicate order (Heinze, 1991:9).

The second criterion then is that shamans serve their community and fulfil vital needs. Shamans accept a life-long commitment. And, thirdly, shamans are the mediators between the sacred and the secular when they translate the "divine" messages into a language understood by all.

To repeat, medicine men or women cannot be called shamans because they do not enter a trance state for their services. Prophets are definitely shamans when they are accessing different states of consciousness. They are indeed, mediators between the secular and the sacred, but their services to the community are limited to divine messages. In other words, prophets are not available on a daily basis to provide solutions for mundane problems.

The many roles of shamans certainly also require artistic

faculties. Divine messages tend to be ineffable, then shamans have to create symbols, metaphors, and rituals to translate and deliver the message, i.e., they shift the attention of their clients through their art.

Mark Levy has invited us to participate in the process of shamanic seeing, dreaming, and performing. His approach to contemporary shaman artists is productive because his delivery is meant to stimulate the creative powers of his readers as well.

Let us listen to what the artists Mark Levy selected have to tell us. Ariadne gave Theseus a red thread to lead him through the labyrinth of the Minotaur; Mark Levy is guiding us safely through the experience of a few of the manifold manifestations of modern art. He has retained the ambiguity of the "divine message," so that readers can interpret the symbols and metaphors presented in the paintings, sculptures, verses or prose, or even performances, according to their own personal expectations and needs.

Ruth-Inge Heinze
University of California, Berkeley

References

Heinze, Ruth-Inge. *Shamans of the 20th Century.* New York: Irvington Publishers, Inc., 1991.

____. *Tham Khwan, How to Contain the Essence of Life, A Socio-Psychological Comparison of a Thai Custom.* Singapore: Singapore University Press, 1982.

Contents

Performing 221

Conclusion 303

List of Illustrations 305

Appendix: 311

Shamanic Techniques to Stimulate Creativity

Bibliography 315

Index 335

Introduction

In the nineteenth and twentieth centuries, ecstasy, the most vital element of religion, has almost disappeared from conventional forms of worship. As a result, some artists have resumed the ancient role of the shaman, "the technician of ecstasy" (Eliade, 1964:4). Shamans have been the intermediaries between ordinary and non-ordinary states of reality. Shaman have visions and record them in poetry, song, and the visual arts for the spiritual and therapeutic benefit of the community. In addition to being seers, shamans are also artists—painters, carvers, musicians, dancers, and storytellers. "Whatever else he may be, the shaman is a gifted artist," said anthropologist Carlton Coon (in Feldman 1982:3). In this book, I will be discussing modern artists who exhibit the qualities of powerful shamans.

It is important to recognize that, in tribal society, one does not elect to become a shaman but is chosen for one's ability as a seer and healer. Sometimes, the individual selected for shamanic initiation has some physical or psychological traits that distinguish him/her from the rest of society. For example, an illness or trauma may make it difficult for an individual to take on a normal role in his/her society. Andreas Lommel argued in his monograph, *Shamanism; The Beginnings of Art*, that "certain shamanistic phenomena correspond to the modern definition of certain mental disorders" (1967:8), but went on to say that it is

Precisely this ability to cure himself and progress from, let us say, a "negative" psychological state to a "positive" and productive one constitutes the difference between him and the modern psychotic (1967:8).

For Lommel, the shaman gets relief from his neurotic condition, among others, in artistic expression.

Lommel's view of shamanism as a kind of neurosis is not shared by other anthropologists today. A.P. Elkin, in *Aboriginal Men of High Degree*, maintained that aboriginal shamans "have taken a degree in the secret of life beyond that taken by most adult males, a step which implies discipline, mental training, courage and perseverance" (1977:66).

In any event, the practice of shamanism requires a high level of sensitivity to maintain contact with the spirit world and this may lead to nervous disorders if the shaman is not properly grounded. Artists also require a heightened sensitivity to themselves, the world around them, as well as to color and form. Like shamans, many artists have enhanced powers of seeing, hearing, and dreaming and move easily between different realities, not experiencing the boundaries that many of us have been acculturated to accept. Artistic as well as shamanic sensitivity, however, is a double-edged sword that opens the individual to all kinds of influences. Artists need to be as firmly grounded as shamans to maintain their emotional equilibrium.

The shamans' successful contact with the spirit world is the source of their visions. The shamans then act on or express the information given in terms their community will understand. To refuse the call of the spirit world puts these selected individuals at great risk.

To my mind, the "call" in shamanism is related to the artistic process. Artists are often compelled to express themselves and the failure to do so can bring about a crisis. Judith Levy, a contemporary New York artist, described it as follows:

I have a strong need to paint; if I don't paint I cry and get bad headaches...and depression sets in. I try to paint every day but sometimes I can't. I've got to paint at least a few days a week not to get crazy (quoted in Stein *et al*, 1986:61).

Like shamans, modern artists are different in character from the rest of society. However, traditional shamans do not feel alienated from the rest of the society; their differences are utilized in an accepted role, while, in materialistic cultures like ours, individuals with the ability to have visions and communicate them are suspect. Modern artists, therefore, frequently feel alienated from the rest of society, regardless of the degree of monetary reward.

Also, unlike traditional shamans, modern artists are not available, on a daily basis, nor do they receive a "call" or attempt to solve mundane problems of individuals or the community. Ruth-Inge Heinze (1991), one of my colleagues who is deeply involved in the study of shamanism, would argue that modern artists/shamans are mainly engaged in either shamanistic or neo-shamanic practices because they cultivate their own knowledge and attempt to heal themselves rather than respond to the daily needs of their contemporaries, i.e., problems with health and inter- as well as intrapersonal difficulties. Yet, modern artists/shamans are interested in transforming, enlightening, and often healing and empowering their audiences as well. Many of these artist/shamans do also enter alternate states of consciousness at will during which they journey to other realms.

Having taken a stand for modern artists as shamans, it should be noted that the individuals I will discuss in this book have trained as artists and consider themselves primarily to be artists who have an important content to convey. The works of art created by traditional shamans, such as African "fetish" figures and Australian Aboriginal paintings of the "Dreamings," are valued primarily for their magical efficacy and only secondarily for their aesthetic qualities.

Furthermore, I wish to emphasize that modern artists function as shamans only for those who look at their art. This may mean a very limited audience, especially if the artists' work is "avant-garde." In this book, I will discuss some of those avant-garde artists.

The relationship between modern artists and shamans is a new topic in scholarship which has only been briefly and unsystematically explored by contemporary commentators. Roland Barthes writes in his *Critical Essays*,

> the avant-garde author is somewhat like the witch doctor of so-called primitive societies: he concentrates the irregularity, the better to purge it from society as a whole. No doubt the bourgeoisie, in its declining phase, has required these aberrant operations which so noticeably label certain of its temptations. The avant-garde is in fact another cathartic phenomenon, a kind of vaccine intended to inject a little subjectivity, a little freedom under the crust of bourgeois values: we feel better for having taken part—a declared but limited part—in the disease (1972:68).

This essentially negative view of modern artists as shamans is shared by art historian Kirk Varnadoe in his contribution to the *Primitivism in Twentieth Century Art Catalogue*. He wrote that the modern artists' exposure to shamanism is generally bookish but insisted that it is a dangerous flight from civilization into irrational "primal determinism" (1984:680). Jack Burnham, in an essay, entitled "The Artist as Shaman," was more sympathetic but focused on superficial similarities between the modern artist and the shaman (1974:139-144). Thomas McEvilley, writing in *Artforum*, was much more informed about shamanism than Burnham or Varnadoe, but he tended to focus on the dramatic aspects of the ordeal in the shamanic practice of contemporary performance artists without taking into account other less harsh and destructive shamanic techniques employed by artists (1953:62-71).

My own knowledge of shamanism is both experiential and scholarly. In 1979 I began practicing shamanic techniques under the direction of Michael Harner, a Professor of Anthropology at the Graduate Faculty of the New School for Social Research. In the course of his study on shamanism of the upper Amazon in the early sixties Harner actually became a shaman and has, subsequently, written a manual, *The Way of the Shaman*, which presents shamanic techniques in a culturally non-specific way for contemporary laymen (1980:1-2). Along with Harner, I firmly believe that in order to understand shamanism one must practice it in some fashion, however elementary. As anthropologist Hans Peter Duerr put it in *Dreamtime*,

> At times we will have to howl with the wolves, and that means that we will have to forget some things [our objective separation from the subject matter]...that prevent us from understanding strange contents. This in no way suggests that we will forget everything for all times, as implied by a consistent relativism. The anthropologist returns home changed but he is not going to be a completely different person, for in that case, it would not be he who had gained the insight (1985:129).

In this book, I will attempt to show how modern artists are using shamanic practices to enter non-ordinary reality. I would like to argue that artists need not be conscious of themselves as being shamans to employ shamanic methodologies. They may use shamanic imagery without being aware of its content. Imagery that reflects non-ordinary reality needs not be tribal art at all. Artists can create new forms that are appropriate to contemporary life and still produce works which have a powerful shamanic content.

Technicians of Ecstasy is not intended to become a definitive history of shamanic art, it is, in fact, a preliminary study. Undoubtedly, scholars who are interested in this topic will come across information about other modern artist/ shamans. Also, there are other artist/shamans who I could have included in this book but their work is similar in style or content to those artists I have analyzed.

Furthermore, *Technicians of Ecstasy* does not necessarily negate previous studies of the artists' lives and work. Other interpretations are quite possible. Nevertheless, I think that looking at these artists from the shamanic point of view yields interesting insights that have not previously emerged. I will cite statements by prominent scholars of shamanism in support of my claims, and I have tested the validity of these statements against my own experience and that of others involved with shamanic practice.

In part, this book has come out of teaching an undergraduate course at the San Francisco Art Institute. I found that art students still are subscribing to the nineteenth-century bohemian myth that in order to have a vision one had to, in the words of Rimbaud, "systematically derange" one's senses. I attempted to expose students of art to an alternative myth of the visionary experience that is more positive—a myth rooted in the grounded practice of shamanic techniques.

I have used the chapter headings—Seeing, Dreaming, Performing—to structure the material that I have collected. These categories will, however, naturally overlap at times. I hope this will not confuse my readers unnecessarily.

While this book is intended for anyone who is interested in modern art and spirituality, it is particularly dedicated to artists who seek visions and want to embody these visions in their work. Indeed, one important goal of this book is to show how we can have visions without self-destructing.

Seeing

Vincent Van Gogh, Paul Cézanne, Giorgio Morandi, Frida Kahlo, Max Ernst, Gordon Onslow-Ford, Robert Irwin, Arthur Tress, and Alex Grey all practiced the shamanic techniques of seeing. They all are visual artists from the late nineteenth century to the present. The lives and work of the poets Arthur Rimbaud and Rainer Maria Rilke influenced twentieth century visual artists and provide valuable insights into the process of seeing.

The shamanic techniques of seeing do not only include hallucinogenic drugs but also solitude, and sensory deprivation. All of these techniques can strengthen the perceptual faculties.

The use of drugs is a traditional shamanic technique for entering non-ordinary reality and drugs have been employed by nineteenth- and twentieth-century artists for similar purposes. In a famous letter to his mentor Georges Izambard, the poet Arthur Rimbaud wrote

> ...I am degrading myself as much as possible. Why? I want to be a poet, and I am working to make myself a seer....It is a question of reaching the unknown by the derangement of all the senses. The sufferings are enormous, but one has to be strong, one has to be born a poet, and I know I am a poet. This is not at all

1

my fault. It is wrong to say: I think. One ought to
say; people think me. Pardon the pun (penser, "to
think"; panser, "to groom") (1967:303).

To have a vision of non-ordinary reality, Rimbaud used
hashish, opium, alcohol, and sex. He wanted to circumvent the
ego and the rational mind. Pierre Petitfils, in his recent
biography of Rimbaud, attempted to build a case on circum-
stantial evidence to show that Rimbaud had no inclination for
debauchery. Petitfils concluded that Rimbaud "had agreed to
it in the interests of 'the rational deranging of all the senses'
which was one of the seer's 'keys'" (1987:139). Petitfils is
referring here in part to Rimbaud's homosexual relationship
with the poet Verlaine which, in that period, was believed to
create an uncommon level of sexual intoxication.

In her magisterial biography of Rimbaud, Enid Starkie
pointed out that, unlike his mentor Charles Baudelaire who

...always kept in the midst of his worst aberrations
[the taking of various intoxicants to enter Les
Paradis Artificiels], a sense of sin; Rimbaud, however, would not feel that for him debauch was vice;
he was certain that he himself was above the reach
of sin (1961:123).

In fact, in the "Bad Blood" section of "Une Saison en Enfer"
(1873), Rimbaud placed himself outside of Christianity,
maintaining that his true ancestors were pre-Christian Gauls.

From my Gaulic ancestors, I have blue-white eyes,
a narrow skull, and clumsiness in wrestling. My
clothes are as barbaric as theirs. But I don't butter
my hair....

From them I inherit: idolatry and love of sacri-
lege....

...I am dancing the witches sabbath in a red clearing
with old women and children.

...We are moving toward the *Spirit*. I tell you it is
very certain, oracular. I understand and not knowing how to explain this without using pagan words,
I prefer to remain silent (1967:175-177).

These lines suggest that Rimbaud was probably aware of the
tradition of the vates or seers of the ancient Gaulish druids.

Rimbaud had a good knowledge of Greek and was well
versed in ancient classics. I think, he was also cognizant of the
tradition of seers in Greek poetry. He had probably read the
following passage from Plato's *Ion*,

For all good poets, epic as well as lyric, compose
their beautiful poems not by art, but because they
are inspired and possessed. And as the Corybantian
revellers when they dance are not in their right
mind, so the lyric poets are not in their right mind
when they are composing their beautiful strains: but
when falling under the power of music and metre
they are inspired and possessed; like Bacchic maid-
ens who draw milk and honey from the rivers when
they are under the influence of Dionysus but not
when they are in their right mind....For the poet is a
light and winged and holy thing, and there is no
invention in him until he has been inspired and is out
of his senses, and the mind is no longer in him; when
he has not attained to this state, he is powerless and
is unable to utter his oracles (quoted in Hofstater
and Kuhns, 1964:54-55).

Thus, for Rimbaud, "All ancient poetry ended in Greek
poetry." He continued in this letter,

> ...From Greece to the romantic movement
> [Baudelaire *et al*.]—Middle Ages—there are writ-
> ers and versifiers. From Ennius to Theroldus, from
> Theroldus to Casimir Delavigne, it is all rhymed
> prose, a game, degradation and glory of countless
> idiotic generations (1967:305).

To my mind, Rimbaud's own experience of seeing is expressed mainly in the fragmentary and highly ambiguous
"Illuminations" (1872) which changed the course of French
poetry in the late nineteenth century. Rimbaud understood
that the visions he brought back necessitated a new language.
Returning from the unknown, Rimbaud argued in a letter, "he
[the poet] will have to have his inventions smelt, felt, and
heard; if what he brings back from *down there* has form, he
gives form; if it is formless, he gives formlessness"
(1967:309).

   As I have already said in the Introduction, verbal or
visual language that reflects non-ordinary reality is not necessarily related to tribal art. Artists can create new forms that are
appropriate to modern life and these forms also have a powerful shamanic content. The "Illuminations" are a series of
stream-of-consciousness flashes which are in part a rendering
of the author's hallucinatory voyages to the lower and upper
realms of non-ordinary reality, comparable to shamanic accounts of these realms. The following passage from the
"Illuminations" is a good example of Rimbaud's encounter
with the lower realms.

> Now hire for me the tomb, whitewashed with the
> lines of cement in bold relief—far underground.
>
> I lean my elbows on the table, and the lamp lights
> brightly the newspapers I am fool enough to reread,
> and the absurd books.

> At a tremendous distance above my subterranean
> room, houses grow like plants, and fogs gather. The
> mud is red or black. Monstrous city! Endless night!
>
> Not so high up are the sewers....Perhaps there are
> pits of azure and wells of fire (1967:219)?

Sitting at a table by the light of a lamp, Rimbaud, probably on drugs, saw the room as a tomb and the levels beyond it as sewers and then a horrible black city. He also provided glimpses of the upper realms. In the "Illuminations," he spoke of "angels whirling their woolen robes in the steel and emerald grasses," "whirls of light," "dream flowers" that "tremble, burst, illuminate" and so forth. Rimbaud's poetic narrative can be related to a shamanic journey, not only in its description of the lower and upper regions but because he saw these realms structured on various levels.

Another shamanic theme of the "Illuminations" is the poet's metamorphosis into animals.

> Reality being too prickly for my lofty character, I
> became at my lady's a big blue-gray bird flying up
> near the moldings of the ceiling and dragging my
> wings after me in the shadows of the evening.
>
> At the foot of the baldaquino supporting her pre-
> cious jewels and her physical masterpieces I was a
> fat bear with purple gums and thick sorry-looking
> fur, my eyes of crystal and silver from the consoles
> (1967:227).

Shape shifting, such as turning into a "blue grey bird," is accomplished by shamans in a state of ecstatic trance when they want to attain the power of animals. Shamans also encounter magical animals that are capable of carrying out a conversation, as Rimbaud indicated in the following passage of the "Illuminations," "A hare stopped in the clover and the swinging flower bells, and said its prayer through the spider's web to the rainbow" (1967:213).

The "Illuminations" were accomplished at great cost. The sufferings engendered by "the derangement of all the senses" created for Rimbaud a veritable "season in hell" in ordinary reality. He felt his vocation as a poet left no other choice. In a section from "Une Saison en Enfer," entitled "Nuit de L'Enfer," he said,

> I swallowed a monstrous mouthful of poison.—
> Thrice blessed be the idea that came to me! My
> entrails are burning. The poison's violence twists
> my limbs, deforms me and hurls me to the ground.
> I am dying of thirst and am choking. I can't cry out.
> It is hell and eternal punishment. See how the fire
> rises up again! I am burning as I should. Come on,
> Demon (1967:183)!

Finally, Rimbaud could not sustain this level of demonic intensity any longer. He abandoned poetry at the age of nineteen for the life of a coffee buyer and gun runner in Africa. He said that if he had continued writing poetry he would have gone mad. In the "Farewell" section of "Une Saison en Enfer," Rimbaud remarked, "I who called myself magus or angel, exempt from all morality, I am thrown back to the earth, with a duty to find, and rough reality to embrace! Peasant" (1967:209)! This sounds as though Rimbaud was forced to find some kind of grounding mechanism in order to keep his sanity. Nevertheless, "Une Saison en Enfer" still contains hallucinatory and prophetic passages that have been relevant for the poet's future life. Wallace Fowlie, a Rimbaud scholar, said that

> At the age of nineteen [in, "Une Saison en Enfer"]
> Rimbaud wrote with an awesome accuracy about

his future. He foresaw his flight from Europe *(je quitte l'Europe)*, the tanning of his skin under tropical suns *(les climats perdus me tanueront)*, his return to Europe with gold pieces in his money belt *(Je reviendrai.... J'aurai de l'or)*, and his state of infirmity nursed by women *(Les fémmes soignent ces feroces infirmes retour des pay chauds) (1967:90)*.

Other than the "derangement of all the senses," there are not many clues about Rimbaud's method of seeing in his writings. According to Starkie, Rimbaud was influenced by Baudelaire's notion that

> only artists who had reached a high state of spirituality would be successful in discovering images, metaphors and analogies for the adequate rendering of their vision. He [Baudelaire] believed that genius lay not in the power of invention, but in the faculty of reception (1961:112).

Rimbaud said about Baudelaire in one of his letters,

> But since inspecting the invisible and hearing the unheard of is different from recovering the spirit of dead things, Baudelaire is the first seer, king of poets, *a real god!* And yet he lived in too artistic a world; and the form so highly praised in him is trivial. Inventions of the unknown call for new forms (1967:311).

In the same letter Rimbaud talked about the necessity of cultivating the soul if the poet is to reach the unknown: "Since he cultivated his soul, rich already, more than any man! He reaches the unknown, and when, bewildered, he ends by losing the intelligence of his visions, he has seen them" (1961:307).

Along with the poems of Baudelaire, Rimbaud was also familiar with Eliphas Levi's *Transcendental Magic, Its Doctrine and Ritual* (1923) which Rimbaud read in the public library of Charleville. Although there are many inaccuracies in this book, as any practitioner of magic or shamanism would be the first to point out, Rimbaud may have absorbed some ideas that had an important influence on his life and work.

"In order to accomplish a thing," said Levi in *Transcendental Magic*,

> we must believe in our possibility of doing it, and this faith must be translated at once into acts. When a child says: "I cannot," his mother answers: "Try." Faith does not even try; it begins with the certitude of finishing, and it proceeds calmly, as if omnipotence were at its disposal and eternity before it. What seek you therefore from the science of the magi? Dare to formulate your desire, then set to work at once and do not cease acting after the same manner and for the same end. That which you shall come to pass, and for you and by you it has indeed already begun....His life [the magi's] must be that of the will directed by one thought (1923:253, 255).

Levi's discussion on the will may have given Rimbaud the idea that, with unwavering faith in himself and enough hard work, he could become an authentic seer. Kenneth Rexroth, the contemporary American poet, said in his essay on Rimbaud's poems,

> There [in the library of Charleville] he discovered not just poetry but the extraordinary claims of the poetics of late Romanticism.

> He immediately applied the recipes to himself, and since he took them literally and acted on them with

superlative vigor and intelligence, the results were astonishing. Not only were they epoch-making—they are still making epochs. The reason is simple: no one before had ever really believed the claims of the poets, and no poet had ever before had either the brains or the muscle to act on such impossible claims if he had believed them (1986:195).

Inspired by the claims of Levi, the Romantics, and Baudelaire, Rimbaud apparently set out to be a seer and even went beyond the Romantics and Baudelaire in this role by the sheer power of his will.

In addition to strengthening the will, Levi gave other practical advice on how to become a seer or magus. Although he did not specifically recommend debauchery as a way of achieving ecstasy, in *Transcendental Magic*, he said that in order to be a magus,

we must be outside the normal conditions of humanity, we must be either abstracted by wisdom or exalted by madness, either superior to all passions or outside them through ecstasy and frenzy. Such is the first and most indispensible preparation of the operator (1923:251).

Levi further explained in *Transcendental Magic* that,

Divinatory vision operates only in the ecstatic state, to arrive at which doubt and illusion must be rendered impossible by enchaining or putting to sleep thought. The instruments of divination are hence only auto-magnetic methods and pretexts for auto-isolation from exterior light, so that we may pay attention to the interior of light alone (1923:453).

In fact, the diviner becomes "completely flooded with an

excess of inner light which completely saturates and hence stupefies, the [external] nervous system" (Levi, 1923:289). In the Qabalah, as Levi pointed out in his discussions of this subject in *Transcendental Magic*, this inner light is also the spark of God and the possessor of inner light is able to see things that are invisible to others. In the "Vagabonds" sections of the "Illuminations," while speaking of his friend, the poet Verlaine, Rimbaud strongly implied that "his primitive state of a sun-child" was the condition of the true poet (1967:233). Rimbaud exclaimed in "Hunger" from "Une Saison en Enfer," "At last, O happiness, O reason, I removed from the sky the blue that is black, and I lived like a spark of gold of *pure light*" (1967:199). Rimbaud may be saying here that he had become an illumine, a living embodiment of Levi's qabalistic concept of "inner light."

Light also has an important significance in shamanism as Joan Halifax pointed out in her book, *Shaman: the Wounded Healer*,

> The nimbus or halo emanating from the heads of these shamans and spirits [in shamanic art] is a visual expression of intellectual energy in its mystical aspect, or of supernatural power. The sun itself is symbolic of the heroic principle of all-seeing and all-knowing, and the indwelling fire of life. The activation of this "internal sun" we have called "solarization" (1982:90).

From shamanism and the qabalistic point of view, seeing is associated with light, and light imagery is found in many of Rimbaud's poems besides "Les Illuminations" and "Une Saison en Enfer."

❖

Turning from a poet to a painter, Vincent Van Gogh was

more explicit about his method of seeing than Rimbaud. He wrote,

> It is looking at things for a long time that ripens you and gives you a deeper understanding. If we study Japanese art, we see an artist who is wise, philosophic, and intelligent, who spends his time—how? In studying the distance between the earth and the moon? No. In studying the policy of Bismarck? No. He studies a single blade of grass. But this blade of grass leads him to draw the plant, and then the seasons, the wide aspects of the countryside, the animals, then human figures....
>
> Come, now, isn't it almost an actual religion which these simple Japanese teach us, who live in nature as though they themselves were flowers? We must return to nature in spite of our education and our work in a world of convention. And you cannot study Japanese art without becoming gayer and happier (quoted in Stone, 1937:389).

In my own development of the process of seeing, I have learned that the first stage is to look at an object for an extended period of time. It is easiest to begin with objects of lesser complexity such as inanimate things, and then progress to plants, animals and humans, in that order. After a period of looking at an object daily for a short duration of time in a meditative frame of mind, a shift from looking to seeing gradually takes place.

As Van Gogh implied, seeing has a religious aspect. Not only does one see the inner structure of the object but one can actually have a dialogue or merge with the object and its environment like those "who live in nature as though they were flowers." The seer moves from an I-It relationship to an I-Thou relationship with the object. Needless to say, this type of religion is far from the orthodox structure of Christianity. Van Gogh was acutely aware of his departure from Christian belief. In a "Self-Portrait" of 1888, Van Gogh depicted himself, in his own words, "as a Bonze, a simple worshipper of the eternal Buddha" with a shaved head and slanted eyes (1958:64). In the same letter to his brother Theo about this portrait, he explained, "It will be necessary for me to recover somewhat more from the stultifying influence of our so-called state of civilization" (1958:64).

The question still remains how Van Gogh was able to move from looking to seeing, how he was able to "stop the world" in Carlos Castaneda's terms[1] and therefore escape "...from the stultifying influence of our so-called state of civilization." By his own admission, Van Gogh subsisted on a terrible diet. "I have lived for four days on twenty-four cups of coffee, with bread," he said in one letter (quoted in Stone, 1937:393). In another series of letters, he claimed,

> If you are well you must be able to live on a bit of bread while you are working all day, and have enough strength to smoke and drink your whack at night—that's all in the bargain—and at the same time feel the stars—the infinite high and clear above you. Then life is after all most enchanted. Oh! those who do not believe in this sun here are the real infidels (quoted in Stone, 1937:374).

> Today again, from seven o'clock in the morning till six in the evening, I worked without stirring except to eat a bite a step or two away. That is why the work is getting on fast. But what will you say to it? And what shall I think of it myself a little while from now? I have a lover's clear sight or a lover's blindness.

> These colours give me extraordinary exaltation. I

have no thought of fatigue. I shall do another picture this very night, and I shall bring it off. I have a terrible lucidity at moments when nature is so beautiful: I am not conscious of myself any more, and the pictures come to me as in a dream (quoted in Stone, 1937:391).

Given Van Gogh's diet, it is hardly surprising that he attained "clear sight" or a "terrible lucidity." In fact, fasting in combination with tobacco juice or alcohol is a typical way of achieving trance states among shamans.

Much has been written about the supposed epilepsy or madness of Van Gogh as the reason for his visions. For me, the best evidence against these claims has been recently put forth by a group of physicians, writing in the *Journal of the American Medical Association*. They argued that the physical symptoms described in Van Gogh's letters were caused by Menière's disease which affects the inner ear. The extreme discomfort of this disease promotes a desire among some of its sufferers to cut their outer ear as Van Gogh actually did. In the words of these physicians,

His voluntary admission to the asylum of St. Remy [following the removal of his ear] hoping to find help for his attacks on vertigo [brought on by Menière's disease] that everyone else thought was a form of epilepsy (epileptoid) and his rational behavior at the asylum as well as before and after the attacks as described in his voluminous correspondence, should forever banish the notion that he was an epileptic or "mad" (Kaufman et al, 1990:493).

So, what was going on? What did Van Gogh experience?

In *The Doors of Perception*, Aldous Huxley remarked that

> each of us is potentially Mind at Large. But in so far as we are animals, our business is at all costs to survive. To make biological survival possible, Mind at Large has to be funneled through the reducing valve of the brain and nervous system. What comes out at the other end is a measly trickle of the kind of consciousness which will help us to stay alive on the surface of this particular planet....Certain persons, however, seem to be born with a kind of by-pass that circumvents the reducing valve. In others temporary by-passes may be acquired either spontaneously, or as a result of deliberate "spiritual exercises," or through hypnosis, or by means of drugs. Through these permanent or temporary by-passes there flows, not indeed the perception "of everything that is happening everywhere in the universe" (for the by-pass does not abolish the reducing valve, which still excludes the total content of Mind at Large), but something more than, and above all something different from, the carefully selected utilitarian material which our narrowed, individual minds regard as complete, or a least sufficient, picture of reality (1963:23-24).

There is strong evidence in Van Gogh's work to suggest that he saw beyond utilitarian reality. In his painting of a pair of old peasant shoes (Illustration 1), for example, he appeared to have uncovered the essence of "shoeness" which is not revealed by ordinary looking. The painted shoes radiate with an energy which the Chinese would call *chi*—the particular underlying life force. This *chi* energy becomes especially pronounced in Van Gogh's later works. In the "Starry Night" (1889), for example, swirling brushstrokes of supersaturated incandescent color seem to explode off the canvas.

   Martin Heidegger, the German philosopher, remarked in his essay *The Origin of the Work of Art*, (1950) that

> Van Gogh's painting is the disclosure of what the equipment, the pair of peasant shoes, *is* in truth. This entity emerges into the unconcealedness of its being. The Greeks called the unconcealedness of beings *aletheia*. We say "truth" and think little enough in using this word. If there occurs in the work a disclosure of a particular being, disclosing what and how it is, then there is here an occurring, a happening of truth at work (quoted in Hofstadter and Kuhns, 1964:665-666).

Heidegger also said in this essay that, in her daily existence, the peasant woman simply wore the shoes without reflecting on their essence (quoted in Hofstadter and Kuhns, 1964:664). As long as they were employed as functional objects their being or essence was never disclosed. Or, using my own terms, the peasant woman may have looked at the shoes when she put them on or took them off, etc., but she did not see them. Heidegger gave a wonderfully poetic description of Van Gogh's uncovery of the being of these peasant shoes.

> From Van Gogh's painting we cannot even tell where these shoes stand. There is nothing surrounding this pair of peasant shoes or to which they might belong—only an undefined space. There are not even clods of soil from the field or the field-path sticking to them, which would at least hint at their use. A pair of peasant shoes, and nothing more. And yet—
>
> From the dark opening of the worn insides of the shoes the toilsome tread of the worker stares forth. In the stiffly rugged heaviness of the shoes there is

the accumulated tenacity of her slow trudge through the far-spreading and ever-uniform furrows of the field swept by a raw wind. On the leather lie the dampness and the richness of the soil. Under the soles slides the loneliness of the field-path as evening falls. In the shoes vibrates the silent call of the earth, its quiet gift of the ripening grain and its unexplained self-refusal in the fallow desolation of the wintry field. This equipment is pervaded by uncomplaining anxiety as to the certainty of bread, the wordless joy of having once more withstood want, the trembling before the impending childbed and shivering at the surrounding menace of death. This equipment belongs to the *earth*, and it is protected in the *world* of the peasant woman (quoted in Hofstadter and Kuhns, 1964:663-664).

Van Gogh's presentation of shoeness is embodied in a visual language that resists translation into a verbal one. And Heidegger's interpretation of Van Gogh's ineffable visual language is certainly subjective and imaginative. Yet, I think, it could be deducted from Heidegger's description that Van Gogh's presentation of shoeness facilitated Heidegger's own process of seeing.

Along with Heidegger, Aldous Huxley also acknowledged the profound presence of Van Gogh's work. Under the influence of mescaline, Huxley

picked up the first volume that came to hand. It was on Van Gogh and the picture at which the book opened was "The Chair"—that astounding portrait of a *Ding an Sich* [the thing in itself] which the mad painter saw, with a kind of adoring terror, and tried to render on his canvas. But it was a task to which the power even of a genius proved wholly inadequate. The chair Van Gogh had seen was obviously the same in essence as the chair I had seen. But, though incomparably more real than the chairs of ordinary perception, the chair in his picture remained no more than an unusually expressive symbol of the fact. The fact had been manifested Suchness; this was only an emblem. Such emblems are sources of true knowledge about the Nature of Things, and this true knowledge may serve to prepare the mind which accepts it for immediate insights on its own account. But that is all. However expressive, symbols can never be the things they stand for (1963:28-29).

Of course, as Huxley argued, no matter how close Van Gogh approached the *Ding an Sich*, his artistic rendering was only an approximation. Yet, the question of whether Van Gogh depicted absolutely the *Ding an Sich* in his paintings or not hardly diminishes Van Gogh's ability as a seer or his heroic attempt to render what he saw.

Van Gogh himself was aware of the discrepancy between nature and his ability to embody it in art. In a letter to Theo he wrote,

To study from nature, to wrestle with reality—I don't want to do away with it for years and years. I should not like to have missed that *error*. One starts with a hopeless struggle to follow nature and everything goes wrong; one ends by calmly creating from one's own palette, and nature agrees with it and follows. But these two contrasts do not exist separately. The drudgery, though it may seem in vain, gives an intimacy with nature, a sounder knowledge of things (quoted in Stone, 1937:307).

Van Gogh's poor diet may have contributed to his abilities as a seer but it also hastened his death. Without the grounding mechanisms that traditional shamans cultivate to counterbalance their visionary states so that they do not become fixed in extraordinary reality and self-destruct, Van Gogh could not sustain the level of intensity that he brought to his life and work. He eventually committed suicide after a frenetic painting career that basically lasted only five years—from 1885 to 1890.

The tragic careers of Rimbaud and Van Gogh had a salutary effect on many twentieth-century artists who used a non-destructive methodology of seeing. Paul Cézanne and Rainer Maria Rilke, whom Cézanne greatly influenced, developed their ability to see through a combination of solitude and prolonged looking. Cézanne maintained in his letters,

> In order to make progress, there is only nature, and the eye is trained through constant contact with her (1976:306).

> I progress very slowly, for nature reveals herself to me in very complex ways; and the progress needed is endless. One must look at the model and feel very exactly (1976:302).

In 1872, at the urging of the impressionist painter Camille Pissarro, Cézanne abandoned his early style, a kind of turgid romanticism, for an approach that demanded a laborious and patient observation of nature. Following the example of Pissarro, as art historian Meyer Schapiro put it, Cézanne began to achieve a new "discipline in seeing" that caused him to eschew his earlier "conventional" style with its references to the masters in the Louvre (1952:26). Cézanne himself argued much later that "The Louvre is a good book to consult but it must be only an intermediary. The real and immense study to be undertaken is the manifold picture of nature" (1976:302-303). He even exhorted his friend Emile Bernard to "render the image of what we see, forgetting everything that existed before us" (1976:316).

Meyer Schapiro called Cézanne's method of seeing one of "radical empiricism" (1952:19). That is to say, he began by suspending or bracketing his received knowledge about natural objects in order to see them for himself. According to Schapiro, Cézanne's attitude toward the subjects of his painting was essentially "meditative and detached" (1952:16); he succeeded after a tumultuous and passionate early life to empty himself of the passion that clogs reception. "Hence," said Schapiro "the extraordinary calm in so many of his views—a true suspension of desire" (1952:14).

The poet Rilke had far fewer art historical sources available to him, yet his famous *Letters on Cézanne* to his wife Clara Westoff in 1907 echo Schapiro's ideas about Cézanne.[2] The poet believed that Cézanne's method of seeing was "passionless." "Cézanne had to start all over again from the bottom" (Rilke, 1985:43). "He sat there in front of it like a dog, just looking, without any nervousness, without any ulterior motive" (1985:46).

Rilke was especially impressed with Cézanne's perseverance and discipline. At the age of forty, partly as a result of Pissarro's influence, Cézanne abandoned his desultory bohemian habits for an austere existence of almost uninterrupted labor which he maintained for the next thirty years. In the *Letters*, Rilke gave an accurate account of Cézanne's daily life.

> ...he would get up at six, walk through town to his studio and stay there until ten; return along the same road to take his meal; eat and set off again, sometimes a half hour's walk past the studio, "sur le motif" in a valley before which the mountain range of Sainte Victoire rose up indescribably with all its

thousand challenges. There he would sit for hours, occupied with finding and incorporating the *"plans"* [Cézanne's word for the kinetic planes he used in his painting] (1985:39).

In the evening Cézanne would continue to work; his social activities with friends became fewer and fewer and his wife and child only visited him sporadically from Paris. Cézanne even missed the funeral of his beloved mother in order not to break the concentration on a painting. In addition to self-enforced solitude, Cézanne increasingly suffered from diabetes. According to Huxley,

> The brain is provided with a number of enzyme systems which serve to co-ordinate its workings. Some of these enzymes regulate the supply of glucose to the brain cells. Mescalin inhibits the production of these enzymes and thus lowers the amount of glucose available to an organ that is in constant need of sugar (1963:24).

Huxley went on to say that under mescalin the ability to "remember and to 'think straight'" is unimpaired while "visual impressions are greatly intensified" and "perception is enormously improved" (1963:25).

Without the availability of insulin (it was first used in the 1930s), Cézanne's erratic blood sugar level may have affected his seeing in a way which was similar to mescalin. Nevertheless, solitary prolonged looking in a meditative state is sufficient to produce heightened powers of seeing. Rilke said that Cézanne stood in front of the landscape and drew religion from it (1985:xxiii-xxiv). "And (like Van Gogh) he made his 'saints' out of such things; and forces them—*forces them*—to be beautiful, to stand for the whole world and all joy and all glory" (Rilke, 1985:40).

Cézanne was a deeply religious man, but his seeing did

not result in the disclosure of the everyday suchness of things
in the manner of Van Gogh. Instead, as several scholars have
indicated, he anticipated the Bergsonian idea of duration and
the related Einsteinian idea of space-time. Day after day, for
extended periods, Cézanne would return to the same spot and
work on the same "motif." He realized that as his consciousness changed over time, the object or objects before him also
shifted their position in space. Similarly, in the *L'evolution
creatrice* of 1907, published in the year after Cézanne's death,
Henri Bergson argued convincingly that the consciousness of
the most static observer continually changes and has an effect
on the perception of objects. George Heard Hamilton maintained in his article "Cézanne, Bergson, and the Image of
Time," that

> in contrast to an Impressionist painting in which the
> surface is the sum of all the visual sensations re-
> ceived at an instant and recorded as quickly as
> possible, the entire pictorial surface of a Cézanne is
> the sum of continuous perceptions of space in the
> mode of time (1956:7).

Hamilton said that, as a result of this,

> Lines, angles and planes which in a conventional
> perspective system define the position of a form in
> a fixed motionless space will exhibit abnormalities,
> discrepancies or structural deformities with refer-
> ence to the traditional appearance of the same form
> in a conventional spatial system (1956:7).

Looking at the Cézanne painting of "Chocquet Seated"
(1877; Illustration 2), we observe that the section of the
baseboard on the left-hand side of Chocquet is lower than the
section of the baseboard on the right-hand side. Assuming that
Cézanne sat up his easel in front of Chocquet at the same place

each day for the long period it took to paint the picture, it is obvious that Cézanne's spatial awareness of the baseboard varied at different points of time and he chose to record the different spatial locations of the baseboard observed at different points of time in his painting. Now, even if Cézanne did not return to the same location in front of the subject every day and moved his easel to the left and then right side of Chocquet or vice versa, he left a record of his spatial sensations relative to his movements over time.

As in the universe of Einstein where time and space are not independent but are fundamentally related, Cézanne's warped perspective manifests shifts of space over time, unlike traditional Western perspective which, in Hamilton's words, represents a "fixed motionless space" from a single unchanging point of view and consciousness. Cézanne's spatial geometry is more like the bent space of Einstein than the Euclidian geometry of Newton. Bergson's and Einstein's ideas about time and space are basically metaphysical; they are not in accord with our normal perception of reality.

It is my belief that Cézanne was able to progress from looking to seeing in his work. He thereby arrived at a metaphysical notion of space-time akin to Bergson's and Einstein's concepts. Unlike Rimbaud and Van Gogh, however, Cézanne's technique of seeing was thoroughly grounded by his direct and daily contact with nature as well as his abstemious living habits, and he did not self-destruct.

In addition to being a strict vegetarian and abstainer from alcoholic beverages for most of his adult life, Rilke's cultivation of solitude, patience, and alertness was a conscious intention on his part to foster the ability to see and hear over a long period of time without poisoning his very sensitive nervous system.

In the *Letters to a Young Poet*, Rilke advised, "The

necessary thing is after all...solitude, great inner solitude. Going-into-oneself and for hours meeting no one—this one must be able to attain" (1962:45-46)

> That mankind has in this sense been cowardly has done life endless harm; the experiences that are called "visions," the whole so-called "spirit-world," death, all those things that are so closely akin to us have by daily parrying been so crowded out of life that the senses with which we could have grasped them are atrophied. To say nothing of God (1962:67).

For Rilke, solitude was necessary to resensitize himself to the spirit world. It is worth remarking here that Rilke's celebration of solitude was a continuation of the German Romantic tradition, beginning in the early nineteenth century. In Caspar David Friedrich's "Monk on the Seashore" (1806), for example, the artist depicted himself alone in a monk's garb in a vast gloomy seascape. Friedrich and other German Romantic painters realized the metamorphosis of the artist into a new role, that of a holy seer who has the ability to apprehend and communicate the spiritual in sublime land and seascapes. This role could only be accomplished in solitude, as depicted in the "Monk on the Seashore."

In traditional shamanism, solitude is a prerequisite of higher insight. The Caribou shaman Igjugarjuk told the Arctic explorer Knud Rasmussen that

> all true wisdom is only to be learned far from the dwellings of men, out in the great solitudes; and is only to be attained through suffering. Privation and suffering are the only things that can open the mind of man to those things which are hidden from others (Halifax, 1979:6).

Rilke, along with the German Romantic painters, believed that the conventional symbols of Christianity had lost their effectiveness and it was the task of the sensitive artist to create new metaphors for the spiritual (1977:16-17). In fact, Rilke's letters are replete with statements against traditional belief systems.

> I have an indescribable confidence in those people that have not come to God through belief but have experienced God through their own race, in their own stock. Like the Jews, the Arabs, to a certain degree the orthodox Russians—and then, in another way, the peoples of the East and of ancient Mexico. To them God is origin, and therefore future as well. To the others he is something deduced, something away from which and toward which they strive as really strangers or as people who have grown estranged—and so they are always needing the intercessor, the mediator, him who translates their blood, the idiom of their blood into the language of the godhead. What *these* people achieve then is indeed "belief"; they must conquer and train themselves to hold for true that which is a true thing for the 'God-descended, and for this reason their religions slip so easily into the ethical,—whereas a God originally experienced does not separate and distinguish good and evil in relation to men but for his own sake, passionately concerned over their being-near-to-him, over their holding- and belonging-to-him and over nothing else (1948:276-277)!

Rilke's negative attitude toward secondary sources is paralleled in shamanism. Not only does the direct experience of the spiritual preclude intermediaries, but this experience transcends conventional ethical categories. Shamans maintain a mode of life which like Rilke's is conducive to having spiritual experiences over a long period of time. It is not the primary goal of a seer to determine what is good or bad. And, in the case of the shaman/seer who is also an artist, the tasteful is beyond categorizing what is good and what is bad. Rilke argued,

> It is not only the *hearable* in music that is important (something can be pleasant to hear without being *true*). What is decisive for me, in all the arts, is not their outward appearance, not what is called the "beautiful," but rather their deepest, most inner origin, the buried reality that calls forth their appearance (1922:164).

In the *Sonnets to Orpheus*, Rilke talked about the necessity of transforming the "makeshift hut" to "receive the transcendent music" [of the God Orpheus] to a "temple deep inside their hearing [he is referring here to the development of the animal's hearing of the forest]" (1922:19).

One of the ways Rilke sought to build a temple deep inside his ear was through prolonged looking. Rilke realized that prolonged looking, if it is to shift into seeing, is a discipline that requires great patience and alertness. In his *Letters to a Young Poet*, he said,

> I am able more and more to make use of that long patience you have taught me by your tenacious example; that patience which, disproportionate to ordinary life which seem to bid us haste, puts us in touch with all that surpasses us (1962:123).

Rilke's idea of patience can also be compared to stalking in shamanism. The alert readiness over a long period of time puts the shaman/warrior in contact with the spirit world. Rilke realized that to maintain this alertness is a lifelong battle. He lamented, in his *Letters on Cézanne*, that "one lives so badly, because one always comes into the present, unfinished, unable, distracted" (1985). Indeed, distraction is the main barrier to seeing, which for Rilke was the main "mission" of the poet. In the "First Duino Elegy" (1912), he wrote,

> Yes—the springtimes needed you. Often a star was waiting for you to notice it. A wave rolled toward you out of the distant past, or as you walked under an open window, a violin yielded itself to your hearing. All this was mission. But could you accomplish it? Weren't you always distracted by expectation, as if every event announced a beloved (1984:151)?

It is the poet's noticing of things which gives them a kind of ontological status. Seeing and recording this seeing are acts of creating the world. As Martin Heidegger argued, in his essay on the poet Hölderlin, "this essence of poetry is the establishing of being by means of the word" (1968:282).

When Rilke was secretary to the sculptor Rodin from 1902 to 1903, the latter advised him to spend several hours each day for several weeks looking at the panther at the Paris zoo. "The Panther," composed in 1907, was a result of Rilke's technique of seeing.

The Panther
In the Jardin des Plantes, Paris

His vision, from the constantly passing bars,
has grown so weary that it cannot hold
anything else. It seems to him there are
a thousand bars; and behind the bars, no world.

As he paces in cramped circles, over and over,
the movement of his powerful soft strides
is like a ritual dance around a center
in which a mighty will stands paralyzed.

Only at times, the curtain of the pupils
lifts, quietly—. An image enters in,
rushes down through the tensed, arrested muscles,
plunges into the heart and is gone (1984:25).

Rilke went from looking at the panther in the zoo to
seeing its psychic state. Like a shaman diagnosing a client for
healing purposes, Rilke went beyond a description of the outer
physical condition of the panther for an account of its inner
condition in metaphorical images. Rilke also saw and celebrated the beauty of even the "smallest things," both in his
poetry and his letters.

> I saw once again that most people hold things in
> their hands to do something stupid with
> them...instead of looking carefully at each thing and
> asking each about the beauty it possesses. So it
> comes to pass that most people don't know how
> beautiful the world is and how much splendor is
> revealed in the smallest things, in some flower, a
> stone, the bark of a tree, or birch leaf. Grown-up
> people, who have business cares and worry a lot
> about trifles, gradually lose their eye entirely for
> those riches which children, when they are alert and
> good children, soon notice and love with all their
> hearts. And yet the finest thing would be if all
> people would always stay in this relationship like
> alert and good children, with simple and reverent
> feelings (1948:59).

According to Rilke, it is not only reverence for things
that enables us to see their beauty, but it is humility toward
them.

> He who kneels, who gives himself wholly to kneel-
> ing, loses indeed the measure of his surroundings,

even looking up he would no longer be able to say what is great and what is small. But although in his bent posture he has scarcely the height of a child, yet he, this kneeling man, is not to be called small. With him the scale is shifted...he already belongs to that world in which height—is depth,—and if even height remains unmeasurable to our gaze and our instruments: who could measure the depth (1948:238-239)?

I think Rilke was linking the ability to see in depth with kneeling. From my own shamanic work in seeing, I also found that looking at an object from below or at the same level is an act of humility which greatly enhances the dialogue with the object.

By 1914, Rilke had developed his ability to see to such an extent that he was able to write to his friend Magda von Hattinberg,

Can you imagine with me how glorious it is, for example, to see into a dog, in passing—*into* him (I don't mean to see through him, which is merely a kind of human gymnastics, where one comes right back out on the other side of the dog, using him as a window to whatever human concerns lie behind him, no, not that)—but to ease oneself into the dog exactly at his center, the place out of which he exists as a dog, that place in him where God would, so to speak, have sat down for a moment when the dog was complete, in order to watch him at his first predicaments and notions and let him know by a nod that he was good, that he lacked nothing, that no better dog could be made....If I were to tell you *where* my greatest feeling, my universal feeling, the bliss of my earthly existence has been, I would have to confess: It has always, here and there, been in this kind of in-seeing, in the indescribably swift, deep, timeless moments of this divine seeing into the heart of things. You see, and when one loved, this was the first thing that fell away—the dog would come along; an inexpressible pain would arise, one no longer had the prodigal freedom to merge with him. There was someone in the background who called you "mine" (that irresponsible word), and the dog would have to introduce himself to that person and ask permission to let you enter him for one imperceptible, secret moment (1987:77-78).

For Rilke, loving the dog in a possessive way would make it impossible to merge with him in the act of "in-seeing." Earlier, in the *Letters on Cézanne*, Rilke had argued,

You also notice, a little more clearly each time, how necessary it was to go beyond love, too; it's natural, after all, to love each of these things as one makes it, but if one shows this, one makes it less well; one *judges* it, instead of *saying* it. One ceases to be impartial; and the very best love stays outside the work, does not enter it, is left aside untranslated: that's how the painting of sentiments came about (which is no way better than the painting of things) (1985:50-51).

In the poem "Requiem," written in 1908, about a year after the death of the painter Paula Modersohn Becker with whom he once was in love, Rilke said, "Let us lament together that someone pulled you out of your mirror's depths" (1984:79). Here he was referring to the fact that Becker, after managing to separate from her husband and spending a productive year in Paris, had succumbed to his pressure to rejoin him. She became pregnant soon thereafter and died in childbirth during the winter of 1907. Rilke reached the conclusion that love for another human being was inimical to seeing and to being a poet. Love clouded "the mirror" by which the artist saw and reflected the world. Like Cézanne, he separated from his wife and gradually reduced his friendships to letter writing. I think Rilke's sacrifice of love and companionship for his work was rather extreme, and his reasons for the eschewal of human relationships may have been an excuse for an inability to sustain them.

However, an inflamed emotional state is not conducive to seeing; it certainly clouds "the mirror" of seeing. In fact, when practicing seeing, it is very helpful to concentrate on breathing from the *chakra* at the solar plexus—two inches below the navel—to calm the mind and emotions.

Rilke was conscious of the importance of the *chakra* at the solar plexus when he said, in his late letters, that it is the focal point of our orientation "as regards the visible as well as the invisible" (1948:320).

He was also aware that breathing has a calming effect on the emotions as evidenced by the following passage in the "Second Duino Elegy" (1912), "But we, when moved by deep feeling, evaporate; we breathe ourselves out and away; from moment to moment our emotion grows fainter, like a per-fume" (1984:157). Breathing was an important part of Rilke's method of poetic creation. In the following passage from the *Sonnets*, he said,

> Breathing: you invisible poem! Complete
> interchange of our own
> essence with world-space. You counterweight
> in which I rhythmically happen.
>
> Single wave-motion whose
> gradual sea I am;
> you, most inclusive of all our possible seas—
> space grown warm.

How many regions in space have already been
inside me. There are winds that seem like
my wandering son.

Do you recognize me, air, full of places I once
absorbed?
You who were the smooth bark,
roundness, and leaf of my words (1986:73).

I think Rilke is saying here that, perhaps in the act of exhala-
tion, the separation between subject and object, inside and
outside, becomes annihilated and there is a union with the
world space. In fact, Rilke mentioned his experience of
merging with the object of contemplation on several occa-
sions in his letters. He hinted at this intermingling with the
object, for example, in his letter to Marie von Hattinberg about
the dog, but he talked about it more specifically in a letter to
Lou Andreas-Salome, his former lover and life-long confi-
dant.

He thought of the hour in that other southern garden
(Capri) when the call of a bird did not, so to speak,
break off at the edge of his body, but was simulta-
neously outside and in his innermost being, uniting
both into one uninterrupted space in which, myste-
riously protected, only one simple place of purest,
deepest consciousness remained. On that occasion
he had closed his eyes so that he might not be
confused, in so generous an experience, by the
outline of his body, and the Infinite passed into him
from all sides, so intimately that he believed he
could feel the stars which had in the meantime
appeared, gently reposing within his breast
(1984:311).

At the point of merging with the object in the practice of

listening and seeing, the seer is no longer aware that he or she is doing the listening and the seeing. In the poem "Gong" (1923-26), Rilke wrote,

> No longer for ears...: sound which, like a deeper ear, hears us, who only seem to be hearing. Reversal of spaces. Projection of innermost worlds into the Open... (1984:283).

When the place of the reversal of spaces is reached, the "innermost worlds" become uncovered and important knowledge is revealed. There is now a kind of love between the observer and the object and the process of looking ceases. Rilke alluded to this cessation of looking in this passage from "The Turning Point" (1913-1916), "For there is a boundary to looking. And the world that is looked at so deeply wants to flourish in love" (1984:135). In the same poem, Rilke went on to say: "Work of the eyes is done, now go and do the heart-work on all the images imprisoned within you."

Although, in his later poems, Rilke began increasingly to work on the "images imprisoned within him" instead of the prolonged looking on a physical object which was the source of such poems as "The Panther," Rilke still employed his ability to see on the images within his heart.

I hope to show later, in my discussion of Frida Kahlo and Max Ernst, that seeing can be directed to an inner as well as an outer object. For Rilke, the ability to see and to listen was an essentially feminine characteristic.

> It is so natural for me *to understand girls and women*; the deepest experience of the creator is feminine—: for it is experience of receiving and bearing. The poet Obstfelder once wrote, when describing the face of a strange man: "it was" (when he began to speak) "as if there were a woman in him—"; it seems to me that would fit every poet who began to speak (1945:181).

Rilke had an actual feminine model for "receiving," Wera Oukama Knoop, the daughter of one of his Munich friends. She was a gifted dancer. At the age of seventeen, however, she was struck with an incurable glandular disease that made her body swell up and made a career in dancing impossible. She then turned to music and finally had to give that up too for drawing which she continued until her death. Rilke had Knoop in mind when he composed the second *Sonnet to Orpheus.*

> And it was almost a girl and came to be
> out of this single joy of song and lyre
> and through her green veils shone forth radiantly
> and made herself a bed inside my ear.
>
> And slept there. And her sleep was everything:
> the awesome trees, the distances I had felt
> so deeply that I could touch them, meadows in
>   spring:
> all wonders that had ever seized my heart.
>
> She slept the world. Singing god, how was that first
> sleep to perfect that she had no desire
> ever to wake? See: she arose and slept.
>
> Where is her death now? Ah, will you discover
> this theme before your song consumes itself?—
> Where is she vanishing?... A girl almost...
> (1985b:21).

I think Rilke was saying here that the example of Knoop's openness entered him, slept in a bed inside his ear, so that it became the key to his own openness "to all wonders that had ever seized my heart."

In another *Sonnet to Orpheus* Rilke used the metaphor of a flower to suggest feminine openness.

Flower-muscle that slowly opens back
the anemone to another meadow—dawn,
until her womb can feel the polyphonic
light of the sonorous heavens pouring down;

muscle of an infinite acceptance,
stretched within the silent blossom-star,
at times *so* overpowered with abundance
that sunset's signal for repose is bare-

ly able to return your too far hurled-
back petals for the darkness to revive:
you, strength and purpose of how many worlds!

We violent ones remain a little longer.
Ah but, *when* in which of all our lives,
shall we at last be open and receivers (1986:81).

It seems to take a little longer for men to be "open and receivers" then women, perhaps because the male temperament is more turbulent. In a letter about the German expressionists (artists whose work is infused with strong feelings), Rilke lamented,

All these voices can hardly help. The expressionist, that inner-man becomes explosive, who pours the lava of his boiling mood over all things, to insist that the chance form in which the crust hardens is the new, the coming, the valid outline of existence, is simply a desperate man and one may let the honest ones among them go ahead and blow off steam. Perhaps through these striking and importunate manifestations...men's eyes will be diverted from the delicate growth of that which really, little by little, will show itself as the future (1948:204).

Once men and women have become receptors, their task is to remain open. It is easy to be "overpowered with [the] abundance" of what one sees and close down again. To quote the famous lines from the first "Elegy," "For Beauty is nothing but the beginning of terror, which we still are just able to endure, and we are so awed because it serenely disdains to annihilate us" (1983:79). If the seer remains open during this terror, the rewards are great. Rilke said,

But as soon as we acknowledge its [life's] dreadfulness (not as opponents: what kind of match could we be for it?), but somehow with a confidence that this very dreadfulness may be something completely *ours*, though something that is just now too great, too vast, too incomprehensible for our learning hearts—: as soon as we accept life's most terrifying dreadfulness, at the risk of perishing from it (i.e., from our own Too much!)—: then an intuition of blessedness will open up for us and, at this cost, will be ours. Whoever does not, sometime or other, give his full consent, his full and *joyous* consent, to the dreadfulness of life, can never take possession of the unutterable abundance and power of our existence; can only walk on its edge, and one day, when the judgement is given, will have been neither alive nor dead. To show the *identity* of dreadfulness and bliss, these two faces on the same divine head, indeed this one *single* face, which just presents itself this way or that, according to our distance from it or the state of mind in which we perceive it—: this is the true significance and purpose of the Elegies and the Sonnets to Orpheus (1984:317).

Indeed, the ability to be open to the awesomeness of existence, its bliss and its terror, is the lifelong task of a shaman. In

Rilke's poem, Orpheus does not only manifest this ability when he embodies the mysteries of the universe in his music, but he is also a trickster, a journeyer between the realms of the dead and the living, and a communicator with animals. Rilke's celebration of Orpheus is a celebration of the shaman.

Giorgio Morandi, like Cézanne, led an austere and solitary existence. Hardly talking to anyone, he lived for forty-five years in the same building in Bologna with his three unmarried sisters and their housekeeper, venturing out only to take long walks and to teach his classes at the University of Bologna where he was a Professor of Etching.[3] As the Italian art historian Luigi Magnini aptly phrased it,

> Painting was his love, the only tie he had with this world....

> If Morandi imposed silence on himself in his relationships with people, he loved to engage in silent dialogue with the world of nature, and he was able to perceive in the most humble of its phenomena like the variations and perfection of the nerve structure of leaves or the curative properties of a plant or fruit, the mystery seen in the inherent law which governs them, intimately corresponding to his own physical and moral being (Des Moines Art Center, 1981:15).

Silence is an important component of seeing. From my own practice of seeing, I can attest that as the dialogue with the object or objects (a dialogue which is usually maintained in silence) deepens over time, one becomes less and less inclined either to listen or engage in idle talk. The practice of seeing promotes a generalized heightening of attention which does not want to be disturbed by chatter.

What topics attracted Morandi's attention? Besides an occasional landscape, Morandi's only subjects were a few dilapidated bottles, canisters, and kerosene lamps which he would endlessly rearrange on a table top, marking their exact position with chalk lines. He looked at these still life objects for about half a century. "You see," Morandi remarked in one of his very few statements, "if I could spend three years looking out of the window up there [at a house], perhaps I could do it" (Des Moines Art Center, 1981:12-13).

The discipline and patience of profound looking was largely absent among his younger contemporaries who were mostly caught up in the fascist or communist passions of twentieth century Italian politics. "The young no longer know how to see," Morandi lamented (Des Moines Art Center, 1981:14). It takes great patience to even look at a Morandi still life properly. The art critic for the *San Francisco Chronicle*, Kenneth Baker, argued in a recent essay on Morandi,

> The placidity of his paintings is a rebuke to the restlessness of our eyes and minds. That compulsive restlessness keeps us from seeing things, including paintings and other representations for what they are. I think he [Morandi] intended to make paintings that can be seen for what they are and which enable us to know seeing for what it is. That is the ambition he shared with Cézanne whose work he revered.

> ...Morandi's painting objectifies the self-discipline we must all learn if we hope for a better world. His art shows us the nature of this discipline—it entails calming the mind and maintaining a relaxed focus on things and tasks at hand. When you make this kind of effort in looking at the paintings, you realize what a crude decision was your initial recognition of their figurative content (Des Moines Art Center, 1981:42-43).

When we concentrate only on the figurative content of Morandi's paintings, i.e., the appearance of the objects at hand, we may not recognize the deeper meaning of his work. Some critics, in fact, believe that Morandi's paintings are banal and boring. In order to understand Morandi's work, it is necessary to slow down, both our mind and our perceptions. Bringing a hurried mind to a Morandi exhibition, we cannot expect to derive anything from his work. Morandi, indeed, tests observers if they are able to appreciate his paintings. The quality of awareness that Morandi engenders in spectators may be carried into their everyday existence. I think this is what Baker means when he said, that "Morandi's painting objectifies the self-discipline we all must learn if we hope for a better world" (Des Moines Art Center, 1981). Of course, to enter Morandi's level and see with his eyes, it may help to live the semi-monastic existence he selected. Our level of seeing is proportionate to the degree that we can slow down our existence. Robert Hughes, another recent commentator on Morandi's life and work, said,

> We owe it to ourselves to be skeptical about saints. Every so often the culture throws up some artist who looks so seraphically indifferent to what Freud listed as the motors of artistic effort—fame, money, and beautiful lovers—that one can barely credit it (1986:160).

Yet, Morandi had to be "indifferent" to fame, money and beautiful lovers if he was to maintain the silence and the slowness necessary to his way of seeing. Also, Morandi himself remarked,

> When most Italian artists of my generation were afraid to be too "modern," too "international" in their style, not "national" or "imperial" enough, I was still left in peace, perhaps because I demanded so little recognition. My privacy was thus my pro-

tection and, in the eyes of the Grand Inquisitors of Italian art, I remained but a provincial professor of etching at the Fine Arts Academy at Bologna (quoted in Roditi, 1961:61).

Morandi's almost Tao-like indifference to worldly acclaim enabled him to survive and to continue painting during the fascist regime in Italy. Arthur Waley once commented on the Chinese Zen Painter, Mu Chi's "Six Persimmons" (Illustration 4), that it was a "passion...congealed into a stupendous calm" (1958:231). This could also be said about Morandi's paintings. It is as though Morandi channeled all his passion into the process of concentrated seeing, arriving at a "stupendous calm" that is reflected in the objects he painted.

Morandi's way of seeing, as embodied in his paintings, has for me stronger affinities with the Zen perception of reality encountered in Chinese and Japanese painting than the still life tradition of Western art. This Zen perception of reality is very close to some aspects of shamanic seeing.

When we compare Morandi's "Still Life" of 1959 (Illustration 3) to Mu Chi's "Six Persimmons" (13th century, Illustration 4), we are struck with the radical simplicity of both paintings. In each, the artist suspended a handful of objects in an indeterminate space. Not only do some of the objects appear to float in a void, they are also interpenetrated by the void. I am reminded of the Buddhist tenet, "form is emptiness, emptiness is form," a tenet which can be tested through the experience of seeing. At the last stage in the process of Zen or shamanic seeing, the boundary line of the object is dissolved and it merges with the background to become an energy field. In Mu Chi's painting, the contour line of the persimmon on the far left is broken and its interior space bleeds into the space of the background and dissolves. In Morandi's painting, the middle area of the bottles and canisters likewise merges with the surrounding foreground.

Cézanne and the Cubists (Picasso and Braque) also used

this technique of allowing a three-dimensional object to merge with its environment in order to reassert the two-dimensional quality of the painted surface. Yet, in the case of Morandi, the dissolution of the object appears to go beyond mere aesthetic concerns; the object/void has a numinous presence that is not found in the paintings of Cézanne and the Cubists. Further similarities between Morandi's and Mu Chi's still-lives are the economy of descriptive formal means, the irregular placement of the objects, and the absence of a recognizable light source. Both Morandi and Mu Chi are not concerned with the detailed appearance of the objects; they are more interested in investigating the essential oblongness of a canister or the squatness of a persimmon. Moreover their objects do not obey the laws of gravity; there is no indication of a ground line for the irregularly placed objects, nor is there any consistent outside light source or any other clues to indicate the time of day or the surrounding environment. Morandi's and Mu Chi's objects exist, indeed, outside of time and space; for them, the physical object is a starting point for a metaphysical investigation into the qualities of thingness. The Italian critic Roberto Longhi was fond of citing the following passage from Marcel Proust to explain Morandi's efforts but it could also be used to express those of Mu Chi.

"The reality to be expressed, I now understood," muses the Narrator, "resided not in the appearance of the subject but in the degree of penetration...the sound of the spoon on the plate, this weighted stiffness of the napkin, had been more precious for my spiritual renewal than all the humanitarian, patriotic and internationalist conversations" (quoted in Hughes, 1986:186).

Morandi's paintings were, in fact, regarded highly by the Strapese, a group of Bolognese artists and critics active during the 1920s. They celebrated the understated poetry of the most ordinary objects—much like the Narrator in the passage from Proust.[4]

Manifesting the poetry of ordinary objects in art doesn't seem much like the work of a traditional shaman, yet Morandi, along with many shamans, devoted his life to extending his powers of perception through solitude, silence, patience, and prolonged looking. Moreover, he presents in his paintings an essentially shamanic mode of apprehending the world; he goes beyond the surface appearance of objects in search for their innermost essence and sees these objects in the context of their space-time continuum—not as isolated, individual things.

Giorgio de Chirico, whose life and painting I am going to discuss extensively in the chapter on Dreaming, wrote an interesting statement about the process of seeing that parallels Morandi's method of shamanic seeing. "One can deduce and conclude that every object has two aspects," he said,

> one current one which we see nearly always and which is seen by men in general, and the other which is spectral and metaphysical and is seen only by rare individuals in moments of clairvoyance and metaphysical abstractions, just as certain hidden bodies formed of materials that are impenetrable to the sun's rays only appear under the power of artificial lights, which could, for example, be X-rays. For some time, however, I have been inclined to believe that objects can possess other aspects apart from the two cited above: there are third, fourth, and fifth aspects, all different from the first, but closely related to the second or metaphysical aspect (quoted in Carra, 1971:89).

In de Chirico's "Seer" of 1915, an eyeless mannequin is seated in front of a blackboard with cryptic writings in chalk. The traditional seer, beginning with Homer, is often portrayed as eyeless because his or her visions go inward. Indeed, the white lines on the chalkboard in de Chirico's painting may relate to the seer's X-ray vision. Another reference to the seer in de Chirico's work is the "Portrait of Apollinaire" (1914) which shows a bust of the poet wearing dark glasses. According to Maurizio Fagliolo dell'Arco,

> The dark glasses have inspired much (usually bad) writing and some attempts at interpretation based on chance. Actually they represent an expedient for visualizing the blinding quality of poetic light (Apollinaire spoke of it in his note on the Orpheus poems), which can be understood also in a hermetic and mysteriosophical vein. They are an attribute of the seer, like Homer blind, but also like the sooth-sayer Tiresias about whom Apollinaire was to write his famous play (quoted in Rubin, 1982:28).

Arco does not mention, however, that in back of the bust of Apollinaire is a dark silhouette of a man who bears spectral white markings similar to those on the blackboard in the "Seer" of 1915. Thus, in the "Portrait of Apollinaire," we may also have a reference to the X-ray vision of the seer.

Frida Kahlo also developed the X-ray vision of a seer after an automobile accident at the age of nineteen in which she broke her spinal bone in three places, smashed her foot and leg, and shattered her pelvis. Although she experienced periods of relative health, she was often in pain and had to undergo thirty-two operations to arrest the slow decline of her skeletal system. As her close friend, the writer Andres Henestrosa once commented, "She lived dying" (quoted in Herrera, 1983:62).

A year after her accident, Kahlo began painting. She said,

> I never thought of painting until 1926, when I was in bed on account of an automobile accident. I was bored as hell in bed with a plaster cast..., so I decided to do something (quoted in Herrera, 1983:63).

> From that time [of the accident]... my obsession was to begin again, painting things just as I saw them with my own eyes and nothing more....Thus, as the accident changed my path, many things prevented me from fulfilling the desires which everyone considers normal, and to me nothing seemed more normal than to paint what had not been fulfilled (quoted in Herrera, 1983:74-75).

Kahlo's accident became an opening into the field of painting. In tribal cultures, the individual who is deflected from his or her "normal" path by accident or disease is also often a candidate for shamanic initiation. According to Joan Halifax, in *Shaman: The Wounded Healer*,

> The realization of power occurs most frequently in the midst of an ordeal, a crisis involving an encounter with death. It comes suddenly, in an instant....The entrance to the other world occurs through the action of total disruption (1982:10).

There is some debate among contemporary practitioners of shamanic techniques and scholars of shamanism as to whether it is necessary to be "wounded" to have shamanic experiences and discover significant healing powers. In contrast to the ideas of Halifax and Eliade, Michael Harner found, during his field work, that sickness or an ordeal is not always a prerequisite to become a shaman in traditional culture. Ruth-

Inge Heinze is in accord with this point. However, based on her own field data, she has warned that intense journeys, undertaken too early during a neophyte's training or embarked upon by uncommitted individuals, may lead to mental or physical breakdowns which do not allow the emergence of healing powers. In brief, not every breakdown leads to deep insights and quite a few victims have been found, incurably wounded, by the wayside.

I think that the "entrance to the other world" through accident or serious illness may partly be the result of a breakdown of everyday routine which enables the individual to have different experiences than "normal" people. To quote Rilke again from the *Letters to a Young Poet*,

> You have had many and great sadnesses, which passed. And you say that even this passing was hard for you and put you out of sorts. But, please, consider whether these great sadnesses have not rather gone right through the center of yourself? Whether much in you has not altered, whether you have not somewhere, at some point of your being, undergone a change while you were sad? Only those sadnesses are dangerous and bad which one carries about among people in order to drown them out; like sicknesses that are superficially and foolishly treated they simply withdraw and after a little pause break out again the more dreadfully; and accumulate within one and are life, are unlived, spurned, lost life, of which one may die. Were it possible for us to see further than our knowledge reaches, and yet a little way beyond the outworks of our divining, perhaps we could endure our sadnesses with greater confidence than our joys. For they are the moments when something new has entered into us, something unknown; our feelings grow mute in shy perplexity, everything in us with-

draws, a stillness comes, and the new, which no one knows, stands in the midst of it and is silent (1962:63-64).

In traditional Australian aboriginal societies, for example, boys are wounded and undergo a descent into the underworld during their initiation into adulthood. In modern cultures, where no traditional initiation rites facilitate entry into non-ordinary reality as part of the maturation process, a life-threatening illness may, indeed, be the gateway to the lower or upper realms.

As a result of her accident, Kahlo was instantly transformed from a typical upper-middle class teenage girl in Mexico City into a woman with heightened powers of seeing. In a letter to a friend, she wrote,

> Why do you study so much? What secret are you looking for? Life will reveal it to you soon. I already know it all, without reading or writing....I was a child [before the accident] who went about in a world of colors, of hard and tangible forms. Everything was mysterious and something was hidden, guessing what it was was a game for me. If you knew how terrible it is to know suddenly, as if a bolt of lightning elucidated the earth. Now I live in a painful planet, transparent as ice; but it is as if I had learned everything at once in seconds. My friends, my companions became women slowly, I became old in instants, and everything today is bland and lucid. I know that nothing lies behind, if there were something I would see it (quoted in Herrera, 1983:75).

I believe that Kahlo's heightened ability to see was sustained by the presence of death in her life. When one is continually threatened with death, it is not only impossible to be occupied with trivialities, but there is an awareness of the importance of the moment which leads to enhanced powers of seeing. The relationship between seeing and death is directly reflected in the "Self-Portrait" (1943) in which Kahlo painted an image of a skull with crossbones on the forehead, midway between the eyes—the precise location of the third eye.

In Carlos Castaneda's *Journey to Ixtlan*, Don Juan found the mark of the shaman/warrior is "to ask death's advice and drop the cursed pettiness that belongs to men that live their lives as if death will never tap them" (1974:35). The notion of asking death's advice or being directed by the presence of death is an important concept in Spanish and Latin American literature.

The poet Federico Garcia Lorca, for example, made a distinction between three kinds of artistic inspirational force: the angel, the muse, and the *duende*. He said that,

> The angel dazzles, but he flies high over a man's head, shedding his grace, and the man effortlessly realizes his work or his charm or his dance....

> The muse dictates and sometimes prompts. She can do relatively little, for she is so distant and so tired (I saw her twice) that one would have to give her half a heart of marble....The muse awakens the intelligence, bringing a landscape of columns and a false taste of laurels. But intelligence is often the enemy of poetry, because it limits too much, and it elevates the poet to a sharp-edged throne where he forgets that ants could eat him or that a great arsenic lobster could fall on his head—things against which the muses that live in monocles and in the lukewarm lacquered roses of tiny salons are quite helpless (1975:44).

For Lorca, however,

The duende [spirit of death] does not come at all unless he sees that death is possible....

With idea, sound, or gesture, the duende enjoys fighting the creator on the very rim of the well. Angel and muse escape with violin and compass; the duende wounds. In the healing of that wound, which never closes, lies the invented, strange qualities of a man's work (1975:49-50).

Frida Kahlo's paintings are filled with images of a wound that never closes. In 1944, after one of her thirty-two operations to arrest the decline of her skeletal system, Kahlo created the "Broken Column" (Illustration 5) showing the artist encased in a brace which holds together the split halves of her body. In the red gash between the halves, a cracked column extends from her pelvic area to her neck. Copious tears run down her face, nails have been driven into her body, and the rents in the earth behind her emphasize her anguish.

"I paint myself because I am so often alone," Kahlo maintained, "because I am the subject I know best" (quoted in Herrera, 1983:74).

Yet, Kahlo's work is not self-indulgent or narcissistic. The Spanish poet Antonio Machado once said,

And I thought also that a man can overtake by surprise some of the phrases of his inward conversations with himself, distinguishing the living voice from the dead echoes; that he, looking inward, can glimpse the deep rooted images, the things of feeling which all men possess (1983:14).

Kahlos's intense and concentrated insight into her own physical and psychic condition went beyond the personal.

The "Broken Column" recalls shamanic paintings of skeletization in which the body is revealed like in an X-ray.

These paintings record the shamanic practice of ritual death and rebirth in a trance/visionary state. The shaman sees his/her flesh stripped by wild animals. The bones are exposed to the healing power of the sun and then the body is put back together again. Because, after a trauma in ordinary reality, shamans can put themselves back together again in a trance state, they gain, through this experience of crisis resolution, the ability to help others. Kahlo's paintings have a therapeutic influence on others and attest to the power an individual can call upon to overcome illness.

Another painting that records the anguish following a spinal operation is the "Little Deer" (1946). Kahlo created a portrait of herself with antlers and the body of a stag. Pierced with arrows, the stag runs through a forest strewn with broken trees and a broken leafy branch—possibly a symbol of her lost youth.

In the shamanism practiced by the Mexican Huichol, the Sacred Deer, *Maxa Kwaxi-Kauyumari*, is the intermediary between the Huichols and the spirit world. *Kauyumari* appears to the shaman in an altered mental state as an instructor and guide. Arrows are also often identified with the horns of *Kauyumari* because, in Huichol myth, *Kauyumari* got its horns when *Tatewari*, the god of the fire, placed his ceremonial arrows on *Kauyumari's* head (Myerhoff, 1974:86). Kahlo's appropriation of the *Maxa Kwaxi-Kauyumari* imagery is no accident. Although the wounded deer is a graphic symbol of suffering, it is also an affirmation of her role as shaman.

André Breton, the surrealism movement's founder, identified Kahlo's painting as being surrealistic.

> My surprise and joy was unbounded when I discovered, on my arrival in Mexico, that her work has blossomed forth, in her latest paintings, into pure surreality, despite the fact that it had been conceived without any prior knowledge whatsoever of

the ideas motivating the activities of my friends and myself. Yet, at this present point in the development of Mexican painting, which since the beginning of the nineteenth century has remained largely free from foreign influence and profoundly attached to its own resources, I was witnessing here, at the other end of the earth, a spontaneous outpouring of our own questioning spirit: what irrational laws do we obey, what subjective signals allow us to establish the right direction at any moment, which symbols and myths predominate in a particular conjunction of objects or web of happenings, what meanings can be ascribed to the eye's capacity to pass from visual to visionary power (1972a:144)?

Although Breton rightly understood that Kahlo's seeing went beyond mere visual power, there is only a superficial similarity between the work of Frida Kahlo and the surrealists. In an attempt to explore the unconscious, surrealist painters such as Dali, Magritte and Leonora Carrington fixed the often disjointed and distorted imagery of dreams in their paintings through illusionistic means. Yet, as Frida Kahlo herself argued, "They thought I was a Surrealist, but I wasn't. I never painted dreams. I painted my own reality" (quoted in Herrera, 1983:266).

Dreaming and the interpretation of dreams is, indeed, an important shamanic practice to gain knowledge, but Kahlo was a seer, not a dreamer. In an altered state of consciousness produced by pain, solitude, and threat of death, she painted her inner psychic terrain with great clarity and precision. Her husband, the artist Diego Rivera, even called her a realist.

Monumental realism is expressed to the smallest dimensions; tiny heads are sculpted as if they were colossal. So they appear when the magic of a projector magnifies them to the size of a wall. When the photomicroscope enlarges the background of Frida's paintings, reality becomes apparent. The web of veins and the network of cells are distinct, although they lack some elements, giving a new dimension to the art of painting....

Frida's art is individual-collective. Her realism is so monumental that everything has "n" dimensions. Consequently, she paints at the same time the exterior and interior of herself and the world (quoted in Herrera, 1983:260).

Kahlo's power as artist and shaman became visible in her ability to express the "exterior and interior of herself and the world" in the most concrete terms.

Max Ernst has also directed his powers of seeing to the interior realms of his psyche and has expressed the content of these interior realms in his paintings, collages and frottages, albeit in more elliptical ways than Kahlo. In *Ecritures*, his memoirs written near the end of this life, Ernst claimed,

Seeing was my first preoccupation [as a child]. My eyes were open not only to the astonishing world that assailed me from without, but also this other mysterious and disquieting world that insistently and regularly gushed forth and faded in my dreams of adolescence. "Clear seeing" became a necessity for my nervous equilibrium (1970:12; French, translation mine).

For Ernst seeing was also a principal function of art. He was quoted by art critic Wieland Schmied as saying,

Direct, true seeing has been lost in the lumber of the centuries. But in every period there have been painters able to recover it. They are the true revolutionaries of art (1973:20-21).

"Direct true seeing" became the motivating force behind Ernst's early to midlife-artistic career, and it was in the process of directing his seeing to the inner realms of psyche that he discovered there was a fundamental relationship between these inner realms and the outside world. In *Beyond Painting*, his writings on art at mid-career (1936), Ernst recalled,

(1897) First contact with hallucination [at age seven]. Measles. Fear of death and the annihilating powers. A fever-vision provoked by an imitation-mahogany panel opposite his bed, the grooves of the wood taking successively the aspect of an eye, a nose, a bird's head, *a menacing nightingale*, a spinning top and so on. Certainly little Max took pleasure in being afraid of these visions and later delivered himself voluntarily to provoke hallucinations of the same kind in looking obstinately at wood panels, clouds, wallpapers, unplastered walls and so on to let his "imagination" go (1948:28).

Looking obstinately, as Ernst did, is essentially a subjective technique of disassociation that goes beyond the ordinary appearance of the object to uncover the contents of his psyche at the particular moment of seeing. In *Ecritures*, Ernst linked obstinate looking, which he also called *regarde irrite*, to trance, clairvoyance and paranoid schizophrenia. "These are states," said Ernst, "that allow us to see and live as if time [ordinary reality] does not exist" (1972:426). Ernst believed that the method of *regarde irrite* was employed by Leonardo da Vinci and quoted the following passage by André Breton in *Beyond Painting*.

Leonardo's lesson, setting his students to copy in their pictures that which they saw taking shape in the spots on an old wall (each according to his own lights) is far from being understood. The whole passage from subjectivity to objectivity is implicitly resolved there, and the weight of that resolution goes far beyond, in human interest, the weight of inspiration itself....The new associations of images brought forth by the poet, the artist, the scientist, are comparable to it, inasmuch as their creation uses a screen of a particular structure which, concretely, can either be a decrepit wall, a cloud or anything else: a persistent and vague sound carries to the exclusion of all others, the phrase we need to hear. The most striking fact is that an activity of this kind which in order to exist necessitates the unreserved acceptance of a more or less lasting passivity, far from being limited to the sensory world, has been able to penetrate profoundly the moral world. The good luck, the happiness of the scientist or the artist in their *discovery* can only be considered as a particular case, not distinguished in its essence from ordinary human happiness. Some day, man will be able to direct himself if, like the artist he will consent to reproduce, without changing anything, that which an appropriate screen can offer him in advance of his acts. This screen exists. Every life contains some these homogeneous entities, of cracked or cloudy appearance, which each of us has only to consider fixedly in order to read his own future. He should enter the whirlwind, he should retrace the stream of events which, above all others, seemed to him doubtful or obscure and by which he was harassed. There—if his interrogation is worth the effort—all the logical principles will be routed and the powers of the objective hazard, making a joke of all probability, will come to his aid. On the screen, everything which man wants to know is written in phosphorescent letters, in letters of desire (Ernst, 1948:11).

According to Breton, Leonardo's method enables the viewer to predict events. One could compare the spots on the wall to the hexagrams of the I-Ching; although the spots are supposedly picked out at random, "a persistent and vague sound carries to the exclusion of all others, the phrase we need to hear." The spots and the hexagrams are, indeed, elements of the "objective hazard, making a joke of all probability" (Ernst, 1948:11).

Along with Breton, Ernst was also aware of the idea of objective hazard. In *Beyond Painting*, he quoted Hume's definition of hazard, "the equivalent of ignorance in which we find ourselves in relation to the real causes of events" (1948:16). The spots seem to have been selected by chance only because the reasons behind the selection are not known. Ernst may even have had the I-Ching in mind when he thought of Leonardo's dots. Hans Arp, his good friend during his Dadaist period, was well acquainted with this text.[5]

The origins of the I-Ching are probably shamanic. When shamans in tribal cultures need information to clarify a situation or foretell the course of events, one of the seeing techniques they employ is to find a stone or another object with markings and they will then interpret these markings. Breton thought everyone can read the markings or this "screen," but it takes a person with heightened powers of seeing to read spots on the wall, the markings on a stone or the hexagrams of the I-ching with a good degree of success.

Since Leonardo's method of *regarde irrite* is intended to provoke the psyche into revealing its interior contents, it is different from other types of shamanic seeing. It is unlike those of Van Gogh, Cézanne, Morandi, or Rilke, in which the starting point is an empirical investigation into the properties of the object(s). Nevertheless, as Breton strongly emphasized in this passage, there is an objective element in the process of *regarde irrite* which goes beyond purely arbitrary subjective association. Ernst was able to gain objective knowledge about the contents of his own psyche which, at times, mirrored the zeitgeist or manifested, in his best works, the archetypes of the collective unconscious.

Ernst's first applied *regarde irrite* to the creation of works of art in the form of collages. He wrote, in *Beyond Painting*,

> One rainy day in 1919, finding myself in a village on the Rhine, I was struck by the obsession which held under my gaze the pages of an illustrated catalogue showing objects designed for anthropologic, microscopic, psychologic, mineralogic, and paleontologic demonstration. There I found brought together elements of figuration so remote that the sheer absurdity of that collection provoked a sudden intensification of the visionary faculties in me and brought forth an illusive succession of contradictory images, double, triple and multiple images, piling up on each other with the persistence and rapidity which are peculiar to lover memories and visions of half-sleep.

> These visions called themselves new planes, because of their meeting in a new unknown (the plane of non-agreement). It was enough at that time to embellish these catalogue pages, in painting or drawing, and thereby in gently reproducing only that which *saw itself in me*, a color, a pencil mark, a landscape foreign to the represented objects, the desert, a tempest, a geological cross-section, a floor, a single straight line signifying the horizon... thus I obtained a faithful fixed image of my hallu-

cination and transformed into revealing dramas my most secret desires—from what had been only some banal pages of advertising (1948:14).

"Two Ambiguous Figures" (1919) is a good example of Ernst's collage technique. Ernst did not glue any of the elements (1948:14) but juxtaposed apparently unrelated images by elaborating advertisements of technological apparatus into two distinctly menacing figures in a claustrophobic box-like space. "Two Ambiguous Figures" has a nightmarish quality which may allude to both Ernst's dreadful experience in the first World War as an artillery officer (the figures appear to be wearing protective goggles or gas masks) and the disturbed period of post-war Germany. In *Beyond Painting*, Ernst related his technique of collage to "the simple hallucination, after Rimbaud." He also quoted the following passage from "Une Saison en Enfer."

I accustomed myself to simple hallucination: I saw quite deliberately a mosque in place of a factor, a drummers' school conducted by angels, carriages on the highways of the sky, a salon at the bottom of a lake; monsters, mysteries, a vaudeville poster raising horrors before my eyes. Then I expressed my magic sophisms with the hallucination of words (1948:14).

Rimbaud's hallucination manifesting in words can be compared to Ernst's hallucination of images manifesting in collages. What he said in *Beyond Painting*, as well as other remarks which I will discuss later, suggests that Ernst was influenced by Rimbaud's idea of the seer.[6]

For the moment, I wish to point out that Ernst's collage technique was also influenced by Nietzsche. In 1909, as a student at the University of Cologne, Ernst became enamored with the work of Nietzsche, particularly *Die fröhliche*

Wissenschaft (The Gay Science; Waldberg, 1958:60). Nietzsche wrote in paragraph 58 of the Second Book,

> *Only as creators!* [italics his]—This has given me the greatest trouble and still does: to realize what things *are called* is incomparably more important than what they are. The reputation, name, and appearance, the usual measure and weight of a thing, what it counts for—originally almost always wrong and arbitrary, thrown over things like a dress and altogether foreign to their nature and even to their skin—all this grows from generation unto generation, merely because people believe it, until it gradually grows to be part of the thing and turns into its very body. What at first was appearance becomes in the end, almost invariably, the essence and is effective as such. How foolish it would be to suppose that one only needs to point out this origin and this misty shroud of delusion in order to destroy the world that counts for real, so called *"reality."* We can destroy only as creators.—But let us not forget this either: it is enough to create new names and estimations and probabilities in order to create in the long run new things (1974:121-122).

For Nietzsche, "so called reality" is an arbitrary mass delusion that is produced by the habitual consensus of naming, a point that is also continually reiterated in Castaneda's books and is known to any shaman who is "professionally" entering non-ordinary reality. Ernst's collages also question the accepted identity of objects. He remarked himself, in *Ecritures*,

> everyone knows that the notion of the identity of objects implies that in each being, in each object, in each idea, the simultaneous or successive presence of an infinity of contradictions....The principal of

ambiguity which is the true essence of my collages, furnished me the means of finding imaginary solutions where everything is permitted and nothing is false (1970:425, in French, translation mine).

The multiple identity of objects in Ernst's collages had an important influence on the formation of the surrealist movement. Breton was keenly aware of the philosophical importance of collage in his "Preface" to the Max Ernst Exhibition of 1921, three years before he wrote the first of his *Manifestoes of Surrealism*. In the "Preface," Breton said that collage is

> the wonderful power to grasp two mutually distant realities without going beyond the field of our experience and to draw a spark from their juxtaposition; to bring within reach of our senses abstract forms capable of the same intensity and distinctness as others; and, while depriving us of any system of reference, to put us out of place in our very recollection—that is what, at the moment, he is concerned with...May it not be that we are thus getting ready to break loose some day from the law of identity (quoted in Ernst, 1948:22).

Breaking loose from "the law of identity" became the raison d'être of the surrealist movement; it precipitated a revolution of consciousness that was to undermine the established intellectual, social and political order. For the surrealists, changing the inner reality of consciousness is fundamentally related to changing the outer order of events. In an essay "Was ist Surrealism?" written in 1934, Ernst said,

> The fundamental opposition between meditation and action (according to Classical philosophy) coincides with the fundamental separation between

the inner and outer worlds. Here lies the universal significance of Surrealism....They freely and boldly move in an undefined land on the frontier between the inner and the outer worlds, which does not exclude the physical and psychic reality (the surreal), and they register what they see and experience (quoted in Schmied, 1973:23).

Although Ernst was only a peripheral participant in surrealist activities, he had great sympathy for the surrealist revolutionary program. In *Beyond Painting*, for example, Ernst argued,

We do not doubt that in yielding quite naturally to the vocation of pushing back appearances and upsetting the relations of "realities," it is helping, with a smile on its lips, to hasten the general crisis of consciousness due in our time (1948:25).

In 1925, Ernst developed a technique, analogous to collage, that also ruptured the identity of objects. Ernst gave an account of his discovering this process of frottage in *Beyond Painting*.

Beginning with a memory of childhood...in the course of which a panel of false mahogany, situated in front of my bed, had played the role of optical *provocateur* of a vision of half-sleep, and finding myself one rainy evening in a seaside inn, I was struck by the obsession that showed to my excited gaze the floor-boards upon which a thousand scrubbings had deepened the grooves. I decided then to investigate the symbolism of this obsession and, in order to aide my meditative and hallucinatory faculties, I made from the boards a series of drawings by placing on them, at random, sheets of paper which I undertook to rub with black lead. In gazing attentively at the drawings thus obtained, "the dark passages and those of a gently lighted penumbra," I was surprised by the sudden intensification of my visionary capacities and by the hallucinatory succession of contradictory images superimposed, one upon the other, with the persistence and rapidity characteristic of amorous memories.

My curiosity awakened and astonished, I began to experiment indifferently and to question, utilizing the same means, all sorts of materials to be found in my visual field: leaves and veins, the ragged edges of a bit of linen, the brushstrokes of a "modern" painting, the unwound thread from a spool, etc....

I insist on the fact that the drawings thus obtained lost more, through a series of suggestions and transmutations that offered themselves spontaneously—in the manner of that which passes for hypnagogic visions—the character of the material interrogated (the wood, for example) and took on the aspect of images of an unhoped-for precision, probably of a sort which revealed the first cause of the obsession, or produced a simulacrum of that cause.

The procedure of *frottage*, resting thus upon nothing more than the intensification of the irritability of the mind's faculties by appropriate technical means, excluding all conscious mental guidance (of reason, taste, morals), reducing to the extreme the active part of that one whom we have called, up to now, the "author" of the work, this procedure is revealed by the following to be the real equivalent of that which is known by the term *automatic writing*. It is a spectator that the author assists, indifferent or passionate, at the birth of his work and watches the phases of his development. Even as the role of the poet, since the celebrated *lettre de voyant* of Rimbaud, consists in writing according to the dictates of that which articulates itself in him, so the role of the painter is to pick out and *project that which sees itself in him*. In finding myself more and more engrossed in this activity (passivity) which later came to be called "critical paranoia," and in adapting to the technical means of painting (for example: the scraping of pigments upon a ground prepared in colors and placed on an uneven surface) the procedure of *frottage* which seemed applicable at first only to drawing, and in striving more and more to restrain my own active participation in the unfolding of the picture, and, finally be widening in this way the active part of the mind's hallucinatory faculties, I came to assist as *spectator* at the birth of all my works....A man of "ordinary constitution" (I employ here the words of Rimbaud), I have done everything to render my soul myself monstrous. Blind swimmer, I have made myself see. *I have seen*. And I was surprised and enamored of what I *saw*, wishing to identify myself with it (1948:7-9).

In a footnote to the above quoted passage, Ernst said that "critical paranoia," a phrase elaborated by Salvador Dali, is a

rather pretty term (and one which will probably have some success because of its paradoxical content) which seems to me to be subject to precaution inasmuch as the notion of paranoia is employed there in a sense which doesn't correspond to its medical meaning. I prefer, on the other hand, the proposition of Rimbaud: "The poet becomes a *seer*,

by a long, immense and conscious disorder of all the
senses" (1948:8).

In frottage as with collage the "intensification of the
visionary faculties" and the "hallucinatory succession of
contradictory images" appear to be the main operating principles. I think, however, Ernst believed that frottage is more
akin to the automatic writing of the surrealists than collage
because the user of this technique becomes a "spectator" at the
birth of his/her work, restraining "active participation in the
unfolding of the picture." Like Rimbaud, who denied the
"active participation" of the ego and rational faculties through
the systematic derangement of the senses, the user of frottage
can avoid "mental guidance" and become a seer. By eschew-
ing authorship (the ego and the rational faculties), the seer
"renders the soul monstrous" (the French word "monstreux"
is closer to the English words "prodigious" or "awesome"
than "monstrous").

Yet, Ernst was hardly a man of "ordinary constitution,"
just as Rimbaud's constitution was hardly ordinary. Ernst was
a natural seer who, since childhood, could provoke a series of
hallucinatory images through the technique of obstinate looking. He therefore employed the raw data of collage and
frottage to good advantage. Indeed, the processes of collage
and frottage merely intensified Ernst's already existing faculty of seeing.

Ernst's principal endeavor in the media of frottage is
"Histoire Naturelle," a collection of thirty-four pencil rub-
bings that he selected from the hundreds he made during the
last six months of 1925. Wheels, birds, and eyes in exotic
landscapes are the most prevalent images in this collection.

In "The Wheel of Light" (Illustration 6), Ernst elaborated the impressions of the grooves in a wooden floorboard
into the radiating spokes of a wheel that doubles as the iris of
an enormous floating eye.

The conflation of the eyes and the wheel, which occurs

also in several other frottages of "Historie Naturelle," suggests for me the archetypal form of the *mandala* that is used as a visualization diagram to access non-ordinary reality.

There is no evidence to indicate that Ernst had any familiarity with mandalas or shamanic imagery, but it is safe to say that the seeing level was an important theme of his work. I think, Ernst acknowledged the latter in a somewhat cryptic comment on "Histoire Naturelle," "As the Universe loses its opacity, it blends with mankind. So to rid himself of his blindness is the first duty of man" (quoted in Schmied, 1973:21). In restraining "active participation" in the creation of a work of art, the form of frottage allowed Ernst to go further into uncovering archetypal contents.

Although there are images that can be related to seeing, for example, the goggled figures in the collage, "Two Ambiguous Figures," a wholly different level of seeing manifested in the "Histoire Naturelle." Ernst went beyond mirroring the psychic malaise of his time. The frottage images have, indeed, a numinous presence that seems to be absent in the earlier collages.

In shamanic art, the bird, which appears quite frequently in the "Histoire Naturelle," is also an important symbol of seeing, because it has the ability to fly over large distances and observe things from above. It is a powerful ally of the shaman/ seer who needs a detached and overall vision of a particular problem or situation.

During the early thirties, following "Histoire Naturelle," images of birds became increasingly important in Ernst's oeuvre. Ernst exclaimed,

In 1930, after having furiously and methodically composed my novel, "La femme 100 têtes," I was visited almost daily by Loplop, Bird superior, a private phantom very much attached and devoted to me (quoted in Spies, 1983:9).

Ever since he was a young boy, Ernst had identified himself with birds and, in middle age, he even began to resemble a bird with his sharp facial features, piercing eyes, and white plumes of hair. In *Beyond Painting*, he wrote about the beginning of his relationship with birds.

> (1906) First contact with occult, magic and witch-craft powers. One of his best friends, a most intel-ligent, and affectionate pink cockatoo, died in the night of January 5th. It was an awful shock to Max when he found the corpse in the morning and when, at the same moment, his father announced to him, the birth of sister Loni. The *perturbation* of the youth was so enormous that he fainted. In his imagination he connected both events and charged the baby with extinction of the bird's life....A dan-gerous confusion between birds and human became encrusted in his mind and asserted itself in his drawings and paintings. The obsession haunted him until he erected the *Birds Memorial Monument* in 1927, and even later Max identified himself volun-tarily with *Loplop*, the *Superior of the Birds*. This phantom remained inseparable from another one called *Perturbation ma soeur, la femme 100 têtes* (1948:28).

I think the death of the bird was a traumatic experience for Ernst because intuitively he thought that it was a physical representation of his power animal in non-ordinary reality. The method of frottage enabled Ernst later to access his power animal in non-ordinary reality.

As I mentioned before, the bird in shamanic art is linked with seeing, so it was a particularly appropriate power animal for Ernst, the seer and proto-surrealist who was a mediator between ordinary and non-ordinary reality in his art. The bird in shamanic cultures is also the vehicle or psychopomp. "La femme 100 têtes" contains a whole section, entitled "The eye without eye, the hundred headless woman keeps her secret" with images of Loplop and eyes.

In his essay on Ernst's collage novels, Evan Maurer affirmed that at least "ten of the eighteen collages in the chapter deal with vision, one of Ernst's most central concerns" (1986:69). The imagery also included depictions of individuals with their eyes closed, apparently having some kind of inward visionary experience. The title of the section itself suggests, indeed, eyeless, interior seeing. All the imagery of the volume was composed of book and newspaper illustrations from the nineteenth century put together and photographed by Ernst. Diane Waldman remarked, in her catalogue essay from the 1975 Guggenheim Museum retrospective of Ernst's works,

> Ernst took the process of collage one step further than anyone had previously done. Rather than disposing the fragments of collage as separate elements upon the picture plane, as the Cubists had done, or allowing them to become a source of shock because of their mundane nature, Ernst created a unified image from the fragments and identified them as a single entity on the picture plane...[so that] the illogical scale of these images produces a disorienting effect that has little to do with the seeming innocence of the individual illustrations (1975:26).

By creating a seamless web of images, however disparate in scale and unrelated to each other, Ernst enabled the viewer to suspend disbelief in the alternate universe he created. Throughout "La femme 100 têtes," objects and animals are distorted in scale, have multiple identities, hover in space, and metamorphose into humans or vice versa.

These are the kind of events that also happen in

shamanic journeys into non-ordinary reality. Ernst's photo-collage novel has, indeed, the intensity, completeness, and consistency of a shamanic journey.

Although "La femme 100 têtes" is a work of great visual and hallucinatory power, no new information about seeing other than that which had already presented itself in frottage became evident in this novel and other works, specifically related to seeing which, with decreasing frequency, were created later. Along with other art historians, I believe that, with some notable exceptions, Ernst's work declined in quality from the mid-thirties onward.

Loplop was largely absent in his later works and it was highly probable that his bird ally had left him. That power animals may leave is a known fact among shamans.

Gordon Onslow-Ford, the artist I chose to discuss next, was, like Max Ernst, interested in surrealism but gradually grew out it. As a young artist he was particularly influenced by André Breton's notion that the use of automatic writing and painting, which circumvents the rational mind and the ego or small self, could create a "Supreme Point" in which a bridge between the subjective interior psyche of the artist and the collective unconscious as well as the objective reality is established (Carrouges, 1974:11-20). Breton even defined surrealism in the first of his *Manifestoes of Surrealism* (1924) as

> Pure psychic automatism in its pure state, by which one proposes to express—verbally, by means of the written word, or in any other manner—the actual functioning of thought. Dictated by thought, in the absence of any control exercised by reason, exempt from any aesthetic or moral concern (1972b:26).

By 1943, however, Onslow-Ford had largely gone beyond the surrealist methodology of automatism for conscious techniques of seeing that would also arrive at this "Supreme Point." "After SEEING and SEEING," Onslow-Ford asserted, "the pioneer painter becomes a SEER with insight into the vast expanses of the inner-worlds and their correspondences to the nature of the universe" (1978:111). Onslow-Ford elaborated these techniques of seeing in his three books, *Towards a New Subject in Painting* (1948), *Painting in the Instant* (1964), and *Creation* (1978).

While living in a Mexican village between 1941-1947, Onslow-Ford came upon a tribe of Tarascan Indians who taught him by example how to develop his ability to see. "I began to purify my formal thinking as a painter," he maintained, "and to approach the visual innocence of the Indian. After the years in their powerful presence I saw in a different way and in a range of forms and colors too daring to have found by myself" (1948:20). Onslow-Ford described the Tarascan way of seeing as follows:

The Tarascan Indians see in a different way than we and have a communion with nature that we have lost. They seem to *comprehend objects rather than see them* [italics mine]. This gives them an astonishing sensitivity to form and color that is manifest in their clothes, so simple and striking in their houses, tools and weapons, made of earth, bone, wood skin, and hair. The things they make and they themselves are of such fine proportion that it was always exciting to watch them. All they did seemed a ceremony. They have not yet taught themselves to see the illusion of three dimensions on two and by comparison I learned how my vision had been biased by the written word, by modern art fashions, and by hangovers from the Renaissance. To remedy this I sat for hours, as they did, in contemplation of objects and scenes before me, a stone, lizards, fanhunters in canoes slinging their spears at wild ducks, a tiny cloud over the horizon that grew into a storm covering the whole sky with explosives (1948:19-20).

Not only did Onslow-Ford realize that seeing begins with profound looking but that a stage of seeing is reached in which the Tarascan Indians "comprehend objects rather than looking at them." This is the stage in which the seer ceases to be an observer and merges with the object. According to Onslow-Ford,

Once I used to think of my world as a place I could visit by switching on the light of the cycloptic eye in the middle of the forehead and looking inward. This intellectual concept was too easy, and during the time I called myself a cycloptomaniac my painting suffered a literary burden. It is clear to me now that I am oblivious of myself and only conscious of my world. I am my world and myself at the same time, and that they were indistinguishable (1948:42).

In addition to the suspension of the self in the act of seeing there is another factor which makes seeing possible. "I am a visionary," wrote Onslow-Ford,

this requires a discipline, a power of relaxation, of gathering the self to the Self, and implies a duty to be honest that is to be able to distinguish between flights of the imagination and real depths. The former leads to fantasies common to children and authors of popular comics, the latter brings visions of things never seen before but immediately recognizable as part of another self (1948:42).

Seeing also goes beyond thinking, as Onslow-Ford remarked.

> In SEEING there is more than the eye registers. It is the mind that SEES.

> SEEING is the mind revealing itself.
> ...

> SEEING happens too fast to be analyzed by thought, but I have the intuition that SEEING comes about through the accumulation of delight.

> Delight is more than pleasure (sometimes tinged with pain) in heartwarming, poignant and astounding circumstances. Delight offers a mysterious hint from the unconscious. As delight follows delight, the mystery mounts and the hints, which at first could be ignored, become an ever-present haunt. This haunt contains a message that seeks to enter the consciousness through dreams, revelatory events in the outer-world and in art (1978:108).

For me, Onslow-Ford's definition of delight comes close to shamanic ecstasy. The shaman/seer/artist goes beyond looking and thinking in a state of deep relaxation to explore the deep recesses of the psyche and the essence of the object. The experience of loss or flight from the self is quite exhilarating.

By the early sixties, Onslow-Ford had developed a painting technique of notation using the circle, line, and dot which embodied both the ecstasy and quickness of seeing. This painting technique was, in part, derived from his training in calligraphy by the Japanese Zen master Hodo Tobase. In his book, *Painting in the Instant*, Onslow-Ford provided the theoretical basis for this technique. "The instant," he stated,

refers to attention. In the instant there is a state of
full attention to what is happening.

In the instant there is a co-incidence of events—
wind blowing, grass growing, brush strokes appear.

All there is, is in the instant (1964:35).

Onslow-Ford's idea of attention related, indeed, to the
Zen practice of attention to the moment. "Awareness of each
moment is indispensable to the way of mindfulness, because
practice is complete only when a person focuses attention on
the present moment: the very moment of existence" wrote
Kazuaki Tanahashi (1985:13) on the philosophy of Dogen,
the great Zen Buddhist of the 13th century. "A moment,"
continued Tanahashi,

> seems to be an extremely small segment of a long
> span of time. Yet past is remembered as past in the
> present moment and future is expected as future in
> the present moment. Each moment carries all of
> time. Thus a moment has an aspect of timelessness.
> In this respect "now" is eternal (1985:13).

This notion of time is also very similar to the shamanic idea of
the dream time—the multidimensional space-time grid that
contains all the events of the past, present, and future. The
shaman enters the dream time to obtain information. I believe
that Onslow-Ford's "painting in the instant" is essentially a
method of seeing that enables him to access the dream time.
Onslow-Ford also fully realized that "painting in the instant"
requires an open mind.

The unknown manifests itself through the open
mind.

If the mind is filled with fears, doubts or ulterior motives while painting, it is the fears, doubt or ulterior motives that become apparent.

If the mind is full of pre-conceived plans, it is only in so far as they are surpassed that the painting will have life. If the mind is buzzing with recent activities, the surface is agitated and the depths are clouded.

The closed mind is personal.
The open mind is impersonal.

When the mind opens, something original can come in. The open mind is not something that can be learned or switched on at will. It happens naturally.

The painters preparation; every time he paints consists in seeing through memory and wish.

It is in the instant that the mind opens (1964:33-34).

The painter must be free from any premeditated intention at the outset of the painting process. That means, "While painting, the painter does not have a goal in mind and he does not seek revelation. If the painter strives for a lofty aim with brush in hand his scope of vision dwindles" (Onslow-Ford, 1978:40). Relaxation, goallessness, openness and clear emptiness of mind are fundamental concepts of both Zen meditation, shamanic seeing, and Onslow-Ford's, *Painting in the Instant*.

Onslow-Ford can be called a seer and a shaman. Although he does not practice traditional meditative techniques, his way of clearing the mind is to remove himself from the visual and auditory pollution of idle chatter, radio, television, and newspapers by living in an almost hermit-like isolation in

Inverness, California, where he deeply communicates with the forest flora and fauna which surround his small house. On a walk with him in the forest, I observed that the artist, now in his seventies, has the acute alertness of an Indian tracker. He himself exclaimed, "What a pleasure it is to be able to walk with eyes all around in the great orchestra of the woods" (1978:119)! For the Zen meditator, "all there is" is ultimately the void, while Onslow-Ford has dedicated himself to seeing the various levels of the dream time, presenting them in his work. The levels are revealed in both his automatic works, drawings and paint pourings, as well as in his line, circle, and dot paintings.

The earlier works are populated by languid semi-transparent biomorphic entities which have some resemblance to the late style of Wassily Kandinsky and the abstract "thought forms" of Annie Besant and C. W. Leadbeater. They are manifestations of mind and emotions on the ethereal level. Onslow-Ford himself described the "Painter and the Muse" (1943), one of the biomorphic paintings, in the following way:

> The Painter-Voyager is floating into the landscape of the Muse. The Painter-Voyager, the Muse and her moon above emit auras; the three meet without touching through a landscape of auras. The landscape is created by the personages, and the personages are created by the landscape; if one were to move, so would the others in sympathy. The painting continues beyond itself in a border in which light colours turn dark, warm colours turn cold and vice-versa, suggesting that the painting is but a drop in an unseen ocean of drops (1978:65).

I think, Onslow-Ford's general interpretation of his biomorphic work which he expressed in *Towards a New Subject in Painting* as "a mass of interpenetrating substance that congeals here and there into nuclei" (1948:44) is less farfetched. The problem with the biomorphic paintings is that they do not support the intellectual explanations that Onslow-Ford gave them, nor are they particularly inspiring from an aesthetic point of view. Onslow-Ford argued that

> Formal qualities are not important....For me, the most vital element of the painting is the subject matter. It is an aspect of inner vision that turns the spectator into a bridge to which the images pass into his everyday life (1948:28).

This echoes André Breton's belief that painting is "a lamentable expedient", a means to tap the deep recesses of the mind rather than an end itself. Breton and Onslow-Ford were ignoring the fact that style and content are intimately related in Western art. "I would like my paintings to carry the spectator from the optical world to the world of vision," asserted Onslow-Ford in *Towards a New Subject* (1948:48). Yet, if viewers are not engaged by the visual style of the painting, there is no chance that they will be carried from "the optical world to the world of vision," especially if they are unfamiliar with the style and content of Onslow-Ford's works. The question of whether he is creating a traditional shamanic painting which has a magical effect on the viewers, irrespective of aesthetic considerations, remains open.

In my opinion, the line, circle, dot paintings are more successful than the biomorphic paintings, as they bring the viewers "to the world of vision." Since Onslow-Ford gradually moved beyond surrealism, he has developed his powers of seeing and painting. He remarked in *Creation*, "The deeper the world the faster the power of awareness needed to catch it" (1978:69). The straight line, the circle, and the dot are, indeed, the fastest lines possible. They need not slow down during the course of their appearance, as Onslow-Ford showed in *Painting in the Instant*. A dot can meet the paper with the greatest intensity. A straight line can move from one point to another as fast as possible. A circular line can rotate at the highest speed (1964:82). The line, circle, dot are also related.

> A line can be the track of a dot. A line can be a circle on edge. A dot can be a line on end. A dot can be a section of a line. A dot can be a section of a circle. A circle can be the orbit of a dot about a dot. A circle on edge can be a line. A section of a circle is a dot. As the view-point changes: A dot can become a line or a circle. A line can become a dot or a circle. A circle can become a dot or a line. Thus in contemplating a line, circle, dot, painting, a mental gymnastic is possible, one element can change into another or is another in profile, on end, on edge, in section or full face line, an endless play of diversity in unity (1964:83).

In "Round See" (1961), one of the better line, circle, dot paintings, the interrelationship between the lines, circles, and dots create an over all infrastructure that orders the seemingly random placement and facilitates the continual metamorphosis of the elements.

James Joyce used the term "chaosmos," a combination of chaos and cosmos to describe Finnegan's Wake. This description is perhaps also applicable to "Round See." In Onslow-Ford's cosmos, there is a breakdown of hierarchical organization; there are no figure ground relationships, no focal points, no perspective, and a reduction of color to yin/yang contrasts of black and white, "...all the colors add their brilliance to each other and become white," as the artist explained (1978:101).

There is no clear separation between space and matter in "Round See." According to Onslow Ford,

> The space *between* and *in* figurations, which once might have passed unnoticed, is now alive. Space

and matter, that once could have been considered separately, now become space-matter (1978:70).

For me, "Round See" is an open-ended metaphor that engenders multiple associations. I am reminded of the rapid interchanges of energy recorded by a sub-atomic bubble chamber, the bright flash at the birth of the galaxy, and the formation of undifferentiated energy into the yin/yang polarities of existence.

The "endless play of diversity in unity," in this painting could also be related to the Buddhist philosophy expressed in the *Avatamsaka Sutras*. In his *History of Zen Buddhism*, Heinrich Dumoulin pointed out,

> The *Avatamsaka Sutras* state impressively the reciprocal relationship and interpenetration of the absolute Buddha-nature and the world of individual phenomena. The Buddha is all, and all is the Buddha. But the inclusive unity does not rob the phenomena of their individual character. Certainly things do not possess a self-nature, for all self-nature is swallowed up in identity with the Buddha, And yet each individual thing has its special meaning in the universe (1963:39).

Dumoulin went on to say that the *Avatamsaka Sutras* do not lack depictions of the "interrelatedness and interpenetration of all things" (1963:39), nor does Onslow-Ford in "Round See." Onslow-Ford's lines, circles and dots are discreet elements, yet they are part of the overall configuration of the painting. I think that, in "Round See," Onslow-Ford has reached a level of mind that is concomitant with the dance and interpenetration of energy underlying all phenomena, on both the microcosmic and macrocosmic levels.

In the early part of *Creation*, Onslow-Ford wrote,

If one could go back to the mind through eon after eon, world within world, one would arrive at the Beginning, the Original Seed, the Absolute Marvel, the most powerful event that has been, is, and will be. Mercifully the Beginning lies deeply hidden from the senses; it is too fast for thought to catch, or to be seen with the eyes (1978:101).

Referring to the line, circle, dot paintings later in the book, he implied that he has embodied this "Original Seed," "Here is the SEED the place of potential into which involution leads and from which evolution can begin" (1978:85). A glimpse of the "Original Seed," what Onslow-Ford also called "an end-less field of live space-matter that is ever-changing" (1978:72), can be a sublime experience that has the capacity to change the seer's life. "As the vastness of the inner-worlds becomes more apparent," said Onslow-Ford, "so personal problems become relatively less important" (1978:30) and "The old painter, who had disappeared into the painting, is reborn very small in person and great in spirit" (1978:98). Most shamans exhibit a similar quality of humility. The awesome experience of the dreamtime has a salutary effect on the ego.

Like Gordon Onslow-Ford, Robert Irwin experienced, during his career, the gradual diminution of the ego. In his series of conversations with Lawrence Wechsler, Irwin men-tioned that he graduated from art school in Los Angeles in the early fifties at the top of his class "without even trying, which is the best way to learn nothing" (1982a:30). Irwin then decided that he had to re evaluate his life and his career which was an unusual step to take for a young Los Angeles man of this generation. He rented a cabin on the island of Ibiza for eight months and did not talk to anyone. Although he had brought along his drawing tools, they remained unused; he just sat on a rock examining the contents of his mind.

Irwin's sojourn on Ibiza was not far removed from the shamanic vision quest that a young man takes in tribal culture. He would go to a remote part of the country and live in isolation for a period of time that is usually shorter than the eight months Irwin spent on Ibiza. Irwin said about this experience on Ibiza,

> I found out that during that period when I was alone for eight months that my head, on a day-to-day basis, is really very superficial. I mean, it responds and bounces around like a rubber ball in a way. But if I gave it no other purposes or activities in the world except simply to sit there and weigh my own feelings, my own attitudes, my own thoughts about things, well, then I began to know something of those things (quoted in Wechsler, 1982a:67).

> ...it's like you peel the layers of that issue and are able to get to a much deeper reasoning of how and in what way this thing makes sense, rather than each time taking on a whole new concept, a whole new aspiration, a whole new idea (quoted in Wechsler, 1982a:68).

Irwin learned that isolating himself helped to empty and clear his mind and he has repeated this technique at various intervals in his career.

He resumed his increasingly successful career as an abstract expressionist painter on his return to Los Angeles and became interested in the work of Giorgio Morandi. "One of the extraordinary things about Morandi's achievements," said Irwin,

> is precisely the spareness of his means. It's always

those same bottles on that same table....But what Morandi did there was to take the same subject over and over again to the point of total boredom, to the point where there was no way you could...be involved with them as ideas....through sheer repetition he drained them of that kind of meaning: they...became open elements within the painting dialogue he was having. And the remarkable thing was that although the content of those paintings...stayed exactly the same, the paintings changed radically. I mean, each painting became a whole new delving into and development of the physical, perceptual relationships within the painting (quoted in Wechsler, 1982a:68).

What impressed Irwin about the work of Morandi was that even though he was a painter of still lives, Morandi was interested in pure formal relationships to a greater extent than the abstract expressionists whose canvases often engendered associations extraneous to the qualities of the painting itself. Examining his abstract expressionist work further, he realized that, among the gestures of his contemporaries, there was no such thing as a neutral gesture. Every mark evoked some kind of meaningful association. "At this point," Irwin maintained,

I began to recognize the difference between imagery and physicality, that everything [every mark in abstract expressionism] had both an imagery and a physicality, and furthermore that for me, the moment a painting took on any kind of image, the minute I could recognize it as having any relationship to nature, of any kind, to me the painting went flat. Now, I don't know where I got that idea but there it was. Imagery for me constituted representation, "re-presentation," a second order of reality, whereas I was after a first order of presence.

...All my work since then has been an exploration of phenomenal presence (quoted in Wechsler, 1982a:61).

Irwin recognized the distinction between appearance or representation and the *Ding an Sich*, or, in Huxley's terms, the difference between Symbol and Suchness. To embody the *Ding an Sich* in art without transforming it into a symbol would, if not impossible, be a task of great difficulty. Those who search for the *Ding an Sich* are usually not artists, they are holy men who need not express ineffable experiences in words or pictures. In André Malraux's *Man's Fate*, the Japanese artists Kama said,

> What the symbol is to the flower, the flower itself, this one (he pointed to one of the drawings) is to something. Everything is a symbol. To go from the symbol to the thing symbolized is to explore the depth and meaning of the world, it is to see "God" (1968:187).

Although, at that time, Irwin was not aware of the dilemma, in searching for the thing in itself, he was embarking on the journey of the seer that would involve his own transformation. In the early sixties, he neither had any idea of the difficulty of his task, nor did he have anyone in Los Angeles to tell him about the difficulties. This may be one of the reasons he succeeded. As Irwin later remarked,

> Like when New Yorkers tell me what's wrong with L.A., everything they say is wrong—no tradition, no history, no sense of a city, no system of support, no core, no sense of urgency—they're absolutely right, and that's why I like it. That's why it's such a great place to do art and to build your ideas about culture. In New York, it's like an echo chamber; its

overwhelming sense of itself, of its past and its present and its mission becomes utterly restricting (quoted in Wechsler, 1982a:51).

Irwin began his "exploration of phenomenal presence" by isolating himself in his studio from 1962-1964. During this time, he completed ten paintings of two lines each. "I embarked on two years of painting those paintings," recalled Irwin,

two lines on each canvas, and at the end of two years there were ten of them. So I painted a total of twenty lines over a period of two years of very, very intense activity. I mean, I essentially spent twelve and fifteen hours a day in the studio, seven days a week. In fact I had no separation between my studio life and my outside life. There was no separation between me and those paintings. Everything else became subsumed to this; this became my whole life, and so the whole question as to whether I had a marriage or whether I had a social life just fell away (quoted in Wechsler, 1982a:70).

"In the beginning," Irwin continued,

all this was not very considered....It was done very intuitively. My concentration was not real good. It was mostly a question of just staying in the studio and simply not going out. Whether I did anything or didn't do anything, whether I was able to work or not, I simply would not let myself leave. But after a while, if you don't let yourself leave, then everything else begins to leave, that is, all your other reasons or ambitions in being there; and if you're very fortunate, you might then reach a point of being completely alone in an intimate dialogue with yourself as acted out in the realm of the painting (quoted in Wechsler, 1982a:71).

Irwin had subjected himself to the discipline of concentration. His ambition and ego were eroding in the process of breaking down the barriers between himself and his painting. As I mentioned before, Irwin did very little painting in the studio during these two years; most of the time he just looked. "I started spending the time just sitting there looking," he said.

> I would look for about fifteen minutes and just nod off, go to sleep. I'd wake up after about five minutes, and I'd concentrate and look, just sort of mesmerize myself, and I'd conk off again. It was a strange period. I'd go through days on end during which I'd be taking these little half-hour, fifteen-, twenty-minute catnaps about every half hour—I mean, all day long. I'd look for a half an hour, sleep for half an hour, look for half and hour. It was a pretty hilarious sort of activity (quoted in Wechsler, 1982a:73).

Fifteen to twenty minutes was his optimum time for looking. Because he was not aware of cultural frames of reference for the task of looking, Irwin called this activity "pretty hilarious." He also found it boring.

> I put myself in that disciplined position, and one of the tools that I used was boredom. Boredom is a very good tool. Because whenever you play creative games, what you normally do is you bring to the situation all your aspirations, all your assumptions, all your ambitions—all your stuff. And then you pile it up on your painting, reading into the painting all the things you want it to be. I'm sure it's the same with writing; you load it up with all your

illusions about what it is. Boredom's a great way to break that. You do the same thing over and over again, until you are bored stiff with it. Then all your illusions, aspirations, everything just drains off. And now what you see is what you get. Nothing more. *A* is *A* and *B* is *B*. *A* is not plus plus plus all these other things. It's just *A*. And suddenly you've got something showing you all its threadbare reality, its lack of structure, its lack of meaning. And then you have a chance to....Boredom's great, It's a silly tool, but finally it's a very good one. There are possibly more sophisticated ways to get at something like that, but when you come from where I came from, you take your tools where you can find them (quoted in Wechsler, 1982a:73-74).

Although looking for fifteen to twenty minutes is boring, as Irwin has pointed out, it is an effective way of emptying the mind as any experienced seer or meditator knows. In fact, a period of Zazen or Zen meditation lasts for about twenty minutes. Moreover, Irwin's statement "A is A and B is B. A is not plus plus plus all these other things" reminds me of the Zen aphorism: "Before Zen, mountains are mountains. During Zen mountains are not mountains. After Zen mountains are mountains again." The mountains don't mean anything, they just are. The shift from looking to seeing, the "threadbare reality," happens suddenly, as Irwin said; it is a kind of mini-satori.

Yet, when Irwin was looking and painting lines on a canvas, he was not engaged in formless meditation like a practitioner of Zen. "Look at that wall carefully," Irwin said to Lawrence Wechsler during one of their conversations,

and you'll of course see that its whiteness is not of just one tone. The light is streaming in from the window, so that it's a brighter white to that side, fading into grays over to this side. There are blues and greens and even purples. It's a little bit more difficult to see the incidental transitions, the low-grade shadows caused by the varying textures, because of the starkness of the contrast between the white wall and the black plank. Still, if I were to daub a slash of red paint in that corner, it would change the whiteness of the entire field. Now, a slash of red paint is a major gesture, and you'd almost need something that extreme to see the contrast in this situation. Because of the extremity of the black-white contrast, for example, its difficult for you to perceive how the whiteness of even a particular spot on the wall changes as you yourself move through the room, or as the sun moves through the day. But as you reduce the incidental contrast, it becomes easier to see such subtle discrepancies. If that plank, for example, were grey instead of black....

Now, what I was doing in those line experiments was to try as much as possible to clear away such incidental distractions. I used, for example, a bright orange paint straight out of the tube for my ground, applied it very evenly over the canvas, trying to avoid any discrepancies in the field while at the same time providing a definite texture. Then I applied the two lines out of the same tube. And it was soon thereafter, when I moved one of those lines that eighth of an inch, that I suddenly realized that the gesture changed everything in the field, not only the composition but even the color! I'd raise that line by the thickness of a sheet of paper, and from across the room the seven foot by seven foot field was no longer the same (quoted in Wechsler, 1982a:71-72).

These statements suggest that Irwin had moved from focused attention on the lines to non-focused attention on both the lines and their surrounding context. Irwin recognized how a slight change of the mark on the canvas or wall can affect the whole field. Non-focused attention is, in fact, a typical shamanic practice in which the seer becomes acutely aware of disturbances within the field.

After considerable practice of non-focused attention, I myself have noticed that any object that seems out of place in the field produces a distinctly irritating physical sensation.

Irwin began to pay an increasing amount of attention to the visual phenomena outside of the canvas, specifically the gallery field in which the paintings were placed. For a show of the line paintings at the Sidney Janis Gallery in New York, Wechsler said that

> he concentrated on trying to control every physical circumstance of the work's presentation. Thus he repainted the gallery walls and floors, smoothed over the cracks, spent hours turning the lights, even tried to "paint out" the shadows cast by guard-rails...to minimize the kinds of distractions to which he had become hypersensitive (1982a:77-78).

Irwin has remarked that the

> New Yorkers [including critics and artists] couldn't see the difference [that his changes in the gallery made on the perception of the paintings]. *They literally couldn't see it* (quoted in Wechsler, 1982a:78).

I believe that they couldn't see it because Irwin was going beyond a purely aesthetic level of seeing.

Irwin has claimed that in looking at the lines "you cease reading and you cease articulating and you fall into a state where nothing is going on but the tactile, experiential process" (quoted in Wechsler, 1982a:76), however, the lines are still marks on canvas that engender associations, e.g., the horizontal lines evoking the horizon lines of a landscape. Irwin still had not made the transition from symbols to the *Ding an Sich*.

In the next series, the "Dots of 1964-67," Irwin attempted to go further in abolishing the mark. He described these paintings as follows,

> In the dot paintings I took a large squarish canvas and painted it an even bright white....Then I put on the dots, starting with very strong red dots, as rich as possible but only about the size of map pins, put them on very carefully, about one quarter inch or so, such that they seemed neither too mechanically nor too crudely applied—either way they would have thereby drawn attention to themselves as patterns— concentrating them toward the center and then dispersing them less and less densely, missing one or two here and there, as they moved out toward the edge. Then I took the exact opposite color and put a green dot between every single pair of red dots, doing the same thing out to the edge, stopping the green maybe just a little before the red so that there was a slight halation of the two colors on the edge. But in the center they essentially cancelled each other out, so that you didn't see either green or red but rather the energy generated by the interaction between the two (quoted in Wechsler, 1982a:88).

From this statement, it appears that Irwin was attempting to fuse the mark into an energy field. In his catalog essay on Irwin's show at the Los Angeles County Museum of Art in 1966, art critic Philip Leider wrote about the "Dots,"

> One is confronted by what at first appears to be an

immaculate white picture plane, about seven feet square, and nothing more. Some time must pass— a minute, or two, or three—before the viewer becomes fully aware of an indistinct, irregularly shaped mass which seems to have emerged out of the white plane (or is perceived within it, or behind it), roughly centered. The colorations is so subdued that there is no possibility of defining what one sees in terms of it, but rather in terms of what it suggests: a quality, an energy, one feels, which will tend, ultimately, to dissolve itself uniformly on the picture plane in a kind of entropic dissipation. The rest—after the elements of the painting have, so to speak, "emerged"—is a history of the hypnotic involvement between the viewer and the elements of color and whiteness before him (quoted in Wechsler, 1982a:91).)

I can attest to my own "hypnotic involvement" with "the elements of color and whiteness," while I was experiencing one of these dot paintings at the Philadelphia Museum of Art for an extended period of time. Yet, I still remained aware of the marks.

Like the line paintings, the dot paintings are not only about presence, they are about seeing. This leads us to Leider's further remark that

What Irwin manifestly wishes to do is *to slow the viewer down*, to prepare him, in effect, for an encounter. A certain measurable duration of time is necessary before one can even see what there is to be seen, so that the viewer will either see it the way Irwin wants him to see it or he will—quite literally—not see the painting at all (quoted in Wechsler, 1982a:91).

The apprehension of these paintings demands that the viewer slows down in order to go beyond the usual process of art observation and reach a level of seeing. "My questions as I finished the dots," Irwin explained to Lawrence Wechsler,

> were fairly simple—I mean very direct. When I finished the dot paintings, they worked very well in creating this physical space which was occupied by a perceptual kind of energy. But you were immediately aware of the confine, because everything that was beginning to happen in those paintings seemed incongruous, being held as it was firmly within that rectangle. And I had never examined the assumption as to why a painting exists within a frame (quoted in Wechsler, 1982a:98-99).

Although Irwin had not yet solved the problem of the mark on the canvas, he became aware of a further problem; the frame acts as a mark in the environment, a figure on a ground.

The "Disk" series, created after much experimentation between 1967-69, was intended to resolve the latter problem. John Coplans, in his essay for the 1968 Pasadena Art Museum, provided a good description of this series.

> In the first place, each of Irwin's new paintings is dependent on the use of its ground, that is, a flat, gray-tinged wall approximately 12 feet high in a suitably sized room or gallery. The wall needs to be at least 12 feet wide, but if possible, should be wider, and there must be sufficient depth for the viewer to stand between 12 and 15 feet back. The ceiling immediately above the wall and the floor immediately in front of the wall are neutralized with paint the same ground color as the wall. All daylight is excluded from the room, and the wall is evenly lighted from top to bottom and side to side by a soft

ambient whitish light of low intensity. Onto the center of the wall, and approximately 72 inches above the ground line, a circular convex disc is mounted onto a concealed male-female tubular arm 20 inches forward and parallel to the wall. The convex shape is 60 inches in diameter..., the convexity is 2-1/2 inches deep, and the thickness of the edge is 1/16 inch....[periods by the author]. The disc is cross-lit from four corners by incandescent lamps (two in the ceiling and two on the floor, placed equidistant from each other and approximately 6 feet back from the wall). All four lamps are of equal intensity...[periods by the author] and the effect of the cross-light beamed unto the disc and the wall is to cast a clearly discernible symmetrical, but elaborate shadow pattern of segments of a circle. Where the shadows overlap at the cardinal points, they are darker than elsewhere. The total shadow pattern is approximately 10 feet high and wide. The ambient light (mentioned earlier) has the effect of softening both the edges and the interiors of the shadows. The result of the cross illumination combined with the ambient light is that the shadow, the disc, and the outer areas of the illumined wall are seen as an entity. Thus the three elements—wall, shadow, and painted disc—are equally positive; the shadow, in fact, sometimes becomes almost more positive than the disc (quoted in Wechsler, 1982a:100-101).

Art critic Melinda Wortz has pointed out that

After some time of looking at these objects in their controlled installations, they seemed to dissolve into the empty space surrounding them. Consequently it then became visually impossible to distinguish figure from ground. The discs enabled us to perceive the substance and void, which is the goal of meditative practice (1981:63).

In my experience of "The Disks," this interchangeability of substance and void, this incandescent void/substance also mirrors the end stages of seeing. As I mentioned earlier, the interchangeability of substance/void has already appeared in Morandi's work but I think Irwin has gone further than Morandi. Irwin has eliminated both the baggage of subject matter and the frame of the painting.

However, "The Disks" were not entirely successful in terms of Irwin's search for presence since they still are essentially paintings and the round shape of "The Disks" invites symbolic associations from his audience and critics. For me, these disks are contemporary versions of Tibetan *mandalas* which function both as symbols of the universe and as seeing tools used in meditative practice to help access the state of formless awareness. Similar mandalas are also found in shamanic art, including Australian bark painting, Huichol yarn painting, etc., where they have a variety of functions, e.g. being vehicles for heightened seeing.

"After the disks," Irwin understood that "there was no reason for me to go on being a painter." Since he could not realize his goal of achieving presence in painting (quoted in Wechsler, 1982a:107), Irwin became involved in other pursuits, such as teaching and a joint art and technology program of Maurice Tuchman, the creator of the Los Angeles County Museum. The program was designed to establish a creative cross-fertilization between artists and scientists.

Irwin was paired with a scientist at the Garett Aerospace Corporation, Dr. Ed Wortz, and both, as Wechsler recorded, got many new ideas from their relationship. Probably the most important spin off was Irwin's six-to-eight-hour stays in a sensory deprivation chamber at U.C.L.A. "There were all kinds of interesting things about being in there which we observed," said Irwin, but the most dramatic had to do with how the world appeared once you stepped out. After I'd sat in there for six hours, for instance, and then got up and walked back home down the same street I'd come in on, the trees were still trees, and the street was still a street, and the houses were still houses, but the world did not look the same; it was very, very noticeably altered (quoted in Wechsler, 1982a:128).

For a few hours after you came out,...you really did become more energy conscious, not just that leaves move, but that everything has a kind of aura, that nothing is wholly static, that color itself emanates a kind of energy. You noted each individual leaf, each individual tree. You picked up things which you normally blocked out. I think what happens is that in our ordinary lives we move through the world with a strong expectation-fit ratio which we use as much to block out information as to gather it in— and for good reason, most of the time; we block out information which is not critical to our activity. Otherwise we might well become immobilized. But after a while, you know, you do that repeatedly, day after day after day, and the world begins to take on a fairly uniform look. So that what the anechoic chamber was helping us to see was the extreme complexity and richness of our sense mechanism and how little of it we use most of the time. We edit from it severely, in time to see only what we expect to see (quoted in Wechsler, 1982a:129).

At this level of seeing, mountains are not quite mountains anymore; Irwin just about reached the point in seeing in which the world is transformed into energy patterns. This is a very advanced level of non-focused attention in which shamanic seers apprehend a web of glowing transparent objects connected by lines of light within their view. It is difficult, of course, as Irwin explained, to get through the day on this level of seeing. Out of habit and necessity the world began to take on a fairly uniform look, "a strong expectation-fit ratio" that seemed solid and permanent (quoted in Wechsler, 1982a:129).

Irwin, the shaman/seer, was learning that the everyday world of solidity and permanence is just a convenient illusion which reminds me of Don Juan telling Castaneda in *Tales of Power*,

> Today I have to pound the nail that Genaro [a Yaqui shaman] put in, the fact that we are luminous beings. We are perceivers. We are an awareness; we are not objects; we have no solidity. We are bound-less. The world of objects and solidity is a way of making our passage on earth convenient. It is only a description that was created to help us. We, or rather our *reason*, forget that the description is only a description and thus we entrap the totality of ourselves in a vicious circle from which we rarely emerge in our lifetime....
>
> We are perceivers....The world that we perceive though, is an illusion. It was created by a description that was told to us since the moment we were born (1994:100-101).

Irwin also related to Wechsler how this new level of seeing became possible in the anechoic chamber.

> We speculated that the difference came from one's having been isolated in total deprivation of audio or visual input. For one thing, what happened is that those two senses changed their thresholds. In other

words, there is a certain way you look and see and listen every day, but when you're suddenly cut off from the world of sight and sound for six or eight hours and then return to it, there occurs a change in the acuity of the mechanism (quoted in Wechsler, 1982a:129).

We heard about the Eskimo shaman Igjugarjuk enduring privation and suffering by isolating himself in the arctic wilderness "to open up the mind to those things that have not been experienced by others." A similar degree of sensory deprivation can apparently be accomplished in an anechoic chamber. "...at U.C.L.A.," said Irwin,

was a particularly fine one; it was suspended so that even the rotation of the earth was not reflected in it, or any sounds being bounced through the earth—a jackhammer five miles away or something. Nothing went into space. And no light at all (quoted in Wechsler, 1982a:128).

Such an elaborate set up, however, does not seem to be necessary to get good results, especially if the experimenter has some practice in meditation. I was lying once in a flotation tank for about one and a half hours and meditated every other twenty minutes. When I got out into the street, there was so much electric energy around me—objects were incandescent masses of multi-colored light flowing into each other—that I had to sit down in my car and do nothing for about half an hour.

Irwin's experience on leaving the anechoic chamber may have been less intense than mine, but it had a very important effect on his thinking and subsequent art work. In his own words, he started questioning that

whole mental structure which allows one to sepa-rate or, in a sense, focus on particular things as

opposed to other things: why, for example, one
focused on objects rather than the light which reveals them. On what conditions, I started wonder-
ing, do we operate with art as a confined element in
the world... surrounded by the world but somehow
not totally or directly attached to it, actually somehow superior to it? It's a highly developed, raised
rationale that this art object exists in. Indeed, we are
oriented to look as such focal points as, in a sense,
more real. And it's because of that we're not really
aware of what takes place otherwise, the so-called
incidentals, the information that takes place between things, the kind of things that happen around,
the multiple interactive relations (quoted in
Wechsler, 1982a:147-148).

Irwin realized that, in order to explore the "multiple interactive relationships" between things, he would have to give up
his interest in the art object. For Irwin, the hardest part

wasn't the loss of my art world identity. It wasn't the
scuttling of my economics. No, it was the loss of a
way of thinking, it was the loss of the physical
things themselves. For twenty years I'd thought in
terms of making objects; I'd worked out my ideas
by working on physical things. I'm a very tactile
person. I think by feel, and not having anything
tangible to handle really threw me for a while. I
mean, I understood how I'd gotten myself into that
predicament—the question simply mandated it—I
just didn't know how to deal with it. I had to train
myself to think in a new way (quoted in Wechsler,
1982a:159-160).

As part of this training, Irwin gave up his studio. He
recalled,

...I felt that if each day I got up and went down the street, the same street basically, and went into the studio, which was a particular scale and size, a room, and so on and so forth, and if I brought with me all my expertise—which is what you can't help but do in a situation like that, bring the things you've learned to be good at (and I'd learned a lot of techniques)—that I would essentially continue to do the same thing. And I didn't know exactly how to resolve that. But what I did was the simplest kind of thing—which was not an answer, but I think fairly reasonable given the dilemma—and that was to get rid of all those habits and practices altogether.

I cut the knot. I got rid of the studio, sold all the things, I owned, all the equipment, all my stuff; and without knowing what I was going to do with myself or how I was going to spend my time, I simply stopped being an artist in those senses. I just quit (quoted in Wechsler, 1982a:156).

To use the words of Don Juan, Irwin had "erased his personal history" by giving up his habits and thought patterns which tied him to a particular way of seeing. Cutting the knot was a way of "stopping the world," a necessary prerequisite for a new way of seeing.

In the early seventies, after he had given up his studio and artistic identity, Irwin spent periods of several days alone in the Arizona Desert. As I have already related earlier, this sequestering of himself in isolation when he had reached a logical conundrum is a technique he employed to break through to a new way of seeing. Shamans would select the same technique for similar reasons and go on a vision quest.

Struck by the sublime presence of the Arizona desert, Irwin marked areas of particular beauty which, he believed, should be noticed. "It soon became clear to me that the mark was a distraction," Irwin maintained, it was about me, about my identity, my discovery. Whereas all that really mattered...was the place's presence. In other words, if I'd taken you out there to a place like that, what you would have perceived was yourself perceiving. You would have been the one dealing with it, and my hand would have been a distraction. Furthermore, I suddenly had this terrible fantasy of thousands of artists coming out and graffitoing the landscape with their art world initials. So I stopped leaving traces (quoted in Wechsler, 1982a:161).

Shamans who visit or dwell in wilderness areas sometimes mark the landscape in the course of their spiritual exercises. They are, however, careful to touch the land rather lightly, leaving only a small but important trace before they move on. I am thinking here of the assemblages North American Indians use to demarcate power spots. These rock configuration are always done anonymously, leaving no evidence of the ego of the creator.

Anonymity is very difficult to attain in contemporary life, especially in the contemporary art world where every gesture is linked with the expression of a particular artist. Irwin was acutely aware of this difficulty as the above quoted passage suggested, "But," as he pointed out, "*this is not an enlightened world.* And the world always draws you back" (quoted in Wechsler, 1982a:189).

It drew Irwin back from the desert and he recommenced his career as an artist, perhaps because he saw a role for himself as someone who could indicate the aesthetics of unmediated presence.

For the 1976 Venice Biennial, for example, Irwin extended a wire in a rectangular pattern around an area that, he thought, was particularly interesting in the way it reflected the light passing through the surrounding trees. This 1976 installation brings to mind John Cages's famous 4' 33" piece that was performed at Black Mountain College in 1952. (Irwin did not know Cage's piece when he set up his 1976 installation at the Venice Biennial.)

Cage had a pianist uncover the keyboard of a piano at the beginning of the piece and close the cover at the end of a period of 4 minutes and 33 seconds, without touching the keys in the intervals. Silence or the "noise" in the room became the concert and Cage's goal was to provoke the listener from "judgement to awareness" of the immediate environment. In such pieces, Cage argued, there is no communication and nothing being said,

> and so contemporary music is not so much art as it is life and anyone making it no sooner finishes one of it than begins making another just as people keep on washing dishes, brushing their teeth, getting sleepy and so on. Very frequently no one knows that contemporary music is or could be art. He simply thinks it is irritating. Irritating one way another, that is to say keeping us from ossifying (1961:44).

Because there is no separation between art and life in 4' 33", Cage realized the notion of presence and made listeners aware of their immediate environment. Although Cage's piece was more radical and irritating than Irwin's in breaking down the separation of art from life, the noises of the room were probably less interesting aesthetically than Irwin's patch of grass. Cage was inspired by his knowledge of Zen, the result of D.T. Suzuki's lectures on the subject at Columbia University, in the early fifties. The goal of Zen is to perform every act with attention so that even the most mundane gesture or encounter with objects has an aesthetic and spiritual quality. The function of the artist and the Zen master is to indicate this idea of "everyday suchness."

Irwin achieved presence in his 1976 installation and, in

the course of the interviews with Wechsler, he often quoted the famous Zen aphorism, "When I point my finger at the moon, don't mistake my finger for the moon" (quoted in Wechsler, 1982a:175). Wechsler did mention the irony of the 1976 installation, where "many people mistook the string itself for the work of art" (quoted in Wechsler, 1982a:175).

The difficulty with the 1976 installation was also one of framing. How was Irwin to indicate presence without the audience focusing on the indicator and the indication?

One of his best solutions to this difficulty was his "Filigreed Line," created in 1979 at Wellesley College. Irwin described this work as follows:

> On my first visit [to Wellesley College] I was struck by the grace of the nature of the campus. How beautiful it all was, and without any intrusion from me. I was struck as well by the challenge made on our claims of "beauty" in art—a challenge that "art" on the whole has avoided by remaining insular, protected by its intellection of the object and frame. The challenge to interact, work directly with nature, has always been a latent question in art, a question brought into focus in "modern art" by the implication inherent in the edict to effect a "marriage between figure and ground." I find it odd that we come to honor the art of artists who author such "concepts" and then don't test the concepts or let them change our lives. I consider such "honoring" meaningless. Such a neglect turns art into decoration.
>
> What would it actually be like to act out "the marriage of figure and ground" in the world?
>
> My proposal "Filigreed Line" was a line of stainless steel [120 feet long, one half inch thick] running along a ridge of grass and in front of the lake. It is

low in profile, only a few inches high in some places and never more than 2' at any point. A pattern of leaflike shapes, taken from leaves on the site, is cut through the steel, creating a light, open feeling which is accentuated by a pattern cut into the surface of the steel. This pattern causes the line, at times, to become lost in the pattern of light on the lake (and in the winter on the snow), to dance along the ridge, coming and going. My best hope for the "line" is simply that it refocus the too-often habituated eye of the passerby to the qualities and pleasures in his or her immediate environment (1985:37).

The line, as indicator, often became invisible. Along with the other works that I have mentioned, Irwin's goal was also to promulgate a non-ordinary, non-habitual level of seeing.

When it is relatively easy to indicate presence in an intrinsically beautiful site, it is much more difficult when the site appears less visually appealing. If Irwin was to truly "refocus the too-often habituated eye of the passerby to the qualities and pleasures of his or her immediate environment," he realized that he would have to select more ordinary sites.

In 1980, at 78 Market Street in Venice (California), Irwin was offered the use of a run-down building in a fairly gritty urban environment (Illustration 8).

My response, "One Wall Removed" was to use the clean white space [of the interior. It was being reconverted into an art gallery]—30' wide, 80' deep, 12' high, with two boxed-in skylights set 2/3 of the way back into the space—by removing the front wall facing the street and stretching in its place a sheer white scrim, in effect creating as a tangible focus the shifting qualities of light and the varying visual densities of the space across the periods of the day. It was quite beautiful.

To press the issues, the building went unmarked and the work unlabeled, thus allowing the casual passerby the full excitement of discovering this uncluttered experience, free for the taking be anyone with "eyes." Perhaps it takes only one such "personal" art experience to alert you to the latent potential for beauty in pure phenomena as well as worldly things (Irwin, 1985:90)?

Not only does Irwin want to break out of habitual modes of looking, but he wishes to change the patterns of perception among the people who encounter his works. By shifting from representation to sight-specific installations, viewers are invited to take an active role in the creation of the work. They are led to become an artist-seer like Irwin who perceives the extraordinary in the ordinary, the beauty in commonplace circumstances. Shamans see for the benefit of their community. Many also attempt to empower their clients by expanding their ability to see and, with that, to heal themselves. In triggering the self-healing powers of their viewers, shamans avoid codependency.

Arthur Tress believes that photography can also change the consciousness of the observer. In an essay, entitled the "Photograph as a Magical Object," Tress wrote,

The photographic image itself has great magical possibilities. Like the ceremonial mask, the ritual incantation, the protective amulet, or magical mandala, the photograph has the potency of releasing in the viewer preconditioned reactions that cause him to physically change or be mentally transformed....A photograph can more often "grab our guts" or arouse our sexual desires than other art forms because of its purported realness, but it can also more subtly stimulate unconscious responses that we are hardly aware of. The grotesque or frightening image may stir forgotten animal instincts of primordial helplessness and fear, reaching back to the basic insecurity of early man and our own personal childhoods. Images of great peace and harmony have the curative possibility of restoring tranquility and balance to a disturbed soul or agitated body. The photographic image which hints at the essential mystery of growing things and the unknown qualities of life itself can make the viewer aware of higher states of nature to which we are faintly sensitive. The magical photograph is simply one that attempts by its mere assertive presence to go beyond the immediate context of the recorded experience into the realms of the indefinable (1986:149).

When photographers create power objects of the intensity that Tress described, the inherent "realism" of photography supports this intensity and photographers become shamans. Tress has acknowledged this role for himself.

Although Tress told me that he is more inclined to produce "grotesque and frightening images" than harmonious ones, his photographs are not malevolent like African fetishes. They are intended to make viewers aware of what can be discovered in their own unconscious. As such, even the most unsettling of his images takes on a healing function.

According to Tress, to be a shaman/photographer, one has to be "acutely aware of the subliminal vibrations of the everyday world which are wrapped up in our unconscious selves." This necessitates an enhanced ability to see which, as it did with Robert Irwin, comes in part out of the creative process. Tress wrote,

> The photographer's intensely heightened sense perception, product of the brutal discipline of constantly seeing at 1/250th of a second, unevenly evolves his visual faculties to an almost superhuman degree (1986:149).

This heightened seeing, however, is not shared by all photographers who take photographs at 1/250th of a second; Tress knows how to slow down and to stalk the "magic moment," as he calls it. In slowing down, he achieved a trance-like state. Speaking about the ideal photographer, Tress ventured that

> Often his best photographs are taken in a trance-like state, where there is an almost mystical communication between his subject and himself, and action is directed through non-verbal gesture and psychic transference. As a trained observer, he can foretell the potential movements of his subjects and perhaps even by mental intimidation and expansion actually causes them to happen. The photographer participates in an almost ritual dance with the world, whereupon his own intense response to its rhythms corresponds to his being able to predict its predetermined patterns (1986:149).

Tress has informed me that he does not perceive connecting lines of light, but he has come close. By breaking the I-it relationship with the objects and entering into a "ritual dance with the world," his movements affect the overall patterns of energy in a way that can alter the outcome of events. This ritual dance with the world is, perhaps, most evident in the "Theatre of the Mind" series of 1976.

Tress invited himself into the homes of families, some of whom he hardly knew, and made documentary photographs of their activities. Through his process of seeing which involves "non-verbal gesture and psychic transference" in the I-thou mode of communication, he was able to set up a situation in which the families revealed their inner psychic condition and relationships. In the words of his friend, photographer Duane Michaels, "Arthur sees rather than looks, and he will see your secrets. I don't know how he does it" (quoted in Tress, 1976:1).

Having visited the home of his friend Ed Berman, for example, Tress photographed Ed ironing the hand of his mother. Later he found out that this depiction correctly mirrored Ed's relationship with his mother. Ed's statement on viewing the photograph was that it was accurate "because I could always do anything to her" (Tress, 1986:14).

Tress has compared his way of seeing as a photographer to the process of the skeletalization in which shamans in a trance state strip off their own flesh or that of a client and uncover the primordial state of being, the bare bones. Tress believes that it is then his task as a shaman/photographer to reanimate the skeletons, to bring them again into some form of life.[7]

He accomplished this literally in "The Presidential Cabinet" (1986) where the members of the United States Cabinet (presumably Ronald Reagan's) are reduced to skulls and then adorned with paraphernalia to reanimate them. Around the skull of the Secretary of the Interior, for example, Tress placed the goggles and tubing of a gas mask and put a plastic crow (an image of death) with a top hat on his head. There is a satirical element in "The Presidential Cabinet" but the series is certainly predicated on the artist's shamanic practice of skeletalization and reanimation in a trance state. "In this series," said Tress, "I have come closest to being a shaman."[7]

Tress's seeing has also been directed inward to focus on

his shadow, the innermost layer of the psyche, which he calls the "basic primal image," "the essence of ourselves" (1986:151). In "The Shadow: A Novel in Photographs" (1976; Illustration 9), Tress depicted himself undergoing a shamanic journey toward illumination. He recounted that it was

> an extended sequence of some ninety-five images of my own shadow shot around the world. The book was meant to be a narrative of my search for identity and style as a photographer, a narrative overlaid with the structure of a visionary voyage of initiation based on ethnographical studies of shamanistic and out-of the body experiences (1988:93).

Tress did not apprentice himself to a shaman during his world travels for the purpose of ethnographic photo-documentation, but he had earlier made contacts with Mayan shamans in Mexico, with shamans among the Lapps, and with Dogon shamans in Africa. He told me that the "Shadow" was the result of both his knowledge of shamanic practices and his own interior seeing in a trance state.[7] "At first," said Tress about his photographic novel,

> the shadow finds himself imprisoned, the world full of pain and suffering partly caused by his own hostility. He leaves in order to explore the world and discover for himself what it has to offer. He travels great distances and meets various guides and ancestor figures. He encounters many difficulties and predicaments which he realizes are his own mental projections, the fears with which he must struggle in order to overcome them. After this perilous undertaking, he acquires the magical ability to change himself into various transformations. Finally, at the end of his wandering, our spiritual voyager has a

great mystical rebirth and illumination. He loses his darkness and is filled with glowing light (1986: 151).

The first stages of the journey in the "Shadow" are about activities in the lower realms. Tress shows a physical shadow of himself as a prisoner behind bars, wandering through an old town and a labyrinth, metamorphosizing into an animal (a bull with horns), encountering ancestors (including his deceased father), and entering a "valley of marvels." Then, after experiencing a variety of initiations, he receives various calls and messages (including a visit from a bird), climbs a ladder into the upper realm, takes a magical flight, undergoes transformations such as having his head transformed into a shadow in the shape of a vortex, and holds a silver disk (actually an old hubcap) that becomes a radiating sun-like ball in his hand. Indeed, the later stages of "Shadow" are a classic narrative of an upper realm journey in which the shaman ascends to the realm of light, has his/her head split open and becomes a radiant being who projects light.

In tribal cultures, such as the Algonkian, Huichol, Australian aboriginals, shaman/seers are depicted with sun halos around their heads. According to Joan Halifax, "The sun itself is symbolic of the heroic principal of all-seeing and all-knowing and the indwelling fire of life" (1982:90). "Solarization," as she called it, however, is more than just an appropriate symbol for the shaman/seer, it is a record of the actual experience of being filled with light.

It is not surprising that Arthur Tress, who dedicated his life to the illumination of himself and of his subjects, has surrounded himself with images of light and solarization in the "Shadow." Of course, these images are also highly appropriate for a photographer who is a master of actual light in the technical practice of his art.

❖

Light is also a principal subject in the paintings of Alex Grey. Before Grey was able to see light in the form of interconnecting light lines and embodied these lines in his painting, he had to move through a long period of darkness, characterized by repeated encounters with death. "When I was ten," Grey recalled,

> I experienced the death of someone I loved when my grandmother got sick and died. I was affected by the fact that I would never see her again, that she would be buried and go away forever. Life took a different texture after that...time became precious.

> But earlier than that, from the ages of five to ten, I was a "mortician" for dead animals in the neighborhood. I had a graveyard in the backyard and would perform funeral dissections on worms, birds, cats, dogs, and everything else. I was interested in dead things and saw that they were different from living things (quoted in Tucker, 1986:105).

Although a gifted draftsman, Grey got in trouble with his instructors at the College of Art and Design in Columbus, Ohio, for bringing an open garbage bag of rotting grass and vegetables as well as one containing a dead dog to class. Leaving school in 1972, without getting a degree, Grey painted billboards for a year and then became active as a performance artist.

> ...I had gotten so riled up about the state of the world and I felt painting wasn't addressing that kind of turmoil and emotional intensity so I left painting for a time and—

> [asked by Brody] Took up with dead animals (quoted in Brody, 1984:1)?

In "Secret Dog," Grey took an animal that had been recently run over and placed it in a bag near a river. Over the course of several days, Grey periodically photographed its gradual decay. In "Rendered Dog," he exhibited a bag of defatted meat in powdered form and another of animal fat—the products of an animal rendering process. Grey said,

> Doing the dog pieces...made me wonder about the nature of consciousness. Life energy, consciousness, awareness seemed to be the things that were removed, and with that came the dissolving or dissolution of the body. It was a meditation on impermanence. If you're really gone, where do you go? And if you don't go anywhere, what does that say about the nature of the universe in which you live? Is it just a material world (1990:19)?

Grey's meditations on the meaning of death continued during the late seventies while he was employed as an embalmer at a mortuary. In "Deep Freeze," he enclosed himself in a freezer for five minutes with a bunch of chilled corpses. In "Monsters," he made a series of thirty black and white photographs of deformed fetuses. In "Life, Death and God," Grey hung himself upside down near a drawing of a crucifix while tied at the ankle to an upside down corpse. And in "Necrophilia," the most gruesome of these performances, he had himself photographed making love to a dead woman whose head was partially chopped off. It is important to recognize that Grey's interactions with the dead were not done out of need to create publicity for himself but in order to overcome his fears.

"I don't consider myself a fearless person," explained Grey,

> It seems that the way I grow is to face fears and so
> I was working with things that scared me the most.

My performances educate me, morally and physically. Even though I never entirely understand the pieces, I knew that I was scared of doing them and that I would probably learn something.

Looking back on my performance work [involving the dead], I relate it to the "shamanic journey"—going to the underworld, facing death, and then coming back with new insight (quoted in Tucker, 1986:105).[8]

"Afterwards [Necrophilia]," said Grey, "I did feel less afraid of death....But I was more afraid of the moral and karmic consequences of my actions" (quoted in Macadams, 1982:44). Indeed, following "Necrophilia," Grey had a series of dreams which dissuaded him from further research with the dead in the underworld. In the first one of these dreams, Grey recalled,

I was making love to a beautiful woman, but as she pulled me towards her, she rapidly aged and died. I saw the sides of the bed grow into a coffin that sealed me up with her. In my second dream, a brainless sage-monster hovered before me like a holographic image. Many different voices were speaking at once through this being, telling me that I wanted to be with them as much as they wanted to be with me, and that I should join them. I felt in this creature an extremely evil presence, and I knew that I was on the edge, very near a point of no return. I started saying, over and over again, "I know divine love is the strongest power," and kept on affirming that belief until the headless figure finally faded away. A bluish light followed shortly after my banishment of the dark apparition, and from it emerged a voice who introduced himself to me as

Mr. Lewis. He told me that he was an inter-plan-
etary angel and was my guide. He reassured me not
to worry. I woke up at this point. It was the middle
of the night, I was covered with sweat and trembling
from fear. A few days later, I had another nightmarish episode in which I found myself inside an
ominously menacing courtroom, before a judge I
could not see and an angry jury, as I faced a woman
who accused me of trespassing her body in my
morgue work. I tried to explain that I was making
"art," but there was absolutely no forgiveness. The
judge told me that from now on I must do more
positive work, and put me on life probation never
again to create such negative art (1990:21-22).

Grey's shift of investigative focus from darkness to
light, however, had already begun before "Necrophilia." In
"Polar Wandering" (1975), Grey underwent a costly and
arduous journey by plane and snowmobile to the North
Magnetic Pole in the Arctic near Resolute Bay. "After arriving
there," remembered Grey,

I felt foolish because I did not know why I had
come. The Pole itself wanders in an unpredictable
path, and at the Pole my compass needle just spun
around. The sun circled overhead all day. I took off
my clothes in the -30° ice desert and ran around in
a circle. I felt like I had dissolved into energy and
become one of the magnetic fields surrounding the
earth (1978/1979:21).

Grey told me that, without being conscious of it, he had been
looking for a primal power spot that would open him up to an
upperworld energy.[9] This experience with a new type of
energy again occurred during a performance entitled "Apex"
(1976) on a roof in Boston.

Covered by a hood to cut off sensory input, Grey suspended himself with ropes and cables in a pyramidal shaped structure for several hours on two consecutive nights. Set up near the structure was a sign that said, "During Apex, I will leave my body and touch you" (1990:22). According to the artist, several individuals reported that they experienced some entity moving towards them or touching them (quoted in Macadams, 1982:45).

In 1976, Grey also began the "Sacred Mirrors," a series of paintings that emerged partly as a record of seeing experiences on an L.S.D. trip which, in his own words, "caused me to redefine my view of consciousness and the self" (1990:31). On this L.S.D. trip, recalled Grey,

> I felt that my body was no longer just a solid, isolated object in a world of separate forms and existential anxiety, but more like a manifestation of the primordial energy of awareness that was every-where present. The mystical experience is not some dreamy fantasy, as anyone who has had one can agree. Psychological research into the mystical experience has yielded the following definition: a sense of profound unity within oneself and with the outside world; a transcendence of space and time or a feeling of being in touch with infinity and eternity; a sense of sacredness, awe or numinosity; a sense of the supreme reality and truth of the insight; the embracing of paradoxes or transcendence of dual-ity; ineffability; and overall positive affect. The mystical experience is a transformative contact with the Ground of Being and, although it is beyond description, it gives people an expanded apprecia-tion of life. During times of cynicism and despair, experiences that empower people to heal conflicts and choose life are especially valuable. I wanted my paintings to visually chart the spectrum of con-

sciousness from material perception to spiritual insight; and to function, if possible, as symbolic portals to the mystical dimension (1990:31).

The twenty-one paintings of the "Sacred Mirrors" project are forty-six by eighty-six inches each and have arched metal frames in which Alex Grey and his wife Allyson symbolically depicted the birth of the universe and the evolution of man and technology. The elaborate frames provide the evolutionary background for the principal subject of the "Sacred Mirrors," a series of frontal life-sized human figures which Grey progressively unraveled from skin to circulatory system to lymphatic system to viscera to nervous system to psychic energy system to spiritual energy system to universal mind lattice to void clear light to various transcendent beings. For Grey,

> This format allows the viewer to stand before the painted figure and "mirror" the image. A resonance takes place between one's own body and the painted image, creating a sense of "seeing into" oneself. The *Sacred Mirrors* may be used as a tool to visualize and focus healing energy to particular parts of the physical and metaphysical bodies (1990:32).

Although audience reactions have not been documented, the paintings probably work well for the average viewer, because, given Grey's profound knowledge of anatomy, he was able to locate and render physical points of distress accurately in the finest detail. In fact, the artist earns most of his livelihood as a medical illustrator.

As a healing tool for the metaphysical systems, however, the "Sacred Mirrors" are more problematic unless the viewer is actively working with these systems. I have not seen any other example of shamanic X-ray art which differentiates the various metaphysical systems with such exactness and finesse. Grey was capable of conveying the most evanescent vision in palpable terms.

This became evident in "The Psychic Energy System," the first of the metaphysical systems portrayed in the "Sacred Mirrors." Not only did Grey depict the seven major *chakras*, he showed also the interpenetration of the ethereal layer, "an oceanic lattice of energy," as he called it, with these *chakras* as a network of delicate white lines in a blue field (1990:36).

In the "Spiritual Energy System," these light lines are thinner and more numerous which is appropriate given the higher vibration of this system. Grey described this painting as follows:

> The *Spiritual Energy System* is an image of heightened awareness. The body has become a permeable channel for the circulation of the subtle and fine energies of spiritual consciousness that are everpresent and interpenetrate the self and surroundings. Parallel lines of force stream through the body extending out of the crown of the head and curling back around to the feet, creating a toroidal flow (1990:36).

In the "Spiritual Energy System," the boundary lines of the body, especially those of the head, legs and fingers, begin to dissolve as the body is opened up to higher energies. In the "Universal Mind Lattice," the only visible remnant of the body is a spine-like central pole, a veritable *axis mundi* that connects the psychic and the spiritual system to a web of curvilinear light lines. These light lines are Grey's version of the level of mind that Gordon Onslow-Ford referred to as the "Original Seed," the dance of energy underlying phenomenal reality that connects all phenomena.

Grey has a graphic recollection of his first vision of the

"Universal Mind Lattice" while wearing a blindfold and earplugs on L.S.D.

> I was part of one vast luminescent, transparent lattice system of love energy. It was as if the veil of supposed "reality" had been stripped from the material world to expose the bedrock reality, the scaffolding of the spirit. I understood it as the intricate interconnectedness of the one and the many on a level of awareness that was infinite and eternal. This was the ethical ground of compassion, where all beings and things are known to be part of us. I knew death needn't be feared because we would eventually return to the profound bliss of this realm (1990:23).

Grey explained that the painting

> portrays an advanced level of spiritual reality that transcends the physical body and all material objects. The Self is seen as a torus-like energy cell, a fountain of consciousness with an infinite, omnidirectional network of similar cells. The Self is distinct from every other cell, and, at the same time, in complete union with all other energy centers in the network. The surrounding cells represent the energy source of every other being and thing....The unified network of energy bodies represented in the painting could be called the Body of God, the Atman in the Brahman, or the fabric of being, beyond space and time (1990:36).

Aside from this significance, the "Universal Mind Lattice," as well as the "Psychic and Spiritual Energy Systems," have light lines radiating an incandescent energy that transcends any physical medium. The light lines in Grey's paintings are comparable in brilliance to those in Huichol yarn and

Australian Aboriginal paintings. The tribal paintings are products of similar seeing techniques, using peyote in the case of the Huichols and the "Strong Eye" in the case of the Aboriginal Australians (see my essay, "Seeing the Light Lines," 1992).

Grey believes that the brilliant light lines of the "Universal Mind Lattice" and the "Psychic and Spiritual Energy Systems" are "repositories of transcendental energy that can 'charge' the receptive, contemplative viewer" (1990:31). This claim is not farfetched. It is generally accepted among connoisseurs of Chinese art, for example, that the energy lines in the great masterpieces of Chinese paintings have the capacity of rejuvenating the viewer.

During his work on the "Sacred Mirrors" series (which was finally completed in 1989), Grey became increasingly involved in the theory and practice of Tibetan Buddhism. He continues to study meditation and visualization techniques under the guidance of Namkhai Norbu, a master of *Dzogchen* teaching. (*Dzogchen* incorporates many of the seeing techniques found in the earlier shamanic practice of Bon.) In his foreword to *Self Liberation Through Seeing With Naked Awareness*, Norbu described the core of *Dzogchen*, originally established by the great Tibetan Guru Padmasambhava,

> It is also called *tha-mal gyi shes-pa*, which means "ordinary awareness"; but this is not our ordinary mind incessantly thinking of this or that throughout the day. In *Dzogchen* we make a radical and fundamental distinction between mind...and the nature of mind...; and here ordinary awareness refers to the latter. The nature of mind is like a mirror which has the natural and inherent capacity to reflect whatever is set before it, whether beautiful or ugly; but these reflections in no way affect or modify the nature of the mirror. There is nothing to correct or alter or modify...What the practitioner does when entering

into contemplation is simply to discover himself in
the condition of the mirror (Padmasambhava,
1989:x).

Grey felt he understood intuitively the connection between
Dzogchen ideas of the mirror and the "Sacred Mirrors" series
before he began *Dzogchen* practices. He even quoted in his
book the above-mentioned Norbu passage to preface his
discussion of the "Sacred Mirrors."

While Grey didn't explicitly explain the relationship
between his "Sacred Mirrors" and the idea of the mirror in
Dzogchen teaching, it could be described as follows: Although the body is a material substance, it is neither fixed nor
immutable but merely an illusion of the mind whose projections can be altered through positive images. For the "Sacred
Mirrors" to work as vehicles for healing, the viewer must enter
a deep state of contemplation to become a pure mirror, as it
were, and reflect the healthy image set before him/her on a
somatic level.

The idea of healing, conveyed by the "Sacred Mirrors,"
is similar to ideas in shamanic healing. In a state of trance,
unclouded by their own emotions, some shamans envision
their client's body as perfectly healthy. This process can help
to bring about a cure. It is fundamental to both shamanism and
Buddhism that the mind has a direct effect on matter.

"Theologue," another Grey painting depicting light
lines can also be related to Buddhist teachings, particularly the
Avatamsaka Sutras, Grey's favorite Buddhist text. In many
passages of this text, surrounded by flames of energy, the
Buddha creates other Buddhas and beings through great
"beams" or "nets" of light.[10]

There are further similarities between the Buddhist
concept of the light lines, "Theologue," and the Navaho
legend of Spider Woman spinning the earth into being from
the rays of the sun. After Donna Henes, a performance and
installation artist in New York, had a vision of Spider Woman

in 1975, she began creating webs, knots and streamers of various materials in parks, museums and other public places as well as continuing her interactive rituals to "weave" people together. She says of her work,

> It's not like inventing forms. When I do these things (in trance] it's more like tracing energy lines that already exist in the space, connecting energy particles. Sometimes it's just making visible what is already existing (1979:24-29).

"During deep meditation," said Grey,

> I entered a state were all energy systems in my body were completely aligned and flowing; it was in this state that I envisioned Theologue—The Union of Human and Divine Consciousness Weaving the Fabric of Space and Time in Which the Self and Its Surroundings Are Embedded. I was wearing a Mindfold which allowed me to stare into total darkness. I stared into an infinite regress of electric perspective grids that radiated from my brain/mind and led to the horizon. A mystic fire engulfed me. Across the horizon all I could see were perspective lines going into deep space. I was seeing both the perceptual grid of my mind on which space and time are woven, and the universal mind which was both the source and the weaving loom. At this moment, faintly, Himalayan mountains appeared. Transparent, but present, they formed a vast and beautiful panorama and then disappeared back into the grid.[11]

Unlike the "Universal Mind Lattice," in which the lines are organic and curvilinear, the lines in "Theologue," emanating from the head region of the seated meditating figure (a doppelgänger for the artist?) at the center of the painting, are geometric. I believe that "Theologue" represents a stage of evolutionary development even prior to the "Original Seed" or the dance of organic energy lines. It is the universe at the stage when it first emerges from undifferentiated energy or pure Being. This idea should be expressed, in the mind of the creator(s), in geometric rather than organic terms.

I think that the concept of light lines expressed in "Theologue" is also held by contemporary physicists who believe that there are no fundamental particles underlying matter but vibrating superstrings (light lines) about 100 billion billion times smaller than a proton. The vibration of the superstrings is concomitant with a particular material form that emerges from it. Superstrings, however, remain a mathematical formulation since physicists have no scientific means to observe them. They do not exist in the usual "physical" realm (Kaku and Trainer, 1987).

Grey's visions also have features which can be found in shamanic texts. When he was in the process of moving from Boston to New York in 1984, which turned out to become a rather traumatic experience, he received spontaneous images of himself in a tunnel through which he traveled to his ritual dismemberment in the lower realm. The painting, "Journey of the Wounded Healer" (1985; Illustration 10) is the result of this vision and his research on this vision in the shamanic literature.

"In the first panel [of the "Journey of the Wounded Healer"]," Grey said,

> we see the self trapped in a dizzying vortex of evolutionary descent, paralleling the hallucinatory descent of the initiate shaman into the underworld or realm of the dead. The prisoner yearns for freedom and becomes sick with the materialist limitations of his genetic chains represented by entrapment in a spiraling DNA molecule [represented by translucent red and green balls, encircling a skeletonized figure].

In the central panel the self explodes and dismembers itself in the mysterium tremendum, a powerful confrontation with forces on all levels of reality: sub-atomic, cellular, planetary, galactic, psychical, spiritual. The energy which animates the All, the force of God, erupts through the embodied self and destroys identification with the sickly contracted ego, opening the self to merge with new powers. An alchemical serpent power with three heads (representing body, mind, and spirit) weaves an integrating and transmuting energy which binds together the new self.

In the final panel, the reintegrated man ascends into the middle and upper worlds, released from the psychic bonds of materialist entrapment and tapped into the light which beams from the mind and heart. As a healer, he wields a crystalline hermetic caduceus with the balanced serpent powers of the unconscious and winged vision of the superconscious. The healer/scientist/artist ascends the crystal mountain of the higher self, a self empowered by the responsibility for healing the future.[12]

Grey's image of the "reintegrated man," radiating energy from the mind and heart is a powerful image of the artist/shaman that can serve as an inspiration to other artists to realize their full potential. It is far removed from the romantic image of the disempowered artist at odds with himself and the world. This image, however, still pervades the contemporary art scene.

One of the ways contemporary artists attempt to realize their full potential is by transcending their habitual ways of viewing. The altered state of consciousness associated with seeing can be accomplished by a variety of methods as the artists in this chapter have demonstrated. To change their patterns of perception, most of the artists only had to withdraw, to some extent, from the social whirl of urban art life and slow down their mental activity.

Notes

1. I will be referring to Castaneda's works throughout this book. I agree along with anthropologist Hans Peter Duerr that "It is difficult to judge just how authentic Castaneda's reports are. At any rate, there is no justification for rejecting out of hand the claim that Don Juan was an Indian and that he was within the tradition of such sorcerers" (1985:81). Despite the inaccuracy of some of Castaneda's statements, he provided excellent descriptions of shamanic states and concepts that are known to shamans. Therefore, I have no hesitation to use his descriptions or refer to them in this book.

2. Rilke based his ideas about Cézanne's life on the artist Emile Bernard's reminiscences of Cézanne in the Parisian paper *L'Occident* of July, 1904.

3. "Late in his life Morandi expressed a mild regret that he had never been to Paris; a visit to London or New York would no more have occurred to him than a trip to the moon," said art critic Robert Hughes (1986:161).

4. For a brief period in his career, from 1918 to 1920, Morandi was part of the Schola Metaphysica, a group of Italian painters including Georgio de Chirico and Carlo Carra who juxtaposed unrelated unusual objects in strange settings. Morandi's Schola Metaphysica works are basically artificial inventions, yet after 1920 his paintings were the result of seeing; he moved from the ordinary to the extraordinary, from the physical to the metaphysical.

5. That Jean Arp was well acquainted with the I-ching was affirmed in my interview with Margaret Hagenbach Arp in May of 1974 at Arp's studio in Meudon.

6. Patrick Waldberg (1958:68) pointed out that there was also a German tradition of seeing, one half a century before Rimbaud. He cited Achim von Arnim, Novalis, Franz von Baader, Gotthilf Heinrich Schubert, and Johann Carl Pasavant as poets who saw themselves as "seers," "visionaries," and "prophets" and believed that they "prepared" Ernst to receive the message of Rimbaud. And Uwe M. Schneede said that Ernst was undoubtedly familiar with Caspar David Friedrich's statement, "Close your physical eye, so that you see your painting first of all with the eye of the spirit" (1973:105).

7. Interview with the artist, San Francisco, April 1990.

8. Grey later discovered a link between his interest in death and Buddhaghosa's *The Path of Purity*. Buddhaghosa was a 5th century Buddhist teacher from Ceylon who recommended that, to overcome their fear and disgust of death, monks should look at burning and decomposed bodies on cremation grounds (see, Buddhaghosa, 1975:87-88).

9. Interview with the artist, New York, May 1991.

10. See, "The Wonderful Adornments of the Teachers of the World," "The Formation of the Worlds," and "Awakening of Light," in Thomas Cleary, trans., (1984:55-149, 182-201, and 282-297).

11. Grey, see caption on the plate of "Theologue," not paginated.

12. Grey, see caption on the plate of the "Journey of the Wounded Healer," not paginated.

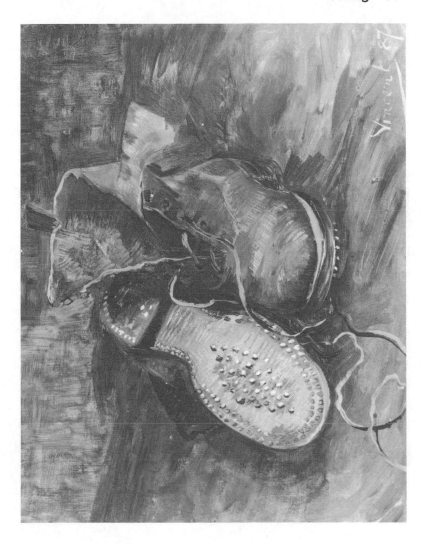

1. Vincent Van Gough
   "A Pair of Boots," 1887
   Oil on canvas
   13 x 16⅛ inches
   The Baltimore Museum of Art: The Cone Collection, formed
   by Dr. Claribel Cone and Miss Etta Cone of Baltimore, ML

2. Paul Cézanne
    "Chocquet Seated," 1887
    Oil on canvas
    18⅛ x 16 inches
    Columbus Museum of Fine Arts
    Howard Fund Purchase

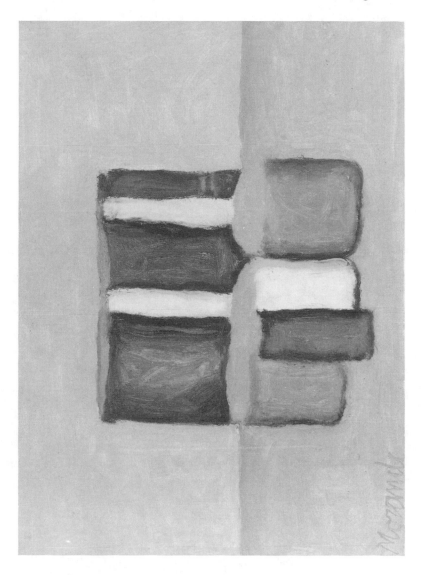

3. Giorgio Morandi
    "Still Life," 1959
    Oil painting
    25 x 35 inches
    Private Collection

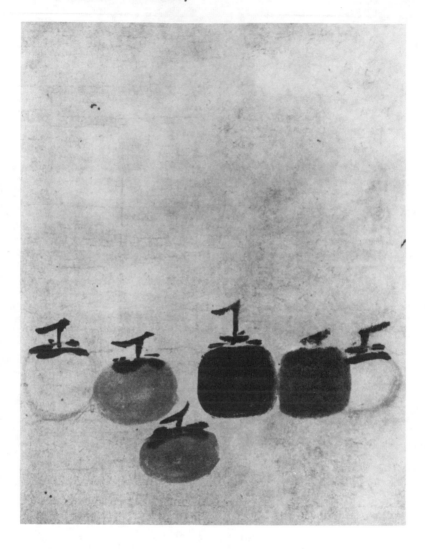

4. Mu Chi
    "Persimmons," late 13th century
    55 x 29 centimeters
    Ink on paper
    Ryuko-in, Daitokuji Monastery, Kyoto, Japan

5.   Frida Kahlo
     "The Broken Column," 1944
     Oil on masonite
     15¾ x 12¼ inches
     Collection of Dolores Olmedo, Mexico City

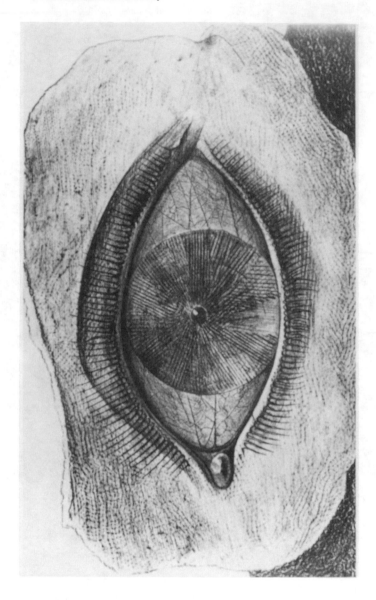

6.   Max Ernst
     "The Wheel of Light,"
     from plate XXIX in the book *Histoire Naturelle*
     published by Jeanne Bucher, Paris, 1926
     9⅞ x 16½ inches
     Frottage reproduced by photogravure

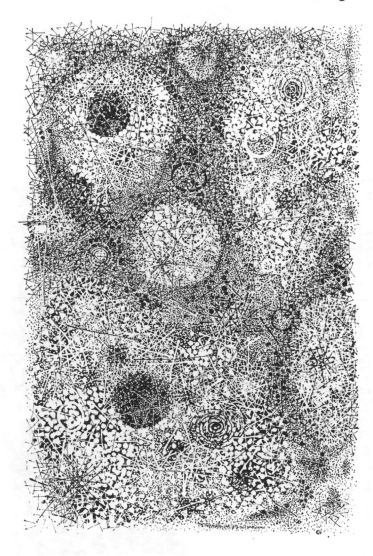

7. Gordon Onslow Ford
    "Round See," 1961
    Acrylic on mulberry paper
    67 x 102 inches
    Collection Gordon Onslow-Ford
    Courtesy Gordon Onslow-Ford

8.   Robert Irwin
     Market Street Studio, Venice, CA, May 1980
     Installation with scrim
     Photo credit, Malinda Wyatt

9. Arthur Tress
   "The Illumination," from the book *Shadow,* 1975
   Black and white photograph
   with permission of the artist

10. Alex Grey
    "Journey of the Wounded Healer," 1984–1985
    Oil on linen
    90 x 224 inches
    collection of the artist
    with permission of the artist

Dreaming

Whether by day, when in a contemplative mood, or by night, when we are sleeping, we all are dreaming. Because we may not remember, some of our dreams never rise to waking consciousness. Scientists have been measuring rapid eye movements (R.E.M.) of sleeping subjects and keep telling us that most of us have up to four or five dreams over a period of one and a half hours each night.

With the advent of rationalism and materialism in Western culture, however, dreams have been generally devalued. Consequently, relatively few individuals make an effort to remember their dreams or interpret and use dreams as source for creative endeavors, healing, knowledge, and inspiration.

The devaluation of dreams began with the Greek philosophers of the Hellenic period. According to Plato, Socrates believed that dreams are the repository of irregular and base desires which go against reason and common sense. Aristotle held that dreams were simply the result of small internal and external movements of the body and could not be a source of knowledge because everybody dreams, not just philosophers.

Freud, although acknowledging the importance of dreams for psychotherapy, agreed with Socrates that dreams are the expression of repressed instincts and desires and, agreeing with Aristotle, proposed that they can be traced to biological causes. Freud also believed that dreams protect rather than disturb sleep, indicating that the true meaning of dreams is hidden in a hermetic symbolic language. Perhaps the real reason why Freud found the symbolic language of dreams to be hermetic is that modern civilization, being fragmented, suffers from a paucity of commonly shared symbols. This also makes the interpretation of dreams more difficult.

However, in ancient Greek, Egyptian, and Hebrew cultures, in Christian and Islamic as well as tribal societies, from Malaysia to Greenland, dreams have provided an important vehicle to access the knowledge found in non-ordinary reality for anyone who is willing to make an effort to remember. Indeed, remembering and programming one's dreams is a very powerful technique of shamanic practice.

As Susan Hiller and David Coxhead pointed out in their book *Dreams*,

> the idea was widespread in the ancient world that the unknown, or God, was more accessible to ordinary people in dreams that in vision by day, in which a more subtle reality has to compete with and overcome the perceptions of the senses (1975:8).

Dream interpretations are usually assigned to wise men or shamans in traditional and tribal cultures, but many "ordinary" dreamers are able to understand much of the culturally shared symbolic content without outside help and without taking recourse to hypnosis or other trance inductions.

Dreaming is as effective as trance in eliminating the will and the ego. In the words of C.G. Jung,

> The dream is a little hidden door in the innermost and most secret recesses of the soul, opening into that cosmic night which was psyche before there was any ego-consciousness, and which will remain psyche no matter how far our ego consciousness

extends. For all ego-consciousness is isolated; because it separates and discriminates, it knows only
particulars, and it sees only those that can be related
to the ego. Its essence is limitation, even though it
may reach to the farthest nebulae among the stars.
All consciousness separates; but in dreams we put
on the likeness of that more universal, truer, more
eternal man dwelling in the darkness of primordial
night. There he is still the whole, and the whole is in
him, indistinguishable from nature and bare of all
egohood. It is from these all-uniting depths that the
dream arises, be it never so childish, grotesque and
immoral (1953:53).

In my experience, shamanic journeys (undertaken in
trance states) and dream journeys (accomplished during sleep
states) are very similar. Both are ecstatic trips out of the body.
In tribal cultures, the soul is believed to leave the body during
dreaming. Anthropologist Edward B. Tylor, in his article,
"The Soul Goes Hunting and Dancing," described soul travel
in tribal cultures as follows,

...Greenlanders...consider that the soul quits the
body in the night and goes out hunting, dancing and
visiting; their dreams, which are frequent and
lively, having brought them to this opinion....New
Zealanders considered the dreaming soul to quit the
body and return, even traveling to the region of the
dead to hold converse with its friends. The Tagals of
Luzon object to waking a sleeper, on account of the
absence to his soul. The Karens, whose theory of the
wandering soul has just been noticed, explain
dreams to be what this *là* [soul] sees and experi
ences in its journeys when it has left the body asleep
(1974:111).

Like the soul on a shamanic journey, in a dream the soul can visit the upper or spirit world, the middle world of everyday reality, and the lower realms which include the realm of the dead. The dreamer can also be visited by another soul from the three realms (Tylor, 1974:112). By "setting up dreaming" (Castaneda's words), the dreamer can choose to visit with a particular soul, when entering the upper, middle, lower realms, can ask for the solution of a problem or creative impasse (dream incubation) or can simply allow the dream to happen. The same choices are available during a shamanic journey, although I have found that "setting up dreaming" is more difficult than directing the soul in shamanic journeys because, in dreaming, the dreamer is less in control.

The first step in "setting up dreaming" is to believe that dreams are valuable. As psychologist Patricia Garfield remarked in *Creative Dreaming*, "Dreamers who regard dreams as important and even vital to success in life will receive and remember helpful dreams" (1974:60). She went on to say that

> In our society there are no cultural pattern dreams required, nor, indeed, much societal reward for dreaming. Only you, the individual dreamer, can encourage your own desired dreams by the pleasures they bring you" (1974:65).

I believe that those individuals who question the materialist/rationalist assumptions of society are the most likely to regard dreams as meaningful. They tend to be outsiders in relation to the dominant ideological system. Some of them are artists.

Let us examine modern artists who "set up dreaming" as part of their creative process. Their method may entail simply writing the dream down and expressing it in visual images (a procedure which greatly facilitates the remembering of the dream). Artists may also ask for specific dreams in a meditative state, employ sophisticated dream interpretation methods and, in rare instances, practice lucid dreaming (i.e., learn how to become aware that they are dreaming and direct the course of their dream).

Henri Rousseau, Giorgio de Chirico, André Breton, Salvador Dali, Louis Buñuel, Man Ray, Carolee Schneemann, Ann McCoy, and Jonathan Borofsky have used one or more of these methods and, therefore, have actively used a shamanic technique of dreaming as opposed to artists whose work is dreamlike.

Although there is a dearth of authentic documentary information concerning the life and paintings of Henri Rousseau, there are a few tantalizing clues to suggest that an important source for his work was dreaming. Yam le Pichon, who took piano lessons from Rousseau's daughter, was told by her that Rousseau had the habit of dozing off in a chair in front of his paintings and then moving his brush across the canvas. Once, on waking, he exclaimed to visitors in his studio that his deceased wife had directed his hand (Le Pichon, 1982:27).

There is no evidence in the extensive annals of dream research to indicate that it is possible to actually paint a picture while dreaming, yet I think it is plausible that Rousseau had a dream helper who guided him in the creation of his work. Dream helpers such as a loved one or a former enemy are found in tribal cultures who engage in dream work (Stewart, 1969:159-167). Often these helpers provide ideas that dreamers can then use in their waking life to solve problems or express them in art.

According to Rousseau's friend, the poet Apollinaire,

> Those who knew Rousseau...recall his taste for ghosts. He had run into ghosts everywhere, and one of them tormented him for more than a year when he was a customs inspector (Le Pichon, 1982:186.)

Whenever our good Rousseau was on duty, his familiar ghost stood ten paces away from him, annoying him, poking fun at him, letting out smelly farts, which nauseated Rousseau. Over and over again, Rousseau tried to shoot the ghost; but a phantom cannot die again. Rousseau also stated that Catulle Mendes had been a great necromancer. "He dropped by my studio one day," said Rousseau, "and took me to a house on Rue Saint-Jacques; on the third floor, there was a dying man whose soul floated about the room in the shape of a transparent and luminous work" (quoted in Rubin, 1968:127-128).

To be sure, Apollinaire was not the most reliable of witnesses, but I think his story at least gives some support to the possibility that Rousseau was open to the spirit world in waking as well as dream reality.

Whether his departed wife actually guided his hand in one of his most important paintings, "The Dream" (Illustration 11), is impossible to determine, yet it seems clear that the painting reflects his experience of dreaming. The painting shows a voluptuous nude woman reclining on a red sofa in the midst of a luxuriant tropical landscape with exotic flora and fauna and a black native playing a flute. Rousseau wrote the following poem about this painting:

Having fallen into a gentle sleep
Yadwigha [Rousseau's nickname for his departed
wife Clemence], in a dream,
Heard the sounds of a musette
Played by a benevolent magician.
While the moon shone down
Upon the flowers, the green trees,
The wild serpents listened to
The instrument's many tunes
(Museum of Modern Art, 1985:252).

Also, as Rousseau mentioned in a letter to the French critic André Dupont,

> This woman sleeping on this sofa dreams that she is transported into the middle of this forest, hearing the notes of the charmer's pipe. This gives the motive for the sofa appearing in the picture (Shattuck, 1968:111).

The sofa that Rousseau referred to in this statement is the one in his studio on which he probably dreamt the subjects for this painting. In any event, several critics mentioned the dreamlike quality of this and other paintings. André Malraux said, "This art is not defined by what he sees...but by...what he dreams" (Le Pichon, 1982:71). For Roger Shattuck,

> Rousseau's realism is that of the remembered or dream image set down directly in paint—an image seeking not to outrage the purely optical arrangement of the world, but to complete it (1968:109).

And, according to art historian William Rubin,

> Rousseau's exotic pictures derive their dreamlike quality from the simplification and conventionalization of forms, which are often rendered with the frontality and strict profile common to primitive, archaic, and other "conceptual" styles. The dream process, being selective, suppresses in a similar way much of the kind of detail associated with the perceptual experience (1968:128).

I agree with Shattuck's statement that Rousseau's painting exhibits a kind of realism, albeit a magical one, and, in general, with Rubin's statement that Rousseau's simplified and "conceptualized" style is appropriate to dream imagery.

Only in rare instances is the quantity of the dream data equivalent to the data given to perception in ordinary reality. Nevertheless, the vividness and clarity of the dream data, however limited, is often greater than that of ordinary reality, particularly if the dreamer sets up dreaming beforehand. Notwithstanding its abstract character, Rousseau's style has an extraordinary clarity which is the product of the precision of the contour lines and the brightness of the colors. This clarity is consistent in both foreground and background, because there is no atmospheric perspective to blur the contour lines or to diminish the intensity of the colors. The high degree of finish, which necessitates a meticulous approach (Rousseau painted from the top to bottom of the canvas, inch by inch) involves the addition of many layers of paint and the elimination of traces of brush work and texture. Such meticulous approach enhances the luster of colors and the clarity of forms. In fact, Rousseau was greatly taken with the finish of French academics, such as Jean Leon Gérome, Bonnat, Adolphe William Bougereau, and so forth, because this finish gave their paintings a sense of hyper-reality.

In some of the paintings of the academics and in Rousseau's work as a whole, the light is evenly distributed throughout the composition, making it impossible to determine both the source of the light and the time of day. As Roger Shattuck pointed out

> ...in spite of impressionist titles...[he] painted only three lights: high noon, moonlight and the uniform floodlighting of a photographer's studio. Even this division is precarious; they resolve into a single mysterious lighting from all sides, shadowless, without high lights, without any power to dissolve color (1968:105).

Rousseau light is the light of dreams; rarely does the dreamer distinguish between different times of day or night and notices the source of the light and shadows.

Despite the similarities between Rousseau's paintings and those of the academics, Rousseau considered himself a naive painter. In a letter to the critic André Dupont, which I mentioned earlier, Rousseau also said,

> I thank you for your kind appreciation, and if I have kept my naiveté, it is because M. Gérome, who was a professor at the Beaux Arts, as well as M. Clément, director of Beaux Arts at the Ecole de Lyon, always told me to keep it. You will no longer find that amazing in the future. And I have been told before that I was not of this century. I will not now be able to change my manner which I have acquired by stubborn application, believe me (quoted in Shattuck, 1968:111-112).

Actually the idea that Rousseau was a naive or primitive artist is a myth that he himself promulgated. Not only was he educated on the Lycée level, an opportunity that was only open to the minority of the French population at that time, but his style has similarities with late nineteenth century avant-garde tendencies such as Gauguin's symbolic style in its abstraction, lack of modeling and natural light, and intense colors. I believe that Rousseau's style is not the result of his inability to paint like the academics or the impressionists (Rousseau produced some very good impressionist studies) but because this style was uniquely suited to embody the visual qualities of dreams.

The preternatural light, clarity, and simplicity of "The Dream" and many other paintings by Rousseau evokes the mood of primordial setting that has been noticed by several commentators. The painter Max Beckmann remarked, "I was thinking of my grand old friend Henri Rousseau, that Homer in a concierge booth, with his prehistoric dream that sometimes brought me very close to the gods." (Le Pichon, 1982:71). And André Malraux said, "his [Rousseau's] greatest paintings link up with a prehistoric past" (1953:510).

I think Malraux and Beckmann, two very acute observers, have sensed that there is a content in Rousseau's paintings which transports the viewer to a place anterior to ordinary time and space.

In dreams and shamanic journeys I have sometimes gone to power spots and landscapes that I have not experienced before in waking reality. The tropical landscape in the "Dream" reminds me of one of these locations, and the desert moonlit landscape of the "Sleeping Gypsy," where a reclining figure seems to dream the surroundings, reminds me of another in its stark silence and archaic simplicity. Rousseau's paintings are as good an approximation of the visual look and sublime mood of these spots as I have seen.

Rubin mentioned, in his analysis of Rousseau, that

> Although...the starting point for most of Rousseau's flowers was sketches made in the Jardin des Plantes, botanists have indicated that the process of reduction and simplification has made it impossible to identify most of them (some appear to be pure inventions) (1968:128).

Yam le Pichon has attempted to identify the sources of many of Rousseau's paintings in the illustrated magazines of that time, particularly a catalogue of animals issued by the Galleries Lafayette that was found in Rousseau's studio. Yet, he was unable to trace the origins of Rousseau's landscapes which have only a superficial resemblance to those of the illustrated magazines. I believe that the source of these "pure inventions" do not lie in Rousseau's waking reality, not even in his visits to the Jardin des Plantes.

Gordon Globus, a transpersonal psychologist and dream expert, argued that there is only an "abstract connection" between "dream life and certain episodes of wake life" and that dreams are more than "the residues of waking life" (1987:62). "We discovered," he said,

that dreaming consciousness is radically more creative and original than Freud thought [he believed
that dreams were a bricolage of waking experi-
ences], that we dream-think up sometimes stupendous worlds each night, that we are capable of
formatively generating by purely abstract means
concrete exemplifications of our meanings, like the
thought of Zeus issues in the concrete Athena
(1987:62).

Because we have no sensory input and our memory functions
are drastically altered, *"we have the capacity"*, said Globus,

for infinite creativity; at least while dreaming, we
partake of the power of immanent Spirit, the infinite
Godhead that creates the cosmos. In waking "we
contract away from infinity," as Wilber says [in
Holographic Paradigm], and take a Heideggerian
"fall" into a limited life-world (1987:62).

Although Globus did not state it so specifically, I think his
concept of dreams is based on the *Holographic Paradigm*. As
Ken Wilber explained,

A hologram is a special type of optical storage
system that can best be explained by an example: if
you take a holographic photo of, say, a horse, and
cut out one section of it, e.g., the horse's head, and
then enlarge that section to the original size, you
will get, not a big head, but a picture of the whole
horse. In other words, each individual part of the
picture contains the *whole* picture in condensed
form. The part is the whole and the whole is in each
part—a type of unity-in-diversity and diversity-in-
unity. The key point is simply that the *part* has
access to the *whole*.

Thus, if the brain did function like a hologram, then it might have access to a larger whole, a field domain or "holistic frequency realm" that transcended spatial and temporal boundaries. And this domain, reasoned Pribam [one of the authors of this theory], might very likely be the same domain of transcendental unity-in diversity described (and experienced) by the world's great mystics and sages (1982:2).

In dreams, the mind functions as a hologram, dreaming up "stupendous worlds at night" that one does not have access to in waking reality. Rousseau's dreaming allowed him to find a primordial power spot which was beyond ordinary time and space in the "larger field." Like every other mortal, Rousseau's dreams probably contained elements of his waking reality, but he was capable of the "big dream" that transcended his own limited experience.

Michael Hoog, in the catalogue for the 1985 Rousseau retrospective at the Museum of Modern Art, argued

This impecunious suburbanite, aware that he had led an unadventurous life, was through the evocation of the "incredible floridas" of Arthur Rimbaud's visions to satisfy his own need for dream, for escape—the same escape Rimbaud and Gauguin had sought in flight and revolt; that Pierre Loti (whose portrait Rousseau painted...) was to realize in the conformist career of naval officer and celebrated novelist; that Redon, Gustave Moreau, Fantin-Latour, and Stephane Mallarmé would find by taking refuge in their inner worlds, Monet beside his pond, Cézanne opposite his mountain (1985: 31).

I think Rousseau's work represents more than merely

the desire among artists of his period to escape from the materialistic confines of late nineteenth century France. As Hoog suggests, Rousseau's landscapes have an hallucinatory intensity that can be compared to Arthur Rimbaud's "incredible floridas." Not only were the visionary landscapes of Rousseau and Rimbaud conceived in a state of altered consciousness, but they also reflect a domain that lies beyond ordinary reality, the domain of shamanic power places. Monet's impressionistic water lilies, Loti's poetic verbal narratives of actual places, and Gauguin's South Sea fantasies pale in comparison to the landscapes of Rimbaud and Rousseau.

Giorgio de Chirico did not know Rousseau personally, but he knew of him through his friend Apollinaire and probably saw "The Dream" in the collection of Ambrose Vollard, Apollinaire's friend. De Chirico had been introduced to Apollinaire and his circle through Ardengo Soffici who was the first critic to associate de Chirico's painting of 1911-17 with dream images. Soffici said about de Chirico's work,

> One could define it as a dream writing. By means of almost infinite escapes—of arcades and facades, of bold straight lines, of looming masses of simple colors, of almost funereal lights and shadows—he ends in fact by expressing this sense of vastness, solitude, immobility and ecstasy which sometimes is produced in our souls by certain spectacles of memory when we are asleep (quoted in Soby, 1966:48).

Apollinaire even quoted this passage in his own review of de Chirico's paintings at the 1914 exhibition of the Salon des Independants in Paris.

André Breton was also very much taken with the dream-like images in de Chirico's work and credited him with having a major influence on his thought, leading to the formation of surrealism. In *Surrealism and Painting*, Breton maintained that the evolution of de Chirico's painting from 1911 involved an "ever-increasing importance" of "the world of the dream" (1972a:63).

Of all the critics who noticed the relationship of de Chirico's work to dreams, William Rubin gave the most extended analysis. "The images in de Chirico's paintings," he wrote,

> are more like those we actually see in dreams than are the images in the paintings of the Surrealists who were influenced by him. De Chirico shuns the fantastical almost entirely. (His mannequins are an exception, but even these probably derive from storewindow figures and tailors' dummies). The mysterious white light in his pictures is less like sunlight (even Mediterranean sunlight) then it is like that "interior light" already noticed in Henry Rousseau's paintings, and its absolute clarity, combined with the simplification and generalization of the shapes it illuminates, produces an apparitional effect closer to dream experience than to anything else. (In his notebooks Leonardo mentions that we see things with much greater clarity in dreams than in waking life).
>
> Sensations of sound, psychiatrists observe, are extremely rare in dreams, and in this connection the Leonardian silence that prevails in de Chirico's pictures is noteworthy. It is, however, a pregnant rather than a calm silence, charged with elusive, nightmarish forebodings. (Writing, in *Sur le Silence*, of the nature of great cataclysms, de Chirico

makes a point of warning us to "beware of the silence" that precedes them.)

The most literally dreamlike aspect of all in de Chirico's art consists of the *extraordinary juxtapositions of ordinary objects* in his paintings. As we know, different contexts and levels of reality constantly mingle in dreams. What makes these minglings striking in de Chirico's art is not so much their presence per se as the quality of the poetry evoked by his particular confrontations—a quality often intensified by exaggerated foreshortenings that bring the objects into hallucinatory proximity with the spectator (Rubin, 1968:131).

For me, the most dreamlike of de Chirico's paintings are the "City Squares" (Illustration 12) in their "silence," "vastness," "solitude," and "clarity." These paintings manifest a languid classical statue on a low plinth (I think it is highly significant that this horizontal female figure is either sleeping or emerging from sleep) in a deserted square surrounded by arcades. Here, de Chirico has established a realm beyond normal space and time that is similar in mood to the one found in Rousseau's tropical landscapes, albeit in the context of a city. Rubin feels that this realm has a "pregnant silence" that engenders a sense of "nightmarish foreboding." De Chirico himself said, in reference to his "City Squares,"

One of the strangest and deepest sensations that prehistory has left with us is the sensation of foretelling. It will always exist. It is like an eternal proof of the senselessness of the universe. The first man must have seen auguries everywhere, he must have trembled at each step he took (quoted in Soby, 1966:248).

For de Chirico and Rubin, the city squares were scary, but for me they have the awesome presence of a power spot. Of course, de Chirico did not have the cultural framework to understand the shamanic content of these places but, I think, he sensed that they cannot not be grasped by logical means.

De Chirico could have been influenced in the creation of the "City Squares" by Nietzsche. In "The Birth of Tragedy," which de Chirico read while a student in Munich, Nietzsche wrote in reference to the exemplary artist,

> through Apollonian dream—inspiration, his own state, that is his oneness with the innermost ground of the world, is revealed to him in a symbolical dream picture" (1968:38).

This "innermost ground of the world" can be identified with Nietzsche's concept of *Stimmung*. De Chirico said in his Memoirs that the true invention of Nietzsche

> is a strange and profound poetry, infinitely myste-rious and solitary, which is based on the *Stimmung* (I use this very effective German word which could be translated into atmosphere in the moral sense)...when the sky is clear and the shadows are longer than in summer, for the sun is beginning to lower (1971:55).

Needless to say, de Chirico's description of *Stimmung* doubles as a description of the "City Squares."

Perhaps the dreaming that produced the "City Squares" was also inspired by Nietzsche. In "The Birth of Tragedy," Nietzsche quoted the following passage from Wagner's "Meistersinger":

> The poets's task is this, my friend,
> to reveal his dreams and comprehend.

The truest human fancy seems
to be revealed to us in dreams:
all poems and versification
are but true dreams interpretation (1968:34).

Nietzsche went on to say, in "The Birth of Tragedy," that

The beautiful illusion of the dream worlds, in the
creation of which every man is a perfect artist, is the
prerequisite of all plastic art, and, as we shall see of
an important part of poetry also. In our dreams we
delight in the immediate understanding of figures;
all forms speak to us; there is nothing unimportant
or superfluous (1968:34).

Unlike Rousseau, de Chirico's "City Squares" appear to
be largely bricolages of his waking experience of the squares,
statuary and arcades of central and northern Italy. They seem
to echo Freud's theory on the origin of dreams and to contain
phallic images such as trains, smokestacks and round towers,
cannons, as well as feminine images such as arcades that
Freud discussed in his *Interpretation of Dreams* (1899).
James Thrall Soby wrote,

For de Chirico's trains are more disturbing than
most Freudian symbols of malaise invented by later
artists. They cut to the core of the ordinary experience. Sometimes they appear in the distance, amid
a silence evoking an almost physical longing for the
reassurance of their sound. Then again they are
animal-like, ferocious and caged, as in *The Anxious
Journey* (1966:49).

For me, de Chirico's images of trains are powerful,
because they are recapitulated from his own dream experience
and are not merely appropriations of Freudian sources. It is

doubtful that de Chirico had any interest in Freud before he met Breton in the early twenties. There are images in the "City Squares" that can be related to Freudian symbols, yet there are a few others that do not relate to Freud or any recognizable image in waking experience. What is the origin of the weird geometrical objects in "The Evil Genius of a King," "The General's Illness," "The Sailor's Barracks"? For me these objects are entities from an alien part of the dream time which do not exist in ordinary reality. They account for the element of "surprise" that Apollinaire noticed in de Chirico's work. I believe that de Chirico obtained these alien entities from his dreams. Indeed, these three paintings have the dreamlike qualities, "silence," "clarity," "vastness," and "solitude" that are found in the other "City Squares."

De Chirico's own references to the dream content of his work are ambiguous. Several of his paintings are given titles such as "The Double Dream of Spring," "The Transformed Dream," "The Dream of the Poet," "The Purity of the Dream," etc.

Some more clues about de Chirico's attitudes toward the dream are found in his unpublished manuscripts (1911-1915). In one of these manuscripts he applauds the work of Max Klinger whose work he much appreciated, saying that Klinger, "psychologically more complex than Böcklin, by combining in a single composition scenes of contemporary life and visions of antiquity, produces a highly troubling dream reality" (Soby, 1966:29). This is exactly what de Chirico did in his "City Squares." De Chirico went on to describe Klinger's etching, "The Agreement," saying that the mythological elements (tritons, etc.) are made "so clear" that "It is a dream and at the same time reality" (Carra, 1971:100).

When dreams are given the status of reality, then waking life has the status of a dream. Indeed, in "The Birth of Tragedy," Nietzsche said that Schopenhauer actually saw the criterion of philosophical ability to be the occasional ability to view men and things as mere phantoms and dream images

(1968:34). And, in 1919, de Chirico affirmed a related idea of Schopenhauer's on the apparitional content of certain sculptures when he said,

> Schopenhauer advised his fellow countrymen not to place the statues of their famous men on high columns or on pedestals, but on low plinths, "as they do in Italy, where some marble men seem to be on a level with the passers-by and seem to walk beside them" (Soby, 1966:247).

I am reminded of Don Genaro's wonderful demonstrations in *Journey to Ixtlan* that human beings and things are apparitions.

There are several other references to dreams in de Chirico's writing. In another of his unpublished manuscripts de Chirico wrote:

> To be really immortal a work of art must go completely beyond the limits of the human: good sense and logic will be missing from it.

> In this way it will come close to the dream state, and also the mentality of children (Soby, 1966:245)

He also celebrated the importance of the dream in a short paragraph, written in 1913, entitled "The Feeling of Prehistory,"

> The problem of what an artist should do becomes more and more disturbing. Nothing is profound enough, nothing pure enough. Everything that has satisfied painters until now to *us* seems child's play; this is why we look behind barriers in search of *something new*. Is it a dream, or a vision? Artists used to like to dream; their sweet souls fell asleep in

the moonlight, to the sound of a flute, on a woman's scented breast (Soby, 1966:247).

Yet, in a statement of 1919, he denied dreams as a "source of inspiration" for his work while, at the same time, saying that he had a "close relationship with dreams."

"We should keep constant control of our thoughts and of all the images that present themselves to our minds," said de Chirico,

> even when we are in a state of wakefulness, but which also have a close relationship with those we see in dreams. It is curious that in dreams no image, however strange it may be, ever strikes us because of its metaphysical strength; and therefore we flee from seeking a source of inspiration in the dream— the methods of people like Thomas de Quincey do not tempt us. Yet the dream is an extremely strange phenomenon and an inexplicable mystery; even more inexplicable is the mystery and appearance that our mind confers on certain objects and on certain aspects of life. Psychically speaking, the fact of the mysterious aspects of objects could be described as a system of cerebral abnormality akin to certain forms of madness....and that this is all the more fruitful when made manifest in an individual gifted with creative talent and clairvoyance. Art is the fatal net that catches these strange moments in flight, like mysterious butterflies, unnoticed by the innocence and experience of ordinary men (quoted in Carra, 1971:87).

I think that de Chirico did not want to fully admit he drew inspiration from dreams, so that he would not cast doubt on his creative abilities as an artist. And he was especially anxious about his creative abilities in 1919 because, from 1917 on, his art began to show a marked decline and he was no longer able to catch those "strange moments in flight" from non-ordinary reality like "mysterious butterflies."

Soby, believing that de Chirico was not in control of his sources of inspiration, said,

> Thus while Picasso's prime creative asset was perhaps his visual alertness, that of de Chirico was his susceptibility to a kind of self-hypnosis. Picasso's control can almost never be questioned. He was and is a great artist who has made creative accidents happen almost at will, a professional born to his art and incredibly deft. De Chirico, contrarily, seems helplessly involved in the strange happenings of his genius, an amateur delighted by bewildering success. One feels that he has watched the objects accumulate in *The Evil Genius of a King* as a child watches the contents of a Christmas stocking pour out on the floor, not knowing what will come next and exclaiming at the miracle of what has already appeared (1966:100-101).1

I do not think that de Chirico's "City Squares" are, even when compared to Picasso, in any way amateurish. De Chirico was able to capture the "fleeting butterflies" of non-ordinary reality in a compelling manner in many of his paintings. Yet, I believe, along with Soby, that he "seems helplessly involved in the strange happenings of his genius" in so far as he had subsumed his ego to non-rational sources such as dreams and the "self-hypnosis" of the seeing process. Indeed, in addition to dreaming there are several paintings in de Chirico's work that relate to seeing, as I have mentioned in the chapter on Seeing. In his unpublished manuscripts, de Chirico quoted Schopenhauer whom he had read as a young artist while studying in Munich. In the quoted passage from *Parerga* and *Paralipomena*, Schopenhauer put forth the theory that

To have original, extraordinary, and perhaps even immortal ideas, one has but to isolate oneself from the world for a few moments so completely that the most commonplace happenings appear to be new and unfamiliar, and in this way reveal their true essence (quoted in Soby, 1966:251).

As pointed out earlier, isolation is an important element in seeing and de Chirico led a rootless solitary existence for much of his youth. Illness also enforces isolation and can, by itself, alter consciousness in the process of seeing. As de Chirico himself wrote,

One clear autumnal afternoon I was sitting on a bench in the middle of the Piazza Santa Croce in Florence. It was of course not the first time I had seen the square. I had just came out of a long and painful intestinal illness, and I was in a nearly morbid state of sensitivity. The whole world, down to the marble of the buildings and the fountains, seemed to me to be convalescent. In the middle of the square rises a statue of Dante draped in a long cloak, holding his works clasped against his body, his laurel-crowned head bent thoughtfully earth-ward. The statue is in white marble, but time has given it a gray cast, very agreeable to the eye. The autumn sun, warm and unloving, lit the statue and the church facade. Then I had the strange impression that I was looking at all these things for the first time, and the composition of my picture ["Enigma of an Autumn Afternoon," 1910] came to my mind's eye. Now each time I look at this painting I again see that moment. Nevertheless the moment in an enigma to me, for it is inexplicable. And I like also to call the work which sprang from it an enigma (quoted in Soby, 1966:251).

Isolation also facilitates the setting up of dreaming. Patricia Garfield said that, based on current experimental studies,

> Relative isolation increases dreaming (and *total* isolation can produce hallucinations in normal people). *Awareness* of dreaming is no doubt increased when there are no social distractions. My own lengthy dream record shows many peaks of dream recall when life is relatively peaceful. Perhaps dreaming is greater in isolation as a compensation for the quiet life. Or, perhaps physical inactivity is responsible for increased dreaming (1974:69).

It is possible that de Chirico's isolation could also have enhanced the recall and subsequent vividness of the dream images in his paintings.

❖

In 1920, André Breton, the founder of surrealism, saw de Chirico's "Child's Brain" in the window of Paul Guiliaume's gallery in Paris. The painting was a veritable revelation to him because he had been looking for an artistic model that expressed non-ordinary reality. The experience of the First World War, in which bourgeois "rationality" led to the destruction of millions of men, and his interest in Freudian dream theory (which he studied as psychiatric orderly during the War) convinced Breton that the subject matter of art could no longer be the expression of external common-sense reality. In the "Introduction to the Discourse on the Paucity of Reality," written in September 1924, shortly before the creation of the first of his *Manifestoes of Surrealism*, Breton argued that "our senses, the very dubious character of their postulates, are poetically speaking, untrustworthy for reference" (1978:24).

"Most poetic creations assume that tangible character of extending strangely the limits of so-called reality" he continued.

> May the hallucinatory power of certain images and the true gift of evocation which certain people possess, independently of the faculty of memory, no longer be misunderstood. The God within us does not...rest on the seventh day. We still have the first pages of Genesis to read. It perhaps remains for us only to hurl on the ruins of the ancient world the foundations of our new terrestrial paradise. Nothing yet is lost, for we know by certain signs that the great illumination follows its course. The perils into which reason leads us, in the most general and debatable sense of the word, in subjecting the spirit to its irrevocable dogmas, in depriving us of the mode of expression which harms us the least—this peril, doubtless, is far from being dispelled. The deplorable inspectors who pursue us even after we leave school still make their rounds of our homes and our lives. They make sure that we always call a cat, a cat and, since after all we accept this to a great extent, they refrain from sending us to the galleys or the poorhouse or the penitentiary. Nevertheless, let us get rid of these officials as soon as possible.— The idea of a bed of stones or of feathers is equally unbearable to me. I can sleep only on a bed made of the pith of the elder tree. Sleep there once yourself. Is it not comfortable? But if you take such a step, where will it lead? Don't you feel that this bed— very simple, except that none are made that way— is suddenly made alluring; that you already prefer it to your own? Then you have not many prejudices on the material which may enter into the composition of a bed. Do I sleep on a bed of elder pith in reality?

Enough! I don't know. It must be true because I said it.

...

Nothing, in my opinion is inadmissable. The frog who tried to be bigger than the ox burst only in the brief memory of the fabulist (1978:26-27).

Breton's statement that reason is a kind of policeman reminds me of Castaneda's description of the "*tonal*" in *Tales of Power*. "The *tonal*," said Don Juan,

"is a guardian that protects something very price-less, our very being. Therefore, an inherent quality of the *tonal* is to be cagey and jealous of its doings. And since its doings are by far the most important part of our lives, it is no wonder that it eventually changes, in every one of us, from a guardian into a guard....

A guardian is broad-minded and understanding," he [Don Juan] explained. "A guard, on the other hand, is a vigilante, narrow-minded and most of the time despotic. I say, then, that the *tonal* in all of us has been made into a petty and despotic guard when it should be a broad-minded guardian" (1974:122-123).

As Breton pointed out, reason insures that we call a cat a cat, but this is only an arbitrary designation, "nothing is inadmissible." Don Juan reiterated Breton's position in shamanic terms when he argued

The *tonal* makes the world only in a manner of speaking. It cannot create or change anything, and yet it makes the world because its function is to judge, and access, and witness. I say that the *tonal* makes the world because it witnesses and accesses it according to *tonal* rules. In a very strange manner the tonal is a creator that doesn't create a thing. In other words, the *tonal* makes up the rules by which it apprehends the world. So, in a manner of speaking it creates the world (Castaneda, 1974:125).

How then does one eliminate the policeman who reinforces the rules? "The task then," said Don Juan,

is to convince the *tonal* to become free and fluid. That's what a sorcerer needs before everything else, a strong free *tonal*. The stronger it gets the less it clings to its doings, and the easier it is to shrink it" (Castaneda, 1974:157).

Then the *tonal* can be

made to give up unnecessary things like self-importance and indulging which plunge it into boredom. The whole trouble is that the *tonal* clings to those things when it should be glad to rid itself of that crap" (Castaneda, 1974:156-157).

Other ways of shrinking the *tonal* are drugs and stopping the internal dialogue. "I've told you," exhorted Don Juan, "that the internal dialogue is what grounds us. The world is such and such and so and so, only because we talk to ourselves about it being such and such or so and so" (Castaneda, 1974:22). According to Don Juan, the *nagual* is the part of us of which there is no description, no words, no names, no feelings, no knowledge. "To even talk about the *nagual* one has to enter the *tonal*, for the *tonal* is the realm of words."

The *nagual*, if I understand Don Juan correctly, is the field of being that makes possible the island of the *tonal*. I think the *nagual* can be apprehended in deep formless meditation and to a certain extent in dreaming which is in greater proximity to its whisperings than waking consciousness. The *nagual*, for example, can be expressed metaphorically in dreams through numinous representations of power spots, as in the case of Rousseau and de Chirico.

Breton's method of shrinking the *tonal* is by projecting products of non-ordinary dream reality on ordinary reality. "I recently proposed," he wrote in the *Discourse*,

> to fabricate, in so far as possible, certain objects which are approached only in dreams and which seem no more useful than enjoyable. Thus recently, while I was asleep, I came across a rather curious book in an open air-market near Saint-Malo. The back of the book was formed by a wooden gnome whose white beard, clipped in the Assyrian manner, reached to his feet. The statue was of ordinary thickness, but did not prevent me from turning the pages, which were of heavy black cloth. I was anxious to buy it and, upon waking, was sorry not to find it near me. It was comparatively easy to recall it. I would like to put into circulation certain objects of this kind, which appear eminently problematical and intriguing. I would accompany each of my books with a copy, in order to make a present to certain persons. Perhaps in that way I should help to demolish these concrete trophies which are so odious, to throw further discredit on those creatures and things of "reason" (1978:26).

In *Surrealism and Painting*, Breton said that

> I certainly hoped that the multiplication of such objects [he is referring here to the one mentioned in the Discourse] would entail the depreciation of those objects of often dubiously accepted useful-

ness which clutter up the so-called real world; such a depreciation seemed to me a prerequisite for the unleashing of the powers of invention which, within the limits of our present understanding of dream process, must surely be vitalized by contact with dream-engendered objects representing pure desire in concrete form. But the aim I was pursuing went far beyond the mere creation of such objects: it entailed nothing less than the objectification of the very act of dreaming, its transformation into reality (1972a:277).

I believe that Breton sensed that the influence of the dream world on waking reality was a way of opening up an individual to the numinous power of the *nagual* (if I may use this term here) which subsequently unleashes powers of creativity. Indeed, it is the contact with the *nagual* in shamanism and philosophies such as Taoism which makes human creativity possible.[1] By giving validity to the reality of dreams, Breton also eschewed the traditional split between the real and the imaginary. "I believe," declared Breton in the first of his *Manifestoes of Surrealism*, "in the future resolution of these two states, dream and reality, which are seemingly so contradictory, into a kind of absolute reality, a surreality, if one may so speak" (1972:14).

By mixing dream and reality, the straightjacket of the *tonal* did not hold. Not only did the *tonal* open to alternative realities, including perhaps the whisperings of the *nagual*, it was also a tremendously enriching and enlightening experience, and it was a revolutionary act. By showing that waking reality of the *tonal* was only one reality and not an absolute reality, the surrealists were defying the political and social power structure that maintained the fiction of conventional reality for its own purposes.

Breton continually affirmed the reality of dreams and did say more about dreams in his later work. In the first of his

Manifestoes of Surrealism, he attacked the dominance of waking reality on consciousness:

> it is in fact inadmissable that this considerable portion of psychic activity [dreaming] (since, at least from man's birth until his death, thought offers no solution of continuity, the sum of the moments of dream, from the point of view of time, and taking into consideration only the time of pure dreaming, that is the dreams of sleep, is not inferior to the sum of the moments of reality, or, to be more precisely limiting, the moments of waking) has still today been so grossly neglected. I have always been amazed at the way an ordinary observer lends so more credence and attaches so much more importance to waking events than to those occurring in dreams. It is because man, when he ceases to sleep, is above all the play-thing of his memory, and in its normal stake memory takes pleasure in weakly retracting for him the circumstances of the dream, in stripping it of any real importance, and in dismissing the only *determinant* [italics his] from the point where he things he has left it a few hours before: this firm hope, this concern. He is under the impression of continuing something that is worthwhile. Thus the dream finds itself reduced to a mere parenthesis as is the night (1972b:10-11).

Breton was lamenting the "parenthesis" or separation of dreaming from waking reality, and the problem of memory in its selective recall of the dream.[2]

    To my knowledge, Breton never attempted to solve the latter problem,[3] but in *Les Vases Communicants* (Communicating Vessels, 1932), a whole book dedicated to his philosophy of dreams, reflections on Freudian theory and extensive accounts of his own dreams, Breton proposed the existence of a capillary tissue in consciousness that dissolves the boundary between dreams and waking reality.

> This fog [the boundary] exists. Contrary to current opinion, it is formed of the thickness of things immediately sensible when I open my eyes. These things that I love, how could I not also hate them for derisively hiding all other things from me? It has appeared to me, it still appears to me, it is everything this book intends that in examining closely this irreflective activity [dreaming], if one passes beyond the extraordinary and badly tranquilizing effervescence apparent on the surface it is possible to bring to light a capillary tissue in ignorance of which one works in vain to understand mental circulation. The role of this tissue is visibly to assure the constant interchange which must take place in thought between exterior and interior worlds, an interchange requiring a continual interpenetration of waking and sleeping activity. My only ambition has been to give an idea of its structure. Whatever the pretensions common to integral consciousness and the delirious details of rigour, it cannot be denied that this tissue covers a sufficiently vast region. It is there that, for man, the permanent transactions of satisfied and unsatisfied necessities are consummated, there that the spiritual thirst— which, indispensably, from birth to death, must be calmed rather than cured—is exalted (quoted in Rosemont, 1978:71).

The interchange between dreaming and waking reality was for Breton the basis for self-transformation and action. Breton, indeed, criticized Freud in *Les Vases Communicants* for getting bogged down in abstract analytical interpretations of dreams, not using the knowledge he learned about dreaming to change his own life. He also criticized Freud's belief that the reality of the dream world is less real than "material reality," for Breton both realities were ultimately illusions. "What is the investigation of real life," said Breton,

> on the pretext that sleep gives the illusion of that life, an illusion discovered on waking, whereas in sleep real life, supposing that it is an illusion, is never held to be illusory? Would we not therefore be authorized because drunks see double to assert that to the eye of a sober man, the repetition of an object is the consequence *of a little different intoxication* [italics his, translation mine] (1932:131).[4]

The idea that dreams and walking reality are both equally real and equally illusory is familiar to anyone who has practiced shamanic techniques on a deep level. Perhaps the best statements on the illusory nature of waking reality are found in Indian mythology about dreams and in yogic practices which in turn grew out of shamanic techniques. For example, in the myth of the sage Markendeya,

> After Visnu had burnt the universe to ashes at doomsday and then flooded it with water, he slept in the midst of the cosmic ocean. The sage Markendeya had been swallowed by the god, and he roamed inside his belly for many thousands of years, visiting the sacred places on earth. One day he slipped out of the god's mouth and saw the world and the ocean shrouded in darkness. He did not recognize himself there, because of God's illusion, and he became terrified. Then he saw the sleeping god, and he was amazed, wondering, "Am I crazy, or dreaming? I must be imagining that the world has disappeared, for such a calamity could never really happen." Then he was swallowed again, and, as soon as he was back in the belly of the god, he

thought his vision had been a dream (O'Flaherty, 1984:111).

According to Heinrich Zimmer, one of the great Indologists,

> These searching reflections of the saint [Markendeya] are a kind of commentary on the idea of Maya, the problem "What is real?" as conceived by the Hindu. "Reality" is a function of the individual. It is the result of the specific virtues and limitations of individual consciousness. While the saint had been wandering about the interior of the cosmic giant he had perceived a reality which had seemed to him congenial to his nature, and he had regarded it as solid and substantial. Nevertheless, it had been only a dream or vision within the mind of the sleeping god. Contrariwise, during the night of nights, the reality of the primal substance of the god appears to the human consciousness of the saint as a bewildering mirage. "It is impossible," he ponders, "it cannot be real" (1962:39).

The continual questioning of what is real and what is illusion in dream and waking reality, expressed in Breton's writings on dreams, is shared by Indian mythologists.

Despite the extensive and sometimes profound rhetoric of Breton on dreaming (of which I have only presented a small part), Breton's application of dream practice to his own life and art was limited, as far as I can determine. The period from 1921 to 1923 was known as the "époque de sommeils" when Breton, Rene Crevel, Robert Desnos, Philipe Soupault and others were holding séances in which they went into trance to produce waking dreams. Yet, when in one of these sessions, Desnos entered so deeply into a trance state that Breton could not wake him (he had to call a doctor to do it), Breton began to emphasize automatic writing as a safe technique that does not necessitate a deep state of trance. In fact, most of Breton's surrealist writings, "Poisson Soluble," "Nadja," "Les Champs Magnetiques" (with Soupault), appear to be the result of automatic writing not dream techniques. And in *Surrealism and Painting*, Breton showed his preference for automatic writing over dreaming. He argued

> that any form of expression in which automatism does not at least advance *under cover* runs a grave risk of moving out of the surrealist orbit.... Automatism leads us in a straight line to this region [of psychic reality]. The other road [of dreaming] available to surrealism to reach its objective, the stabilizing of dream images in the kind of still deception known as *trompe l'oeil* (and the very word "deception" betrays the weakness of the process), has been proved by experience to be far less reliable and even presents very real risks of the traveler losing his way altogether (1972a:70).

I think, however, the real reason why Breton eschewed the role of dreaming in art was that he was afraid of the whisperings of the *nagual* that could be experienced in dreaming. Perhaps his ego was too enormous for him to contemplate a radical self-transformation. To be sure, in 1924, the year of the formation of the surrealist movement, Breton established the "Bureau de recherches surrealistes." It was set up in part to investigate altered states of consciousness such as dreaming. Every one of the fifty or so members of the surrealist movement, at one time or another, made a point of recording their dreams. In *La Revolution Surrealiste*, the major surrealist periodical, some of the surrealists, and a few outsiders such as de Chirico (whose favorite dream had been solicited by Breton) provided accounts of their dreams. Yet, no dream analysis or theoretical discussions can be found in *La Revolution* besides some rather uninteresting "textes surrealistes." In the first issue, Breton even cautioned his fellow artists not to try to recapitulate a dream image in paintings, given the distortions of memory in dream recall. On the whole, I would say that *La Revolution Surrealiste* neither advances the knowledge of dreams nor shows how they can be used to good advantage in art.

Although practically all surrealists experimented with dreams, dreamwork does not seem to have had a major affect on their art and life, which is not surprising, given Breton's ambiguous attitude toward the dream. Salvador Dali and Louis Buñuel, however, have created major works based on their practice of dreaming.

In his autobiography, *The Secret Life of Salvador Dali*, the artist wrote,

> At this period, the early twenties, I had just begun to read Sigmund Freud's Interpretation of Dreams. The book presented itself to me as one of the capital discoveries of my life and I was seized with a real vice of self-interpretation, not only of my dreams but of everything that happened to me, however, accidental it might seem at first glance (1942:167).

Dali was so enamored with Freud's theories that, in 1939, he journeyed to London to meet Freud (shortly before the latter's death). He apparently made a good impression on Freud who, prior to this encounter, had scant regard for surrealists.[5]

In addition to interpreting dreams, which helps to establish their importance for the psyche and makes them easier to remember, we learn from *The Secret Life* that Dali set up dreaming in a number of other ways. He said that during "the course of his life," in the twenties and thirties, he recorded his important dreams. Moreover, he would occasionally put the painting on which he was currently working on an easel at the foot of his bed so that he would look at it immediately before going to sleep and be likely to dream about it. This is, in fact, a classic technique for programming dreams.

Dali's style was particularly suited to the precise rendering of dreams. Already as a young art student in Madrid he had rebelled against the abstract avant-garde tendencies that were filtering into Spain from France. He applied his extraordinary coordination of eye and hand to precise representational transcriptions that approached the verism of Messonier and Zurbaran, his technical mentors. In the "Conquest of the Irrational" (1932), he maintained that,

> My sole pictorial ambition is to materialize by means of the most imperialist rage of precision the images of concrete irrationality. The world of imagination and the world of concrete irrationality may be objectively evident, consistent, durable, as persuasively cognoscitively, and communicably thick as the exterior world of phenomenal reality. The important thing, however, is that which one wishes to communicate: the irrational concrete subject. The pictorial means of expression are concentrated on the subject. The illusionism of the most abjectly *arriviste* and irresistible mimetic art, the clever tricks of a paralyzing foreshortening, the most analytically narrative and discredited academicism, can become sublime hierarchies of thought when combined with new exactness of concrete irrationality as the images of concrete irrationality become the Real, the corresponding means of expression approach those of great realist painting (1969:113)

Along with Breton, Dali's goal was the infinite expansion of reality by endowing "the world of imagination" and "irrationality" with substance. Yet, as Dali himself admitted, the concretization of the irrational

> offers two serious inconveniences: 1. They cease being unknown images, because by falling into the realm of psychoanalysis they are easily reduced to current and logical speech albeit continuing to offer an uninterpretable residue and a very vast and authentic margin of enigma, especially for the greater public. 2. Their essentially virtual and chimerical character no longer satisfies our desires or our "principles of verification" first announced by Breton in his *Discourses on the Paucity of Reality*. Ever since, the frenzied images of Surrealism, desperately tend toward their tangible possibility, their objective and physical existence in reality. Only those people who are unaware of this can still flounder about in the gross misunderstanding of the "poetic escape," and continue to believe our mysticism of the fantastic and our fanaticism of the marvelous (1969:114).

Dali understood that the fixing of dream images tends to reduce their enigmatic power, a problem that Breton never fully realized in his statements on dreaming. Nevertheless, Breton, who saw himself as a kind of scientist of the interior realms, had an interest in eliminating the mystical aura that surrounds dreams by transforming them into durable entities. Dali, a much more flamboyant person than Breton, to say the least, found it inconvenient (probably for the promotion of his work) that "the mysticism of the fantastic," is reduced by the fixing of dream images.

The best of Dali's "hand painted dream photographs," as he called them, were created in the late twenties and early thirties. "Sencitas" (1927), for example, manifests a large torso-like image in the background surrounded by disembodied fragments of recognizable and non-recognizable images that seem to whirl all over the canvas.

Although the small jewel-like details are of great clarity, it is difficult to comprehend these images. In my opinion, this painting is a representation of the extremely disjointed and fragmented imagery that occurs during hypnagogic states— the almost hallucinatory states that occur between the waking and sleep stage. I know of no other artist who has captured the delirium of hypnagogic states in such a convincing manner.

Dawn Ades, a scholar of Dali's work, gave the following analysis of his work of 1929:

> In *Dismal Sport* [a painting that Dali specifically mentions when he talks about putting paintings at the foot of his bed], The *First Days of Spring, Illumined Pleasures* and *The Great Masturbator* he paints a stretch of undifferentiated land as a vista stretching away and out of sight to the horizon. This landscape is usually monochrome: in the *First Days of Spring* and *Dismal Sport* both it and some of the objects and figures are a dull grey, against which the brilliance of other objects stands out with all the force of a Technicolor dream. Within this landscape structure, which...immediately creates a sensation of great depth emphasized by the presence in the background of tiny figures, the foreground objects and figures are placed in apparently unrelated groups and huddles. This suggests the dreaming mind at work, where certain things may happen or be seen with clarity but at the same time other things are going on just out of sight or on the margins of consciousness, "at the back of one's mind." Odd or apparently illogical connections are made between disparate objects or groups of objects, and people or things can metamorphose unexpectedly into something else, for no apparent reason (1982:75).

Ades' points are well taken; Dali understood that the dreamer tends to focus on only a few images when there is much more going on in the dream. Other images become larger and more brilliant as the dreamer shifts his or her attention. Nevertheless, Dali's paintings of 1929 are too complex in their number of details to be merely the product of dream recall. It is obvious, as several scholars have pointed out, that Dali borrowed images of these paintings from descriptions of psychological states in Freud and Krafft-Ebing's writings.

Yet, there are works by Dali that appear to be representations of the artist's actual dreams. When he had been three or four years old, Dali saw a decaying lizard being eaten by ants and began to have recurring dreams of this event. One such dream has been reproduced in a film (on which Dali collaborated with Luis Buñuel), "Un Chien Andalou." In one of the most striking images in the movie ants are crawling on a hand. In "The Persistence of Memory" (1931, Illustration 13), ants crawl on two of the four limp watches which are placed on a monolithic block in the foreground. Other limp watches are wrapped around the branch of a desiccated tree and a curious bird-like head/torso in a landscape that recedes into infinite space. The images of decay and forlorness are accentuated by the stark forbidding landscape and the dark strip of sky on the upper register of the painting.

Both Freud and Jung saw images of putrefaction marking an early stage of the self-transformation process—a period of fermentation and a link with primordial, unconscious forces. Given Dali's great creativity in the late twenties and thirties, it is not surprising that these images would find their way into "The Persistence of Memory" and many other paintings of this period. Whatever the interpretation, "The Persistence of Memory," in its simplicity, clarity, and numinous imagery, is for me the painting which most approximates a dream.

It was no accident that Dali was selected by Alfred

Hitchcock to do the dream sequence in Alfred Hitchcock's "Spellbound." When they arrived at the dream sequence, Hitchcock said, in an interview with François Truffaut,

> I was determined to break with the traditional way of handling dream sequences through a blurred and hazy screen. I asked Selznick if he could get Dali to work with us and he agreed, though I think he didn't really understand my reasons for wanting Dali. He probably thought I wanted his collaboration for publicity purposes. The real reason was that I wanted to convey the dreams with great visual sharpness and clarity, sharper than the film itself. I wanted Dali because of the architectural sharpness of his work. Chirico has the same quality, you know, the long shadows, the infinity of distance, and the converging lines of perspective (Truffaut, 1966:117-118).

Unfortunately, very few of Dali's designs were used in the final version of the movie, which Hitchcock called "just another manhunt story wrapped up in pseudo-psychoanalysis" (Truffaut, 1984:165). I think, however, that Hitchcock's hiring of Dali for the film shows that Dali had a well deserved reputation for his ability to present dreams in visual terms.

Louis Buñuel, probably more than any other film maker, surrealist or otherwise, realized the inherent ability of the cinema to present dreams and maintained an ongoing interest in dreams throughout his life and cinematic career. In his autobiography, *The Last Sigh* (1983), Buñuel wrote,

> If someone were to tell me I had twenty years left, and ask me how I'd like to spend them, I'd reply:

"Give me two hours a day of activity, and I will take
the other twenty-two in dreams... provided I can
remember them" (1983:98).[6]

I love dreams, even when they're nightmares,
which is usually the case. My dreams are always full
of the same familiar obstacles, but it doesn't matter.
My amour fou—for the dreams themselves as well
as the pleasure of dreaming—is the single most
important thing I shared with the surrealists. *Un
Chien Andalou* was born of the encounter between
my dreams and Dali's. Later, I brought dreams
directly into my films, trying as hard as I could to
avoid any analysis (1983:92).

For the making of "Un Chien Andalou" (Illustration 14),
said Buñuel,

We [Dali and Buñuel] simply acquired the
psychoanalytical practice of remembering our
dreams. We had no script, but every morning would
tell each other our dreams and select a few images
of each to put into the film (quoted in Aranda,
1976:60).

The sharing and retelling of dreams early in the morning
is an important aid to remembering them. Such practice can be
also found in tribal cultures.

We learn from his autobiography that Buñuel liked to
arrive on the scene to start the film very early in the morning,
around 6:00 a.m., to prepare for the day's shooting and Dali
could have joined him then. According to Buñuel, "Un Chien
Andalou" began with two dreams, "He [Dali] dreamed obses-
sively of a hand crawling with ants. I dreamed of a slit eyeball"
(Mellen, 1978:66). These dreams are incorporated directly
into the film. In two of the most powerful sequences, at the

beginning of "Le Chien Andalou," a man slits a woman's eye (in actuality a cow's eye) with a razor as thin, knife-like clouds cut across the surface of the moon. Later, the cyclist, who is the principal protagonist of the film, is shown looking at his hand. In the final version of the screen play, Buñuel wrote:

> Quick close up of the cyclist's hand: the palm is crawling with live ants.
> Cut back to the cyclist still staring at his hand.
> Cut back to medium close-up of the young woman getting up from her chair, and cut again to show her going over where the man is standing. Medium close-up of the two of them, standing together as she looks inside his hand. A second magnified close-up of the palm crawling with ants, which come from an apparent dark hole in the centre of the man's palm. Cut back to the two people; the young woman now looks very alarmed.
> The man pays no attention to her and continues to stare at his hand in fascination. He finally turns his head towards her and looks at her briefly, as though waking up from a dream (1963:96).

These striking dream images have been interpreted along Freudian lines by several critics (e.g., Edwards, 1982:59). Buñuel, along with many other Spanish intellectuals during the twenties, had read Ortega y Gasset's Spanish translation of Freud's *Psychopathology of Everyday Life* (1921) and probably other works by Freud as they were translated into Spanish already in the twenties. Nevertheless, Freudian psychology does not explain the intentions of the film. Buñuel said,

> To produce in the spectator a state which could permit the free association of ideas, it was necessary to produce a near traumatic shock at the very begin-

ning of the film; hence we began it with a shot of an eye being very efficiently cut open. The spectator entered into the cathartic state necessary to accept the subsequent events of the film (quoted in Aranda, 1976:67).

In other words, Buñuel was trying to shock the viewer into a state of non-ordinary reality. He was aiming at a "realistic" depiction of "irrationalism," as he argued in the following statement:

Although I availed myself of oniric [*sic*] elements, the film is not the description of a dream. On the contrary, the environment and the characters are of a realistic type. Its fundamental difference from the other films consists in the fact that the characters function, animated by impulses, the primal sources of which are confused with those of irrationalism, which, in turn are those of poetry. At times these characters react enigmatically, in as far as a pathological psychic complex can be enigmatic.

The film is directed at the unconscious feelings of man and therefore is of universal value, although it may seem disagreeable to certain groups of society which are sustained by puritanical moral principles (quoted in Aranda, 1976:57-58).[7]

"Un Chien Andalou" is not a dry analytic description of a dream state but concretizes the irrational consciousness of the characters in a language that approaches that of a dream. "When we were working on the script of *Un Chien Andalou* with Dali," said Buñuel, "we had only one rule: Keep only the pictures that we cannot explain rationally" (Mellen, 1978:92).

Jacques Brunius, a French writer and an assistant to Buñuel on his next film, "L'Age d'Or," argued that the language of cinema is intrinsically related to dreams. The lights going out in a movie theatre can be compared to closing one's eyes.

> Then, on the screen, as within the human being, the nocturnal journey into the unconscious begins. The device of fading allows images to appear and disappear as in a dream; time and space become flexible, shrinking and expanding at will; chronological order and relative values of time duration no longer correspond to reality, cyclical action can last a few minutes or several centuries; shifts from slow motion to accelerated motion heighten the impact of each (Mellen, 1978:107).

Most of these elements that Brunius mentioned can be found in "Un Chien Andalou." "The structure of the film," said Spanish film critic Francesco Aranda,

> has, moreover, an interior cohesion not easy to account for immediately. It is true that the narrative is not continuous, that events happen helter-skelter, that there are non-real jumps in time and space, that the characters doubt, retract, repeat themselves, very much as in dreams. Yet at no point does the spectator feel lost, or worry that the succession of events is arbitrary. Everything appears linked by a fatality (1976:65).

Indeed, one of the basic concepts of both Freudian psychology and surrealism is that the unconscious may not obey the laws of rational logic but has its own logic. This is probably a reason why Breton, who did not know Buñuel at that time, on seeing "Un Chien Andalou," declared, "Yes, this is a Surrealist film" (Edwards, 1982:19). Moreover, there is a sequence in the film that appears to embody Breton's idea about circulating dream objects in ordinary reality to disrupt the *tonal* or common sense hold of this reality. As the screenplay described it,

> ...Dissolve to the head of a girl seen directly from above. This shot is taken as though from the iris of an eye: the iris opens to reveal a group of people standing around the girl and trying to push their way through a police barrier.
>
> In the middle of the circle, the young girl is using a stick to try and pick up a severed hand with painted fingernails which is lying on the ground. A policeman goes up to her and begins rebuking her. He leans down, picks up the hand, wraps it up carefully and puts it inside the striped box which had been hanging around the cyclist's neck. He hands the box over to the girl; she thanks him and he salutes.
>
> As the policeman gives her the box, she seems completely carried away by a strange emotion and is oblivious of everything that is going on around her. It is as though she were listening to some distant religious music, perhaps music she heard when she was a child (Buñuel, 1963:87).

I have seen "Un Chien Andalou" fifteen times and this sequence still retains its unsettling ability of pulling me out of common sense reality and opening me to the whispering of the *nagual*. In part this is because Buñuel's seamless rendering of this dream sequence meshes perfectly with the inherent suspension of disbelief afforded by the medium of the cinema.

Man Ray is another artist who fabricated numinous

objects based on dreams. In 1920, before Breton had wrote the "Introduction to the Discourse on the Paucity of Reality," the first surrealistic text which mentioned the phenomenon of dream objects, Man Ray discovered a plaster cast of a child's hand in an art supply shop, covered it with green paint and inserted it in a flower pot. In an interview with critic Pierre Bourgeade in 1972, Man Ray recalled the reason for this object: "I dreamed once that, as I walked down the street, hands came out from the road and I had to thread my way through the hands" (Bourgeade, 1972:116, French, translation mine).

The imagery of this dream brings to mind one of my shamanic journeys in which hands impeded my progress down a road to the underworld. I had asked for information on why I was not able to accomplish any creative endeavors at the time so I took this vision of hands sprouting from a road to mean that many people were making demands on me, making it difficult to pursue my own creative work. It is interesting that 1920, the year before Man Ray moved from New York to Paris, was a slow period in his creative life during which he transformed only a few ready made objects into art.

Man Ray's next and last dream object was "Le manche dans la manche" (1921) which can be literally interpreted as "the handle in the sleeve." The source was a dream of an empty milk bottle and a hammer that were lying side by side. Man Ray fitted the handle of the hammer into the neck of the bottle, echoing the words of the title. He mentioned to his friend Arturo Schwarz, "when I see an opening I want to put something into it, right away" (Schwarz, 1977:161). Indeed, as Schwarz explained,

> If we remember that *manche* is French slang for being in a state of erection, and that bottle is a French female symbol, Man Ray's joke is all the clearer. Moreover, "handle" in French is masculine in gender and "sleeve" is feminine (1977:161).

While a dream of an empty milk bottle and a hammer doesn't appear to resound with important knowledge, it may have had a profound meaning for Man Ray that went beyond punning on "Le manche dans la manche." Often, there are elements in a dream or a shamanic journey which appear absurd at first, but become more significant upon closer investigation. In *Psychopathology of Everyday Life* (1901), which Man Ray may have read by 1920, Freud argued that there is nothing in a dream or mental life which is random and undetermined.

Although Man Ray did not manufacture dream objects after 1921, dreams played an important part in his work of the late thirties. He told Bourgeade,

> I always have by my bed a notebook with pen and ink. Even when I travel. At night, before falling asleep, if I have an idea, I immediately make a drawing. And in the morning when I wake up, if I had a dream, I sketch it immediately. Many of the "Main Libres" drawings are drawings of dreams (Bourgeade, 1972:115, in French, translation mine).

"Les Main Libres" (1937), he is referring to, is a series of drawings which have been illustrated by poems of Paul Eluard and seem to forecast France's debacle during the Second World War.

For many shamans, dreams are an important source of information about the future and it is not surprising that a sensitive individual such as Man Ray, when seriously involved in dream work, would also pick up information about the future. The poet W.H. Auden once said that the artist can be likened to an extended set of antennae that pick up shifts in the vibratory field of the Zeitgeist before denser individuals are able to do so. In fact, many artists, along with Man Ray, had premonitory dreams about the Second World War.

In "Les Mains Libres," there are several striking images

that foretell disaster. "Le Tournant" (The Turning Point, Illustration 15) shows a huge hand gripping a rugged rocky promontory at the turn of a mountain road. A person traveling around this mountain bend would encounter some kind of enormous human or quasi-human monster. By showing a fragment of this monster, rather than the whole thing, one can only imagine the whole, therefore multiplying the terror.

"L'Angoisse et l'Inquietude," as the title implies, is another disturbing drawing in which Man Ray depicted crossed hands that appear to be cutting off the growth of a tree. In "Pouvoir," an enormous hand of a man tightly grasps the torso of a struggling woman. In "L'Espion," a hand is pierced with a cone-shaped object. And in "Reve," a locomotive cascades through the top of some tall city buildings.

Premonitory and troubling dreams also influence "Le Beau Temps" (1937), Man Ray's largest and most elaborate painting during the late thirties. The basic elements of the painting are: in the foreground, near an open book with strange geometric symbols, two quasi-human individuals composed of machine-like geometric fragments, stand on each side of a door on which blood drips in a thin stream from the keyhole. In the middle ground on the left side of the figures are two three-pronged pitchforks propped up in front of a broken brick wall. On the right of the figures is a billiard table with a river traveling in a snake-like pattern across it, and a lighted studio with an easel and a man and woman embracing. Two fighting animals are shown on the roof of this studio. "Now and then," related Man Ray in his autobiography, *Self Portrait*,

> I'd drive out to my little house in St. Germaine-en-Laye, where workmen were making some changes and stay a couple of days. One night I heard distant guns, and when I fell asleep again, dreamed that two mythological animals were at each other's throats on my roof. I made a sketch of this and incorporated it in the dream painting which I called *Le Beau Temps* (Fair Weather) (1988:241).

In a discussion with Arturo Schwarz, Man Ray further commented on this origin of the painting.

> One night I dreamed that two mythological animals were fighting on the roof of the house in the country in Saint-Germaine-en-Laye, where I used to spend the weekends. When I awoke in the morning I immediately recorded the dream image by a drawing, changing a few details. In the drawing—as well as in the painting—the mythical animals became a bull biting an alligator on the neck; in the dream the animal wasn't biting, he was using his horns (Schwarz, 1977:71-72).

The machine-like figures in the front are another product of dreams. "When I was a child," said Man Ray, "I often dreamed of strange people that were geometric forms walking in the street, or pushing a cart. I was fascinated by color in my dreams and these personages were very colorful" (Schwarz, 1977:72). The two tridents were also the result of a dream that Man Ray had about two trees in his garden that had been transformed into sharpened pitchforks (Schwarz, 1977:72). Whatever the personal meaning of the dream-induced images in "Le Beau Temps," of which there are probably more than Man Ray verbally spelled out, their menacing nature belies the title of the painting. As Man Ray pointed out in *Self Portrait*,

> All in all, Paris in spring [of 1937] was paradise again; one could not help being optimistic, since nature was true to herself, ignoring all threats. In May, the barometer had settled permanently on fair, like my last painting, Fair Weather, at least, like its title. I could not, like Whistler, say that nature was imitating me, as there were a few disquieting elements in my work which were not literally borne out by the title. The painting was less prophetic than it

was a recording of the past, like a barometer with a chart in which one can read what has gone before, deducing the tendency for the future (1988:242).

After the Second World War, philosophical ideas such as existentialism with its emphasis on rationality, political praxis, and conscious decision-making in the creative process, tended to preclude dreaming as source for the arts. Yet, following the debacles of the Sixties—including the Vietnam War, the student rebellions in the United States and France, the failure of Marxism, and so forth—a veritable crisis in consciousness occurred which was similar to Breton's experiences after the First World War. Consequently, artists began again to "set up" dreaming, and one of the first artists to do so was Carolee Schneemann. "Since the early '60s," said Schneemann,

> I've been using dream as an active process in my film and performance works. I keep pens and paper next to the bed and often find dreams will generate ideas or images directly related to the problems of particular works in process. Hypnagogic messages often guide and define the work; drawings which occur persistently on waking indicate the tenacity of a new work emerging (1988:1).

Schneemann is referring here to "scrawl drawings, marks, and symbol clusters," as she called them. She draws them on the wall near her bed while half asleep (1988:1). "At other times," she maintains, "during the most concentrated submersion in a film or performance work, complex 'score instructions' unravel directly from dream to consciousness" (1988:1). Part of this unraveling of dream to consciousness involves a shift of consciousness while in a highly receptive or, to use her words, "permeable" state. She feels a build-up of energy at her solar plexus which needs release, along with the dream images, in a sensory and kinesthetic form; otherwise she would feel very uncomfortable. The original dream images may be quite personal and disturbing but Schneemann feels that she had no choice but to express them for an audience. This was her calling as an artist/shaman.

"Eye Body" (1963)" marked the beginning of Schneemann's shift from painting and environmental work to performance. Here, Schneemann interjected her own body into a loft installation consisting of large interlocking color panels, lights, mirrors, moving umbrellas and other motorized parts.

> I had an overwhelming desire to merge the move-
> ments of my body with my own internal energy in
> a state of trance, and to create with my body a
> physical manifestation of the construction I was
> building (interview with Schneemann, December
> 1990).

In *More than Meat Joy*, the monograph she authored on her work, Schneemann wrote about "Eye Body,"

> Covered in paint, grease, chalk, ropes, plastic [from
> her interaction with the materials of the site], I
> establish my body as visual territory. Not only am
> I an image maker, but I explore the image values of
> flesh as material I choose to work with (1979:52).

The most powerful image of "Eye Body," which was docu-mented by a photographer, is that of small garter snakes writhing on the recumbent body of the naked artist. The viewpoint here is frontal and direct; Schneemann looks at us unflinchingly with her mouth slightly open in a slight state of trance while putting her hands behind her head to fully expose her torso. This image was based on a series of dreams Schneemann had of herself, in which she was positioned the same way as in the photograph with serpentine forms enclosing her head and torso. Schneemann believed that in "Eye Body" she became the vehicle for a primal archaic feminine force who was manifesting her erotic power while ceasing to be merely a sexual object for men. "I felt compelled to 'conceive' of my body in manifold aspects which had eluded the culture around me," remarked Schneemann (1979:52). In fact, she was probably the first female artist since the Second World War to challenge the supremacy of the male gaze with an uncompromising image of pure feminine power.

Eight years after "Eye Body," Schneemann was able to associate the central image of herself in this performance with those of neolithic Snake Goddesses, including bare-breasted Minoan women holding snakes in their hands while in a state of rapture and clay figurines from the Balkans (about 4,000 BC) with snakes enclosing the breast and belly region. The snake symbolized, in early European folklore, the feminine guardianship of unfolding life energies as well as the special relationship of women with the mysteries of the underworld. Of course, the Christian patriarchy transformed the snake, along with images of female sexuality, into symbols of evil.

Given the repressiveness of Western society in the early sixties, I am not surprised that Schneemann, with her advanced consciousness of the physical body, was directed to reclaim female images and symbols through her dreams and internal physical sensations.

"Meat Joy" (Illustration 16) which followed soon after "Eye Body," further exploded the sexual status quo of the early sixties. Schneemann described the origin of this performance as follows:

Meat Joy developed from dream sensation images gathered in journals and stretching back to 1960. By February '64 more elaborate drawings and notes accumulated as scraps of paper, on the wall over my bed, in tablets. I'd been concentrating on the possibilities of capturing interactions between physical/metabolic changes, dream content, and my sensory orientation upon and after waking: an attempt to view paths between conscious and unconscious organization of image, pun, double-entendre, masking, and the release of random memory fragments (often well-defined sounds, instructions, light, textures, weather, places from the past, solutions to problems). I found the transition between dream and waking, envisioning and practical function, became so attenuated that it was often difficult to leave the loft for my job or errands. My body streamed with currents of imagery: the interior directives varied from furtive to persistent: either veiling or so intensely illuminated ordinary situations that I continually felt dissolved, exploded, permeated by objects, events, outside the studio, the one place where my concentration could be complete (1979:63).

From this statement, it appears that, in the intense beginnings of "Meat Joy," Schneemann's body became a "communicating vessel" in which she was able to fuse waking life and dream life. Schneemann has told me that this streaming of images, an ongoing part of her creative process, was concomitant with what Wilhelm Reich had called "streamings," the flood of energy occurring after orgasm in individuals with high orgastic potency.

According to Reich, whose writings have been an important source of conceptual reification for Schneemann's experiences, people with high orgastic potency have less character armor than those without it. That means they are more open to the world as they do not have the physical structure—stiffness, heaviness, etc.—connected with defense mechanisms. Armoring, according to Reich, is the product of a repressive familial, social, and political environment. For the most part, Schneemann's world was much different.

Schneemann has fond memories of growing up in rural upstate Pennsylvania among parents who took great satisfaction in their sexuality.

> [We'd]...all lie in bed on Sunday mornings, they would teach me to read the comics....I remember the deep intimacy, sensuousness and delight. I built my own erotic fantasy life with various invisible animal and human lovers inhabiting my sheets, bed....
>
> The animals were sexual creatures and I identified that part of my nature with them. Nudity was also clear and direct. We turned hay as adolescents. In the afternoons after working we would just take off our work clothes to swim naked in the river (quoted in Gadon, 1989:295-296).

As a very young child Schneemann also began to draw. "Drawing and masturbating" she said,

> were the first sacred experiences I remember. Both activities began when I was about 4 years old. Exquisite sensations produced in my body and images that I made on paper, tangled with language, religion, everything that I was taught. As a result I thought the genital was where God lived (quoted in Gadon, 1990:295).

From that period on, artistic receptivity and expression have been both erotic and sacred as well as being opposed to the cultural conventions of society for Schneemann. She recognizes that sacredness is a way of tapping into what she later termed "an electrical cosmic energy pulse" during the erotic/creative state (1975:23). In short, the erotic/creative state is both a means of empowerment and going beyond ordinary reality for Schneemann.

"Meat Joy" was one of Schneemann's great affirmations of the liberating potential of the erotic/creative. She described the performance as follows:

> Meat Joy has the character of an erotic rite: excessive, indulgent, a celebration of flesh as material: raw fish, chickens, sausages, wet paint, transparent plastic, rope, brushes, paper scrap. Its propulsion is toward the ecstatic-shifting and turning between tenderness, wildness, precision, abandon: qualities which could at any moment be sensual, comic, joyous, repellent. Physical equivalences are enacted as a psychic and imaginistic stream in which the layered elements mesh and gain intensity by the energy components of the audience. (They were seated on the floor as close to the performance area as possible, encircling, resonating.) Our proximity heightened the sense of communality, transgressing the polarity between performer and audience (1979:63).

The essential movements of "Meat Joy" came out of one of Schneemann's dreams in which she saw naked men and women interacting with raw meat during an orgiastic ceremony. Without being aware of it, Schneemann had produced an ecstatic ritual that, in a comparatively subdued way, approached the Dionysian rituals of ancient Greece which involved the eating of raw meat in a state of erotic frenzy. Although "Meat Joy" did not involve actual sexual intercourse and the eating of raw meat, it celebrated the transforming power of flesh like the Dionysian rites.[8] According to E.R. Dodd in *The Greeks and the Irrational*, participants in

Dionysian rites were both supremely repulsed and exalted by these festivals (1951:277). Participants and audience of "Meat Joy" had similar reactions. "Still, I was astounded," said Schneemann,

> when in the midst of *Meat Joy* [during the Paris performances of 1964] a man came out of the audience and began to strangle me. Steeped in the writings of Wilhelm Reich, I understood what affected him but did not know how to break his hold on my neck. I was saved by three middle aged women who realized this assault was not part of the performance and jumped him as one (1979:27).

In Reichian terms, the man in the performance was too repressed to handle the enormous energies generated by the performance. Instead of allowing these energies to dissolve his armor, he transmuted them into violent action.

"Interior Scroll" (1975) also engendered very strong reactions. "People are just as confused and upset about it now as when I did it," remarked Schneemann in a recent interview.

> I felt that I definitely didn't *want* to do it. It was a dream image again. I woke up and had this old image of a figure—I drew it right away as I saw it in the dream—pulling a coil out of its vagina; and the message of the dream was the value of interior knowledge, that everything I've ever done and everything I've ever known comes through my erotic self and this was absolutely to emphasize that and position it physically (Peterson, 1990:20, 22).

Performing in front of a group of artists at a summer event in East Hampton, New York, Schneemann extended a long accordion-like strip of paper with a typewritten text from her vagina which she then began to read inch by inch. The text enumerated the supposed intellectual insufficiencies of women artists in the course of a dialogue between a structuralist film maker and Schneemann. The artist pulling the paper from her vagina was the crucial part of the performance. The image of the artist pulling the paper from her vagina, as Schneemann recollects,

> seemed to have to do with the power and possession of naming—the movement from interior thought to external signification, and the reference to an uncoiling serpent to actual information (1979:235).

Many of the women in the audience were profoundly moved by Schneemann's acknowledgement of "vulvic knowledge," her words for the process of signification emerging out of the female genital self. In patriarchal culture, it is assumed that this process of signification is a rational activity but Schneemann's research on the images of ancient Goddess culture following her dream led to an entirely different conclusion.

> I related womb and vagina [in this images] to primary knowledge, with strokes and cuts on bone and rock by which I believed my ancestor measured her menstrual cycles, pregnancies, lunar observations, agricultural notations, the origins of time, factoring, of mathematical equivalences, of abstract relations. I assumed the carved figurines and incised female shapes of Paleolithic, mesolithic artifacts were carved by women—the visual-mythic transmutation of self-knowledge to its integral connection with a cosmic Mother—that the experience and complexity of the personal body was the source of conceptualizing, of interlocking with materials, of imaging the world and composing its images (1979:34).

The connection between knowledge and the vagina in "Interior Scroll" was not only empowering for women. According to Schneemann,

> ...A banker who was a close friend was deeply affected. Sex for him was very confused—mixed up with dominance, power, control—so that yielding, dissolving sensitivity and female erotic experience were tainted and destructive for him; he would lose power if he identified with that aspect of himself. He was in bliss over this piece and exclaimed, "I finally understand...the transparence of the direction of all my life! It's the umbilicus, it's the rainbow, it's the ticker-tape, it's the unfolding, the secrets that should be revealed because then you get to real secrets rather than the degraded ones (quoted in Peterson, 1990:22).

I think this banker was trying to explain his realization that unfolding information, the stuff of his own life, is the product of a real secret, the generative and erotic energies which both men and women possess.

In "Fresh Blood" (1981-1988), the real secret, uncovered by Schneemann, is the power of menstruation and menstrual blood which is taboo in most patriarchal cultures. "Fresh Blood" was the product of the following dream, narrated in the second section of the three-part performance. The artist was in a cab in London with three men on route to a concert when one of them declared that he is bleeding. "We wonder," said Schneemann,

> how this cut came about, confined as we were. I have a sudden fear it might be from my umbrella; perhaps I inadvertently jabbed his leg getting into the taxi. He smoothly opens the trousers along the crease over his thigh: we can see vivid, fresh "flowers" of blood spurting here (1988:9).

Schneemann also related that the night of the dream she was menstruating and that the dream was about the futile desire of men to menstruate. "But in reactive male mythologies," exclaimed Schneemann in the performance,

> the men wound each other to "spill blood," [to have] blood revenge, blood lust, bad blood between them. This grandiose blood in contradistinction to proportionate periodicity of menstrual blood (1988:12).

Throughout *The Wise Wound* (1978), a book that Schneemann discovered much later, Penelope Shuttle and Peter Redgrove pointed to many tribal cultures where menstrual blood is magic blood because it ensures fertility. In wanting to have access to this magic blood, men undergo initiation rites which inflict wounds and ersatz vaginas secrete blood. In societies where menstruation is looked upon with fear and men do not have initiation rites, they are usually involved in wars which lead to heavy bloodshed. Shuttle and Redgrove also showed the connection between menstruation and dreaming in *The Wise Wound*. Since menstruation is a highly receptive time for women, it is regarded as an optimum time for shamanic activity in tribal cultures, a time particularly for prophetic dreaming and access to important information for the group. One important implication of "Fresh Blood" is that dream recall and vividness are also enhanced during the menstrual period.

In the first part of "Fresh Blood," Schneemann affirmed the role of the dream body as opposed to the mental body in her body. Physical activities, such as menstruation, are, for her, the sources of dreams and should not be analyzed according to male constructs. As Schneemann exclaimed in this section of "Fresh Blood,"

> she is aware of dismantling those analytic authoritarian hierarchies which male conventions pro-

jected into the scope and implication of her creative imagination—even our dreams and unconscious recognitions were subjected to pervading male interpretations

our realm of symbolic event has been confirmed by the male creative will when integrated into his own work his own words (the Muse for instance) our unique biological experiences have been permitted definition as a masculine invention his description of a female psyche and persona...

our creative work our dream works our dreams were habitually denigrated ignored if not corresponding to what the male imagination required as antagonist or consort or complement

his dream of us is so culturally pervasive that we still ask: are we dreaming ourselves or dreaming the dreams of men dreaming us?

perhaps maybe perhaps it's possible for all of these considerations refer to the "dream body"—which incorporates—"mind" an implicit emphasis denied to the primacy of body in Freud's use of "dream-mind" so refer to "dream-body" not "dream-mind" (1988:7-8).

These stream of consciousness meditations were intentionally non-grammatical and were linked to visual images along with the gestures of Schneemann who held a transparent umbrella and was partially clad in red pajamas (the color of blood). The concept behind these linkages was to mimic the remembering dream-body which continues the actual dream process.

In working with Oscar Köllerström [a psychiatrist

who combined traditional analytical disciplines with Zen practice and paranormal techniques] I learned to follow the *remembering-dream body* as part of *dream process* itself—so that the flow and branching of associations, equivalences were valued for whatever kind of attachments they could trigger. Not hierarchial, not aesthetic and *not* predictable (1988:1),

explained Schneemann in the preliminary notes of "Flesh Blood." In the visual images themselves, which included Schneemann's own drawings, she explored and expanded the morphology suggested by the original and other dreams during her menstrual period, showing the relationships between flower petals, a man's thighs, spurting blood, vaginas, vector shapes, Tantric trees, volcanoes, vertical penises, umbrellas, and so forth. Besides the images, texts, and gestures, the sound of Schneemann's voice was also important in establishing the dreamlike mood of the performance. Projected through a reverberation device, it seemed as though the performance was being narrated by another voice that was directing the event. In having the performance come to life as though it were an actual dream, "Fresh Blood" enhanced the authority of the original shamanic revelation.

In "Cat Scan," another complex performance involving the juxtaposition of images and the physical movements of performers and objects, the revelation came through a cat in a dream. Schneemann described the origin of "Cat Scan" in an interview with William Peterson in *Performance* magazine as follows:

It's quite wonderful and it happened in Austin, when I was out here for my teaching interview last Spring [1989]. I had the dream when I slept at Deborah Hay's studio which is one of those big white, sort of Buddhist places [it had a powerful image of the Buddha in the living room where Schneemann slept on a mat, brackets mine]....When I woke up the next morning, I was feeling just fine; it was a bright day and I bounced through the kitchen...then I looked out the window and there was a cat crossing the street and coming up to Deborah's lawn and I said, "I'll come help in a minute but first I'll go out and meet this cat." So I went out on the lawn and reached down and petted the cat and all of a sudden the world just went...inside out! It all sort of tumbled around me and I realized that I had a very intense message from Cluny [her cat that had recently died from a rat bite] and it was one of the overwhelming ones.

...When I touched this strange cat, suddenly the whole thing [the dream] came flying back. In the dream I had my big red plastic notebook and it was slightly larger than normal; it had sleeves inside it with pockets; and in the dream I was in Austin getting ready for the interview and going to write some notes. I opened the book and there in the middle of it was Cluny's arm—paw up to the elbow—it was his fur and his shapes and his marks and everything but slightly larger than life size and I started to cry when I saw it, and I said, "Thank you. I'm so glad that you could show me something of yourself." And he said, the way these ghostly things talk to you, "This is all I can give you right now." And I was stroking him and I said, "It's wonderful, thank you," and he said, "It's for you to use." I said, "use? How do you use it?" And he said, "Sit down just like this *[she sits up with a straight back]* and lift it up and hold it in your hands. Now just close your eyes and let it go on your knee and then go up here [*raising her right arm, palm opened, from her knee, diagonally across her chest, placing her hand on her heart,* brackets by Peterson]. So I started to do that and my arm turned into his arm. I started to do that on the lawn, sitting there and then—I'm going to ask you to try it and see what you think. It produces the most incredible state of wholeness; it's extremely releasing, it opens these two axes—and who know's what's going on with the chakras. I gave this action to my performers when I went back to my rehearsal [for Cat Scan]. I didn't say a word about it. I said just relax your arm and very slowly bring in your hand, very slowly let it come up and bring in against your chest, just concentrate (quoted in Peterson, 1990:13).

Schneemann showed me this technique during our interview and I experienced an immediate feeling of warmth, relaxation and an opening of my heart *chakra*. I have no doubt that Schneemann had a classic shamanic experience in which she contacted a powerful being who gave her an important technique to share with others. In the original dream, Schneemann saw a scepter or rod with a cat's paw at the end of it moving from the knee to the heart which led her to believe there was an Egyptian connection to this technique. Cats were, indeed, deified in Egyptian culture but Schneemann has not been able to find a scepter with a cat's paw in Egyptian art. Further gestures for "Cat Scan" came to Schneemann in subsequent dreams about Cluny.

To summarize, "Cat Scan" and Schneemann's other performances have put her body "where the dream is." Schneemann's dreams, indeed, often contain important messages which are conveyed through the non-intellectual impact of her powerful physical performance.

❖

The work of Ann McCoy is less physically oriented than Schneemann's but this artist, like Schneemann, had some important experiences as a young girl that shaped her role as an artist/shaman. Growing up in the American Southwest, McCoy witnessed the march of the penitents as they flogged themselves while being led by a skeleton on a cart. And she saw the snake dances on the Hopi mesa where hundreds of Indians danced bare-chested in the snow. The march of the penitents and the dances of North American Indians were quite different from the activities of the materialist white civilization around her in the fifties. "I was greatly impressed," said McCoy,

> by the Pueblo Indians who still believed in the importance of dreams, visions, and the inner life....For me our "rational" commonsense view of reality is not the whole picture (1987:108).

McCoy thinks that her Irish Catholic background with its heavy pagan underpinning predisposed her to experiencing alternate modes of consciousness and holding spiritual beliefs. "As psychological types," McCoy has argued, "the Irish tend to be intuitive and believe in non-rational functions, the supernatural, and the unconscious," tendencies which can be found among "the writers from Swift to AE (George Russell). For me the epic quality of the oral tradition translates into [my] epic mural-sized work that has a story to tell" (quoted in Gould, 1989:68).

The stories McCoy tells, in her large scale pencil drawings, are based on her own dream experiences which accelerated in frequency and intensity during Jungian therapy. Her analysis began as a cure for twenty years of severe alcoholism. "The images in my works are not appropriated in the usual post-modern sense. I am not interested in simulation or plundering the past for nostalgic reasons," argued McCoy.

The images in my works come from dreams, from the collective unconscious, the psychic reservoir of human experience which is transpersonal. For me the artist stands between two worlds, an outer world which makes us understand everything as the effect of physical and physiological forces, and an inner world which shows us everything as the effect of spiritual agencies (1987:108).

In the words of art historian Suzi Gablik, "McCoy's art brings the dream to the viewer in much the same way as a soothsayer would have a dream for a whole group" (A.C.A., 1988:5).

What distinguishes McCoy's dreaming from that of others and established her as an artist/shaman was the effort she put into her dream work and her ability to record her dreams in an aesthetically compelling, narrative form. McCoy uses dream incubation techniques she had learned from C.A. Meier, her analyst and an expert on dream practices in pre-Classical Greece. According to Meier, in his monograph *Healing Dream and Ritual*,

the Greeks, especially in the early period, regarded the dream as something that really happened: for them it was not, as it was in later times and to "modern man," in particular, an imaginary experience. The natural consequence of this attitude was that people felt it necessary to create the conditions that caused dreams to happen. Incubation rites induced a *mantike atechnos* (prophecy without system), an artificial *mania* in which the soul spoke directly, or, in Latin, *divinat* (1989:iii-iv).

In a catalogue for a show of her work in 1988 at the A.C.A Gallery in New York, McCoy wrote,

...Keeping a journal of my dreams has been a twenty

year practice. For me, the voyage into the dream world is akin to Platonic *anamnesis* or "remembering." I think of certain types of dreams as letters from the gods, or from an autonomous universal intelligence (collective unconscious) in which past and present merge to give the dreamer valuable insights for the future (1988:12).

Keeping a dream journal as part of the remembering process is only one of the "conditions that cause [McCoy's] dreams to happen." Although she makes little money from her art work and survives mainly through grants, McCoy goes to Zurich several times a year to visit Meier. In effect, the journey to Zurich, which requires much self-sacrifice, has become a pilgrimage to an important place of incubation where she is usually rewarded with "big" dreams. In fact, the word "incubate," from the Latin *incubare*, originally meant to sleep in a sacred sanctuary. McCoy's journeys to Zurich could certainly be said to parallel those of the ancient Greeks to the sacred Asclepian incubation sanctuaries where pilgrims received personal and prophetic transpersonal messages from gods and goddesses in their dreams.

It is important to recognize that Meier, along with most Jungian analysts, does not interpret his clients' dreams. As James Hillman, a leading Jungian psychologist, argued,

> The healing cults of Asclepius depended upon dreaming, but not dream interpretation. This implies to me that dreams can be killed by interpreters, so that the direct application of the dream as a message for the ego is probable less effective in actually changing consciousness and affecting life than is the dream still kept alive as an enigmatic image (1979:122).

The Jungian method involves analysis without interpretation.

According to Hillman,

> Analytical tearing apart is one thing, and concep-
> tual interpretation is another. We can have analysis
> without interpretation. Interpretation turns the
> dream into its meaning. Dream is replaced with
> translation. But dissection cuts into the flesh and
> bone of the image, examining the tissue of its
> internal connections, and moves around it in bits,
> though the body of the dream is still on the table. We
> haven't asked what does it mean, but who and what
> and how it is (1979:130).

"Moving around it in bits," for the Jungian analyst and the
client primarily involves amplifying the symbols of the dream
and noticing the relevance of these symbols to events in
everyday life. McCoy amplifies the symbols in her dreams by
uncovering their mythological contents through extensive
research. "Those [dreams] which are reoccurring or are of
special relevance," said McCoy,

> are catalogued and traced down in the world's
> iconography. I also pay attention to synchronistic
> acausal events which I feel are related to the images
> of the dreams (1987:108).

McCoy's drawings and sculptures are, indeed, depictions of
her original dream images which are sometimes elaborated
and amplified in a traditional iconographical vocabulary without destroying the initial power of the image. "It is only be
retaining and enhancing the original power of the image," said
McCoy, "that the artist can take back his or her role as a
redeemer and healer of the psyche from the theologian"
(interview with McCoy, June 1989). "The events which led to
the making of 'The Temple of Isis' (Illustration 17)," McCoy
recalled,

came from a dream fragment. In a dream I was handed an ancient instrument by an unknown woman. The next day I was looking up a word in my dictionary, I saw a picture of a sistrum, the ancient instrument from my dream. The synchronicity of the events was underscored the following afternoon when I found a brochure from an Egyptologist in the street. I entered his shop and saw a sistrum in the case. When I told him about my dream, he sold me the sistrum at a greatly reduced price, and informed me it was the first he had ever had. The sistrum was thought to contain the magical properties of Isis, and when rattled was believed to make the Nile rise and fall. This votive rattle meant to keep the worshipper in a state of spiritual attentiveness (1987:108).

The sistrum is held by several figures in "The Temple of Isis," an immense, nine foot by fifteen foot, colored pencil drawing from 1987. I should mention here that McCoy hung large sheets of paper on her studio walls and drew images from her dreams soon after she had absorbed and amplified them. In fact, there are no significant elements in her murals which are not the direct result of dreams and dream work. McCoy even had to wait at times for the appropriate dream to complete the drawing.

In addition to the inclusion of sistrums in "The Temple of Isis," McCoy made actual working sistrums out of bronze which she used in a way similar to the dream "arrows" employed in many tribal cultures. By placing this power object close by when she went to bed, it frequently acted in dreams as a reminder to remember the dream.

In another dream that related to the creation of "The Temple of Isis," McCoy saw a goddess wearing a robe of gold and blue silk which McCoy touched as it moved in the wind. "I felt charged by the numinous presence [of the dream]," declared McCoy, "and happy for weeks afterwards, during which time still another dimension was added to the task" (A.C.A., 1988:16). In part, this dimension consisted of a dream in which she unearthed large clay cows from an excavation site while a friend read from a text about a female deity who had undergone resurrection. These dreams led McCoy to a meditation on Isis who she identified with the goddess in the blue silk robe and on Hathor, the sacred cow who is associated with Isis.

McCoy became so taken with Isis that she journeyed to Pompeii to visit one of the last remaining temples of the deity. "I arrived in the midst of a thunderstorm," described McCoy.

> The place was deserted of its usual visitors. An old man with an umbrella appeared to lead me through the sheets of rain to the tiny temple. I entered through a hole in the back wall and spent the day alone inside there. The atmosphere was mysterious. Lightening bolts shot through the storm-blackened sky and off the rim of the volcano.

> On either side of the temple altars were carved with serpents entwined about staffs—symbols of the divine physician Asclepius. The association of Isis to Asclepius and healing seemed appropriate, for it is she who healed Osiris, who found and integrated the sacred parts of him. It was through dreams and work on this temple drawing that Isis was helping to resurrect a buried part of myself (A.C.A., 1988:16-17).

Along with images of Isis, including one of the goddess breast-feeding her son Horus, representations of a lightening storm, and the temple also figured in the drawing, as well as several other symbols relating to Isis myths. McCoy gave me a brief account of how the images of "The Temple of Isis" can have healing effects on viewers, both women and men who resonate with goddess imagery, even without being familiar with the iconography of Isis.

Personally, however, I was more affected by "Kore," a pencil drawing of 1986 which depicts a fish-headed goddess surrounded by floating fetuses, a young girl, temple ruins, wolves, birds and other symbols for reasons that were not clear to me at the time. "Kore" was based on the following dream of McCoy's:

> I am with a group of archaeologists on the restoration of a temple site. I tell the workers how important this work is, and how we must care for the temple once it is completed. My guide around the temple precinct is a draped woman whose veil hides her face. As we speak, she bends down and lifts her skirts to expose her legs, which are covered by fish scales—rainbow coloured, like those of some tropical fish. I find myself more fascinated then repelled. Now she is moving ahead of me. She turns her head and I realize that on her neck are gill slits. Fins protrude from behind her ears....

> As the fish goddess and I spoke, a procession led by a radiant child, entered the temenos. On the temple ground were large vials containing fetuses in different stages of development (A.C.A., 1988:13, 16).

McCoy believes that the images of the fish goddess and girl child, in combination with the bottled fetuses (an archetypal symbol of Mercury, the "golden child"), signify the return of the goddess and the development of the feminine aspect in man, as embodied by Mercury.

While I think that McCoy's interpretation of the dream has meaning in terms of my own personal attraction to the image of the fish goddess (I saw "Kore" during a period in which I was becoming more in tune with the feminine aspects of my own psyche) and perhaps also in terms of the Zeitgeist, the images of "Kore" worked for me on a deeper non-intellectual level because, to use a phrase of Hillman's in describing the dream image, "they are experienced as fully real," satisfying an "instinctual requirement" (1979:123).

The "reality" of McCoy's painted images is accomplished by a style that embodies many of the characteristics of the dream in the fragmentation of elements, levitation of objects, discrepancies of scale, fade-out effects, and so forth. Furthermore, the medium of colored pencils, while allowing McCoy to directly record her dreams without the intermediary of brushes and pigments, gives the images an evanescent effect which is well suited to some dreams. At the same time, the large scale of the images heightens their impact on the viewer.

"Coeur de Lion," similar to "Kore" in style and format, contains a central numinous image of an androgynous figure with the head of a male lion and human arms, legs and a torso which is opened up to reveal the heart. Surrounding the lion-headed figure are wolves devouring a corpse, floating chalices, a fountain, and so forth. According to Mc Coy, this drawing is the result of years of rotting and dismembering dreams, including dreams of a king being cut and ground up with a mortar and pestle and wolves tearing off the artist's own flesh. "The rotting corpses in my path," said Mc Coy, "were things I had to finish decomposing in my life. For the descent, the putrefaction, precedes learning and new life" (Gould, 1989:71).

In addition to representing her own psychic process, McCoy pointed out to me that the figure of "Coeur de Lion" is an important symbol in alchemical texts of transformation; the metamorphosis of the old dysfunctional self into the new lion-hearted one through dismemberment and reconstitution. One could say, with some certainty, that the alchemical concepts of *putrefactio* (rotting), *mortificatio* (dismemberment), and *coniunctio* (coming together) were founded on the ancient shamanic practice of tearing apart the body in trance and then having it put back together. In alchemy as well as in shamanism one is never quite the same afterwards; otherwise this procedure would have no purpose.

In her most recent paintings, drawings, and sculptures, created during her stay at the American Academy in Rome in 1990, McCoy's symbolic power concentrated on single numinous images. Much of this new work is based on recurring dreams of foot baths and Roman baths. McCoy amplified these dream images as follows.

> The Asclepian sanctuaries included baths where the afflicted took cleansing baths before entering the abaton, (inner chamber) to dream. The ground plan of the Epidaurian thalos resembles a labyrinth with water flowing through it. The baths are important in several ways, first, for ritual cleansing, entering the sanctuary with good intentions. Second, springs call to mind the chthonian aspect of the healing deity. Here underworld is equated with dreamworld (A.C.A., 1988:21).

McCoy first became aware of an underground labyrinth when she explored Native American Indian ruins in the shafts and tunnels of her father's tungsten mines and kivas as a young girl. "Life to me," she recalled,

> seemed to involve a kind of excavation. Later I realized this excavation was excavation of the psyche. Perhaps because of the great kiva restoration, I sensed early the importance of the *temenos* and sacred chambers beneath the earth. Later I connected this to the Abaton of the Asklepian Sanctuary—the underground chamber one entered to have healing dreams of the divine physician in the classical world (Gould, 1989:67).

The dream world is also related to the upperworld. According to Karl Kerenyi who made an extensive study of the divine physician Asklepius, the Epidaurian thalos is "more or less a copy of the heavenly cosmos" that unites above and below (1959:105). "Vasca," one of McCoy's most impressive new sculptures, consists of a huge copper tub with large wings of the same material extending from its sides. McCoy hopes that this tub would be used for ritual bathing, "an opportunity for dissolution and rejuvenation," as she put it, "prior to dream incubation" (telephone conversation with McCoy, June 1991).

She also chose copper for its specific energy-conducing properties—a means of propulsion, as it were, to the lower and upper worlds. The form of "Vasca" is appropriate to its function as the tub looks like a boat in which the dreamer can travel on the waters of the underworld or be transported by the wings to the upperworld.

Journeys to the upperworld and underworld are also evident in Jonathan Borofsky's dream-inspired installations. Before creating these installations, however, Borofsky was involved in an interesting project which facilitated his later work with dreams. In 1968, dissatisfied with his own paintings and sculptures and the values of the New York art world, he underwent an emotional crisis and discontinued his usual art production. He began writing down numbers consecutively on sheets of 8 1/2 inch by 11 inch graph paper. "I came to numbers in the late sixties," Borofsky recalled,

> as a way to kind of focus my mind, to have a mind activity. I had done painting and sculpture, a lot of thinking and writing down of my thoughts that led to number sequences: 1, 2, 3, 4, 5. It was a kind of action of mind to hand to paper. Something inside

told me that if I stuck to it long enough it would
teach me something....It's a form of structure, it's a
form of order....the brain tends to want to chatter on,
to continually make discussion regardless. This is a
way of taking that chatter, bringing it down to one
clear simple format. Ultimately the goal is a quiet
mind (quoted in Jarrell, 1920:52).

Borofsky continued this meditative discipline of counting for the next four years and it became his exclusive "art"
activity, surpassing a count of 2,000,000 and accumulating a
four-foot stack of graph paper which he compared to
Brancusi's "Endless Column"—an *axis mundi* that leads the
individual to a higher state of being. Borofsky still counts for
about one or two hours a day. He believes that the control of
his mental activity opens his mind to dream imagery—the
main source of his painting and drawings from 1972 to 1982.
"My images," remarked Borofsky,

come from two sources: inner and outer. The deepest inner source is, possibly my dreams. Other
images come from my subconscious, such as telephone scribbles and drawings that I make on the
beach. All these I see as photographs of different
states of mind (quoted in Rosenthal and Marshall,
1984:148).

During the period of 1972 to 1982, said Borofsky, "I was very
conscious of writing down my dreams in the morning when I
woke up and looking at them for whatever they teach me about
this world or any other world" (quoted in Jarrell, 1990:52).

In addition to recording the night-time dream material,
Borofsky would lie in bed every morning in a semi-dream
state, rapidly drawing on slips of paper many of the images
that passed through his consciousness. These drawings were
stuck on walls and further elaborated into paintings and

sculptures for his first major exhibition at the Paula Cooper Gallery in New York in 1975. "I was making so much work," recalled Borofsky,

> that it felt natural to jam it all into one space. This arrangement represented my attitude that everything is good—there was no real selection process, or if there was, it was minimal. I didn't pare my output down to the ten best objects and put them under glass or frame them in preparation for a sale. My show wasn't about that, but about bringing in all that I had been thinking about, all that I had been working through in the last year (the little scraps of paper as well as the finished paintings). The show seemed to give people a feeling of being inside my mind. But it was also not unlike walking into a supermarket (which was a major dream I had earlier) where there is just so much stuff all over, colors and boxes of food, and prices and numbers, and things hanging off the ceiling. It's just that kind of experience.
>
> In part, the idea in my 1975 show was to reproduce some of the feeling that was in my studio. My work was very personal. I tried to illustrate the workings of my mind-dreams and various psychological states. Both conscious and unconscious were exposed for the sake of making human connections with others who had similar states of mind—a sort of psychological comparing of notes (quoted in Rosenthal and Marshall, 1984:106).

In revealing the contents of his inner mind with a minimum of selection, Borofsky urged viewers to value the contents of their inner mind, however mundane these contents may initially seem. Borofsky believed that the archetypal reveals itself through personal "little" dreams. "In fact," argued Borofsky,

> I thought, maybe the more personal I get, the more archetypal. I wanted to do those dreams, not like Dali, Tanguy and those people, but "I was walking with my mother down the street and some gangsters chased us." It seemed open, and it seemed it could be made fun of, but I didn't think of that too much (quoted in Simon, 1981:159-162).

Unlike de Chirico or Dali, Borofsky doesn't focus on bizarre or extraordinary dream material, nor does he convey his dream contents in a highly refined and idiosyncratic style. As critic and curator Richard Armstrong wrote in an *Artforum* review,

> Jonathan Borofsky's immense influence on so wide a spectrum of contemporary artists (both in this country and in Europe) derives more from the permission he gives himself to do everything imaginable (and from having the guts to do it) than from any identifiable plastic style. He may be the least stylized artist of his generation (1984:75).

The intentional downplay of technical abilities in Borofsky's drawings and paintings (he received an Master of Fine Arts Degree from Yale), indeed, reduces barriers between his work and the audience and reinforces the "every person" content of his work as he likes to characterize it. To be sure Borofsky's intentional naiveté was regarded as an avant-garde stance in the seventies. Borofsky believes that his naive approach was reinforced by one of his dreams in which Salvador Dali wrote him a letter saying, "Dear Jon, There is very little difference between the avant-garde and the commonplace" (Borofsky, 1981). In fact, conflation of the avant-garde and the commonplace in Borofsky's style is well suited to his idea of the dream world in which it is difficult to make distinctions between ordinary and extraordinary dreams.

In 1975, Borofsky remained alone in his New York studio, painting a large wall. "I worked all the time," said Borofsky,

> especially during the night and early morning hours when the city was quiet, and I would sleep in the same room some ten feet away. By working directly on the walls of this white room, I felt like a twentieth century cave painter (quoted in Rosenthal and Marshall, 1984:109).

This methodology allowed for a continuous flow between dream and waking state. Borofsky also realized that he could continue the flow of his dream images and semi-awake states of early morning by remaining in a meditative attitude throughout the day. Given Borofsky's artistic process, no significant distinction can be made between images that are directly inspired by dreams or by day dreaming. Borofsky's wall and those that followed all have the numinous dreamlike presence of a cave painting as a result of his creative process as well as a formal language involving simple renderings of shape and color, exaggerations of size, and juxtapositions of unrelated images.

"At the end of the month," continued Borofsky about this first installation,

> all I could think about was painting the wall white again, which I did almost immediately, but not before a friend took some slides of what had been done.

> Still, wall drawing seemed very exciting, and I wanted to bring this attitude into the art world—

drawing images directly on the wall. I later found a tool, the opaque projector, to help me, and I started to make hundreds of small drawings that could be carried in my briefcase to each exhibition and projected on the wall (quoted in Rosenthal and Marshall, 1984:109).

The transfer of the drawings to the wall were accomplished rapidly in a trance-like state, echoing the semi-awake or meditative condition of their origin. Borofsky placed his images all over the walls, corners and ceilings of the gallery or museum and varied sizes greatly so that viewers usually could not apprehend them at first glance or analyze them intellectually. According to art critic Jeffrey Deitch,

Borofsky wants his work to communicate on a pre-rational level, enter the viewer's mind at the first glimpse, bypassing the "brain chatter" and aesthetic scrutinizing that contemporary painting sometimes encourages. In order to have as little interference as possible between his mind and the viewer's, he began working directly on the wall in the period after his Paula Cooper show (1976:99).

Deitch's points are well taken, although I would say that Borofsky's communication is non-rational rather than pre-rational; besides affirming the worth of "every man's" inner mind and promoting the self-awareness of that mind, his goal is to affect his audience on a profound non-rational level.

A good example of this intention was his 1977 wall painting of a Shinto priest (Illustration 18) for the Men's Shelter in the Bowery near his studio in New York. "I felt very nervous," remembered Borofsky,

closed in, and self-conscious in the men's shelter because I was with a bunch of sick men who were lying in bed. I was talking to them, trying to make them comfortable, trying to make me comfortable and to figure out why the hell I was doing this in the first place. I didn't think I could do a whole installation—and the room was already an installation, for me anyhow; it was as if there was nothing I could add. I thought I would try to do a very beautiful image in this rather difficult space. At first, I was going to do the Blimp (which for me was a very beautiful image) on a light blue background. It was just at the last minute, again with the potential of installation, that I projected the Shinto priest on the wall. It just seemed to be what I had to do. I wasn't sure the image was going to be right for these men, or what should be in a hospital, but I thought I had to do this subject. For me it is a healer, a healing image and it is about meditation, but it is questionable what sense it makes—a Japanese Shinto priest in a hospital wing for homeless men. It was incongruous—for I ended up putting a very acidy green behind it on walls that were stained yellow and ugly (quoted in Rosenthal and Marshall, 1984:115).

Borofsky needed not have worried about the incongruity of the Shinto priest image. One art critic who visited the shelter reported that this image had a positive impact on the men who lived there (Bourdon, 1977:8).

Borofsky mentioned that he had considered using the blimp image, for he felt that levitating and flying images have a psychologically uplifting influence on viewers, following his own dream of flying over a strange landscape in 1978. To be sure, flying in dreams is very exhilarating, especially for people who do not have any other way of journeying to the upper realms. Borofsky's painting of his flying dream as well as flying figures and objects in his installations support the desire of many viewers to be freed from their earthly moorings and to venture into other worlds. Borofsky also linked flying with seeing—a relationship well understood by shamans. He explained that his "Flying Figure," a life-size sculptural self-portrait suspended in space over the Basel Kunsthalle in 1981

> is looking down on the planet, sort of surveying. I don't feel like I'm trying to escape the world, as much as trying to get above it for an overview of larger issues—to try to see it as a whole—the tensions and the beauty, the touch of God. I want to see both together, to understand the workings of the planet (quoted in Rosenthal and Marshall, 1984:161).

Some of Borofsky's flying men are permeated by holes. He explained the origin of these "molecule men" as follows:

> I was on a conceptual sidetrack—taking a wooden chair and drilling holes into it, trying to make it disappear. I tried to get space to penetrate the chair, so that it wasn't so much a chair any more, but literally a dematerialized object....Then I decided to make a cutout of myself out of masonite. So I had a photo taken of me with a briefcase, traced the photo on masonite board, cut the piece out, and started drilling holes in it. I was concerned with lightness, though I know how heavy we are, centered on the ground, subject to gravity. The opposite is being free, flying or whatever. I was drawing the man with holes in it on a plane, and the stewardess asked me what it was. I didn't know—it was just my silhouette with holes in it. Another stewardess said "molecules" as she walked by. That was important for me to hear at the moment. From that point on he was "the molecule man" (quoted in Simon, 1981:164).

These "molecule men" are quite impressive in content as well as style for Borofsky manifests the desire of almost every person to inhabit a non-material universe. Borofsky also understands that our essential nature is permeable, "They [the molecule men] explore the idea that we are all made up of pockets of air and water" (quoted in Rosenthal and Marshall, 1984:80). This physical permeability in the doppelgänger's of the artist may also be a metaphor for Borofsky' own psychic permeability—his openness to the subtle and evanescent information passing through his consciousness.

The fragmented human figure with the long ears of a rabbit, another doppelgänger, can be found in Borofsky's dream books and installations. "I think that's me," Borofsky claimed, "but I also think that's me as an animal....It's about hearing, about the sensitivity of animal ears, like radar" (quoted in Simon, 1981:164). "At other times," said Borofsky, "these ears become antennae that can pick up energy or reach into space" (quoted in Rosenthal and Marshall, 1984:75). The fragmentation of these figures also relates to the permeability of the artist's "molecule men". According to Borofsky,

> By coming apart, and then rejoining itself, the image is about fragmentation and losing one's sense of the body or the physical world, which one might do if one is focused on hearing....So it might not be so much exploding the system, as coming apart and pulling it back together (quoted in Rosenthal and Marshall, 1984:179).

Borofsky has made an interesting connection between dismemberment and hearing, the necessity of being opened in order to hear and the requirement of pulling the psyche together again if one is to hold and communicate this hearing.

There are other dismembered figures in Borofsky's oeuvre besides the rabbit-headed individual. They include a man who removes his head, another whose head is split in half, and still others with ribbons and other stuff exuding from a broken skull. These men are generalized portraits of the artist and may refer to the transcendence or disruption of the intellect in Borofsky's methods as an essential prerequisite for the expression of spiritual meaning. "Art is for the Spirit," the title and inscription in large block letters of one of Borofsky's paintings, sums up Borofsky's approach.

In "Art is for the Spirit" (1973), he depicts himself on an earth globe suspended in the cosmos with his arms stretched above his head, indicating his connection with the upperworld—the general realm of the spirit. Aside from the ascent and connection to the spiritual upper world, Borofsky's work mirrors his descent to the lower realms. "I dreamed," wrote Borofsky,

> I was being followed. I stepped down into a hole in the ground and started to work my way downward into the earth. I realized that if I was going to make it, I would need some help (1981).

In the drawing accompanying the dream description, Borofsky shows himself crawling downward through a long spiral tunnel. Tunnels such as these are frequently encountered on shamanic journeys, along with power animals who are called upon to assist the traveler. Borofsky did not have such assistance on this particular journey but on his dream journeys he was given important gifts to help him through life.

One of the most significant of these gifts was a red ruby which he drew, painted, and sculptured in many of his installations. "I dreamed, I found a red ruby," Borofsky related. "It seemed very beautiful. I tried to make a red ruby [in the dream] and as I painted it I began to think of it as my heart" (quoted in Simon, 1981:162). The ruby has many meanings in Borofsky's work.

In a war-damaged building in East Berlin that used to be the headquarters of the Gestapo, Borofsky covered the walls with rubies to neutralize the bad feelings emanating from the place and to provide a feeling of warmth in the dismal surroundings. Painted rubies on the walls of the Basel installation accompanied the "Flying Figure" which, according to critic Marc Rosenthal, appeared to be "representative of celestial orbs that establish a heavenly host for the Flying Figure and guarantee its safe journey" (quoted in Rosenthal and Marshall, 1984:16).

In one of his Paula Cooper shows Borofsky placed a sculptural version of the ruby on top of the counting piece, counterbalancing the conceptual aspects of the counting. "In that particular case," argued Borofsky,

> I think the connection is obvious. You have this huge stack of counting that's been going on for over 11 years. Very conceptual—the left part of my brain obsessively rational and linear—then suddenly at the last minute I'm trying to think of where to put this little red ruby I've finally made, which is cast of translucent resin. I don't want to just put it on a shelf because I think someone gonna walk off with it. It's the best color in a ruby I've managed to get out of several I've cast so far. So I think I'll put it right on top of the counting, under the protective plexiglass case. The next day, I look at it, and I realize what I've done. That side of me which is the core of feeling—the heart, the spirit—is connected up with the conceptual side of me which is the counting. I've put the two together, physically and symbolically (quoted in Simon, 1981:163).

In still another installation at M.I.T, the artist created a wall drawing where, in Borofsky's words, "the figure is sort of holding and looking at its own head and the ruby is kind of popping out" (quoted in Simon, 1981:163). "...[T]he body looking at its own head and the ruby between them," continued Borofsky in the same interview with Joan Simon, "implies self-awareness and a state of looking to oneself for purification and a state of perfection (quoted in Simon, 1981:163).

I am reminded of the goal of inner perfection that is attained through meditation and self-contemplation in Vajrayana Buddhism. It is symbolized by the "diamond" or vajra in Indian and Tibetan art. Despite all the possible meanings of the ruby in Borofsky's work, the practice of making a dream gift available for the spiritual and therapeutic benefit of the community is also a classic shamanic endeavor. Indeed, all artists discussed in this section— Rousseau, de Chirico, Breton, Dali, Buñuel, Schneemann, and McCoy— have embodied their dream gifts in images that continue to reverberate among viewers. Their images, including some of Borofsky's, are often disturbing, but they are effective because they reveal knowledge and deep psychic conditions which further the inner awareness of their viewers.

Notes
1. I think the Tao and the *nagual* are similar. They are both formless energy fields that cannot be described analytically. Creative ideas in Taoism can be obtained by accessing the Tao through meditation and quietism.

2. Breton's concern with selective recall could have come from Freud's idea that the "manifest content" of the dream constitutes a censorship of the true or "latent content" in order to protect the dreamer from waking up.

3. In the first of his *Manifestoes*, Breton said that "From the moment when it is subjected to a methodical examination, when, by means yet to be determined, we succeed in recording the contents of dreams in their entirety (and that presupposes a discipline of memory spanning generations: but let us nonetheless begin by noting the most salient facts), when its graph will expand with unparalleled volume and regularity, we may hope that mysteries which really are not will give way to the great Mystery" (1972b:14). One way to mitigate the effects of selective recall is to wake up immediately after having the dream and write it down. This is a technique that Breton employed, as evident in *Les Vases Communicants* (1932). He, indeed, noted the time of night in the accounts of his own dreams.

4. This is my translation of "Qu'est -ce que ce proces intente à la vie reele sous pretexte que le sommeil donne l'illusion de cette vie, illusion decouverte a

l'éveil, alors que dans le sommeil la vie reele, a supposer quelle soit illusion, n'est en rien critiquee, tenue pour illusoire? Ne serait-on pas aussi fonde, parce que les ivrognes voient double, a decreter que pour le'oeil d'un homme sobre, la repetition d'in object est la consequence d'une ivresse un peu differente?" (Breton, 1932:131). There is very little difference between my translations and the others. It is difficult to render Breton's ungrammatical French prose into clear English syntax.

5. For an account of Dali's encounter with Freud, see, Rubin (1968:216).

6. Buñuel, in a later passage of his autobiography, made no distinction between waking and sleeping dreams. He wrote, "Waking dreams are as important, as unpredictable, and as powerful as those we have when we're asleep" (1983:98).

7. Dali maintained that the purpose of the film was, "To disrupt the mental anxiety of the spectator, and to reveal the principal conviction which animates all Surrealist thought: the overwhelming importance of desire" (quoted in Aranda, 1976:64).

8. In the early sixties in Vienna, Hermann Nitsch disemboweled animals, poured their warm blood over the stage and, using blood-smeared naked men, reenacted the crucifixion in his "Orgien-Mysterien Theater." He believed these "actions" would have a therapeutic effect in allowing the audience to release their desire to kill in a place relatively safe for humans (but not for animals). Thomas McEvilley (1983:62-71) linked Nitsch's work and that of similarly violent "body" artists such Paul McCarthy, Rudolph Schwarzkogler, etc., to Schneemann's "Meat Joy" and to shamanic initiation rites. The exploitation of violence and blood along with the suffering and death of animals for dramatic effects, however therapeutic for some people, has little in common with authentic shamanic therapies and initiations and has no relation to Schneemann's joyful rituals.

11. Henri Rousseau
    "The Dream," 1910
    Oil on canvas
    69½ x 99½ inches
    The Museum of Modern Art, New York
    Gift of Nelson A. Rockefeller

12. Giorgio de Chirico
"The Soothsayer's Recompense," 1913
Oil on canvas
53½ x 71 inches
Philadelphia Museum of Art
The Louise and Walter Arensberg Collection

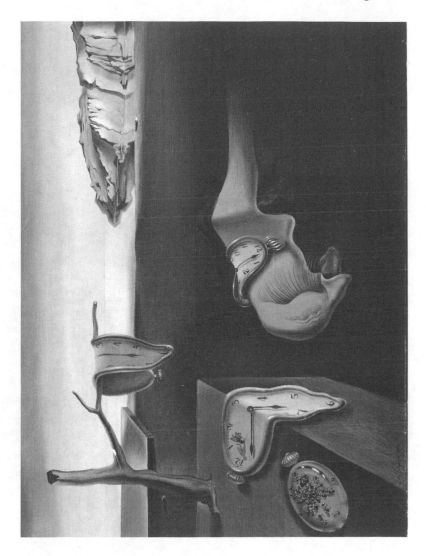

13. Salvador Dali
    "The Persistence of Memory," 1931
    Oil on canvas
    9½ x 13 inches
    The Museum of Modern Art, New York
    Given anonymously

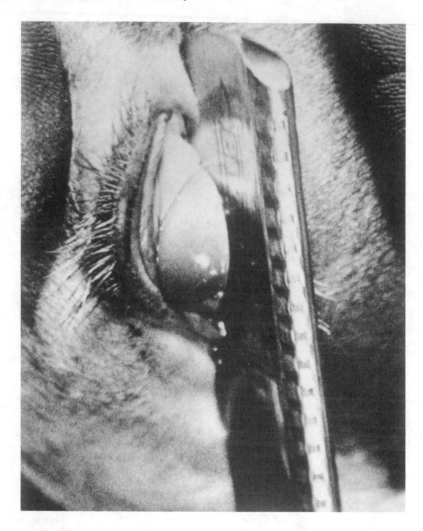

14. Louis Buñuel
    Still from the film "Un Chien Andalou," 1928
    The Museum of Modern Art, New York

15. Man Ray
"Le Tournant" (The Turning Point)
from the book *Les Main Libres,* Paris, 1936
India ink
25 x 19¾ inches

16. Carolee Schneemann
     From the performance "Meat Joy" May 29, 1964
     Festival de la Libre Expression, Paris
     Courtesy Carolee Schneemann

17. Ann McCoy
    "Temple of Isis, Pompeii," 1987
    Pencil on paper on canvas
    9 x 15 feet 8 inches
    Photo Credit: Ivan Dalla Tana

18. Jonathan Borofsky
     "Shinto Priest," 1977
     Installation at the Men's Shelter
     in the Bowery, New York
     Ink, dayglow paint on wall
     5 x 3½ feet

Performing

Hugo Ball, Yves Klein, Joseph Beuys, Mary Beth Edelson, Karen Finley, Rachel Rosenthal and Sha Sha Higby either had little training in traditional theatre or they wanted to go beyond the boundaries of traditional theatre to express their experiences of non-ordinary reality. Most of them started their careers as painters or sculptors and then decided to perform in front of audiences. Their performances do not reflect the art of traditional shamanic cultures, and they may not think of themselves as shamans but they employ shamanistic techniques to enter non-ordinary reality.

For me, the most important antecedent of contemporary performance artists employing shamanistic practices is the Dadaist poet Hugo Ball. Dadaists used sound poems, chance techniques, automatic drawing, and dreaming to evade the rational mind and enter non-ordinary reality. According to the Dadaist poet and artist Hans Arp,

> Dada aimed to destroy the reasonable deceptions of man and recover the natural and unreasonable order. Dada wanted to replace the logical non-sense of the men today by the illogical senseless....Dada denounced the infernal ruses of the official vocabulary of wisdom....Dada is direct like nature. Dada is

for infinite sense and definite means (1972:238).

Dada emerged during World War I when millions of men were being sent to a senseless death. Given this carnage, it is not surprising that a small group of highly intelligent and sensitive artists began questioning the accepted order of values along with the usual forms of artistic expression. One group which included Arp, Ball, Emmy Hemmings, Tristan Tzara, Marcel Janco, Richard Huelsenbeck, and others moved to Zurich to avoid the draft and the military climate of Germany. It was in Zurich that Ball invented the sound poem which he recited in a series of performances at the Cabaret Voltaire (Illustration 19). In his autobiography, *Flight Out of Time*, Ball said that

> In these phonetic poems we totally renounce the language that journalism has abused and corrupted. We must return to the innermost alchemy of the word, we must even give up the word too, to keep for poetry its last and holiest refuge. We must give up writing secondhand: that is, accepting words (to say nothing of sentences) that are not newly invented for our own use. Poetic effects can no longer be obtained in ways that are merely reflected ideas or arrangements of furtively offered witticisms and images (1974:71).

Ball believed that to arrive at the "innermost alchemy of the word" and to be able to use the word as a magical incantation, it is necessary to jettison its meaning, especially because its meaning has been "debased by journalism" (nationalist propaganda). By sacrificing the common sense of the word, the poet has the possibility of reaching, in the words of Arp, "infinite sense." According to Ball, the sound poem is a "living art" that is "irrational, primitive, and complex": "it will speak a secret language and leave behind documents not of edification but of paradox" (1974:49).

To my mind, the sound poem becomes a kind of *mantra* in which the same or similar vowels are repeated over and over again. "We have loaded the word with strengths and energies that helped us to rediscover the evangelical concept of the 'word' (logos) as a magical complex image," Ball argued in *Flight out of Time* (1974:68). "In mantra chanting," maintained the poet Gary Snyder,

> the magic utterances, built of seed-syllables such as OM and AYNG and AH, repeated over and over again, fold and curl on the breath until—when most weary and bored—a new voice enters, a voice speaks through you clearer and stronger than what you know of yourself; with a sureness and melody of its own, singing out the inner song of the self (quoted in Rothenberg & Rothenberg, 1983:94).

The word Dada, supposedly taken at random from a dictionary, can itself function as a *mantra* loaded "with strengths and energies." As Ball wrote in his autobiography,

> How does one achieve eternal bliss? By saying dada. How does one become famous? By saying dada. With a noble gesture and delicate propriety. Till one goes crazy. Till one loses consciousness. How can one get rid of everything that smacks of journalism, worms, everything nice and right, blinkered, moralistic, europeanized enervated? By saying dada. Dada is the world soul, dada is the pawnshop. Dada is the world's best lily-milk soap, Dada Mr. Rubiner, dada Mr. Korirodi, Dada Mr. Anastasius Lilienstein.
>
> ...Dada Johann Fuchsgang Goethe, Dada Stendhal, Dada Dalai Lama, Buddha, Bible, and Nietzsche. Dada m'dada Dada mhm dada da. It's a question of

connections, and of loosening them up a bit to start with.

...Dada is the heart of words (1974:220-221).

Yet, said Ball,

I want my own stuff, my own rhythm, and vowels and consonants too, matching the rhythm and all my own. If this pulsation is seven yards long, I want words for it that are seven yards long (1974:221).

Ball's most famous public performance of his sound poems was at the Cabaret Voltaire in the winter of 1916. He recalled in *Flight Out of Time*,

I invented a new genre of poems, "Verse ohne Worte" [poems without words] or Lautgedichte [sound poems], in which the balancing of vowels is weighted and distributed solely according to the values of the beginning sequence. I gave a reading of the first of these poems this evening. I had made for myself a special costume for it. My legs were in a cylinder of shiny blue cardboard, which reached up to my hips so that I looked like an obelisk. Over it I wore a huge coat collar cut out of cardboard, scarlet inside and gold outside. It was fastened at the neck in such a way that I could give the impression of a winglike movement by raising and lowering the elbows. I also wore a high, blue-and-white-striped witch doctor's hat.

On all three sides of the stage I had set up music stands facing the audience, and I put my red-penciled manuscript on them; I officiate at one stand after another. Tzara knew about my preparations, so there was a real little premiere. Everyone was curious. I could not walk inside the cylinder so I was carried onto the stage in the dark and began slowly and solemnly:

gadji beri bimba
gandridi lauli lonni cadori
gadjama bim beri glassala
gandridi glassala tuffm i zimbrabim
blassa galassas tuffm i zimbrabim...

The stresses became heavier, the emphasis was increased as the sound of the consonants became sharper. Soon I realized that, if I wanted to remain serious (and I wanted to at all costs), my method of expression would not be equal to the pomp of my staging....I feared a disgrace and pulled myself together. I had now completed "Labadas Gesang an die Wolken" [Labada's Song to the Clouds] at the music stand on the right and the "Elefanten-karawane" [Elephant Caravan] on the left and turned back to the middle one, flapping my wings energetically. The heavy vowel sequences and the plodding rhythm of the elephants had given me one last crescendo. But how was I to get to the end? Then I noticed that my voice had no choice but to take on the ancient cadence of priestly lamentation, that style of liturgical singing that wails in the Catholic churches of East and West.

I do not know what gave me the idea of this music, but I began to chant my vowel sequences in a church style like a recitative, and tried not only to look serious but to force myself to be serious. For a moment it seemed as if there were a place, bewildered face in my cubist mask, that half-frightened, half-curious face of a ten-year-old boy, trembling and hanging avidly on the priest's words in the requiems and high masses in his home parish. Then the lights went out as I had ordered, and bathed in sweat, I was carried down off the stage like a magical bishop (1974:70-71).

From Ball's account, it is evident that, like the shaman's drum, the sound poem induces a trance state. Moreover, Ball's utterances were very much like the magical incantations of shamans in their remoteness from ordinary speech. In order to have any effectiveness, the anthropologist Bronislav Malinowski believed that magical speech must have "a very considerable coefficient of weirdness" (quoted in Rothenberg & Rothenberg, 1983:112). To be sure, Ball's dress and actions in the Cabaret Voltaire performance enhanced this "coefficient of weirdness."

Although Ball was a devout Catholic who lived a very ascetic life, he was by no means an orthodox Christian and his writings manifested an affinity with the role of the shaman. In *Flight Out of Time*, he wrote,

There are primitive peoples who remove all sensitive children from daily life at an early age and give them a special education as a clairvoyant, priest or doctor by order of the state. In modern Europe these geniuses are exposed to all the destructive, stupid, confusing, impressions (1974:108).

There is neither evidence in the autobiography nor does the limited information on his life indicate that he was one of these geniuses, but he realized that he approached the shaman's role as an artist. It is a fact, argued Ball, "that modern artists are gnostics and practice things that the priests think are long forgotten; perhaps even commit sins that are no longer thought possible" (1974:101). "What constitutes our mind and spirit?," Ball said later in *Flight Out of Time*, "Where do we get belief and form from? Do we not steal the elements from all magical religions? Are we not magical eclectics" (1974:111)?

Yves Klein also exhibited a considerable "coefficient of weirdness" in his art and life. For his antics in France during the fifties, he has somewhat disparagingly been called "a Dada" by American and French critics. According to McEvilley, who wrote an important catalogue essay on Klein for his retrospective at the Guggenheim Museum in the Winter of 1983, Klein had also been associated with Rosicrucianism and Zen Buddhism. For me, however, Klein's work can best be explained in terms of shamanic practice.

Jean Tinguely, Klein's best friend and occasional artistic collaborator, disclosed that "He [Klein] always talked about two things; he talked about levitation, and he talked about just vanishing" (McEvilley, 1982:62). As early as the summer of 1948, when Klein was twenty, he and his friends Claude Pascal and Arman would meditate for many hours on the roof of his apartment house and, as McEvilley said, talk "of leaping from the roof and flying into the full moon ahead" (1982:28). This desire to fly was in part inspired by Max Heindel's "Cosmogenie," a text explaining Rosicrucian practices. It became on ongoing concern for Klein during the remainder of his short life. Klein's mother maintained that he would read this book for hours every day during the period between 1948 and 1952 (McEvilley, 1982:26).

Heindel had written in 1908 that the Age of Matter was waning and would be replaced by an Age of Spirit in which humans would be able to escape matter at will and fly through spiritual realms. Klein believed that he would be able to attain a state of "immaterial sensibility" which would enable him to fly if he seriously practiced for seven years the breathing and meditation exercises outlined in Heindel's book. Klein's wife, Rotraut Ecker, reported,

> He was sure he could fly. He used to tell me that at one time monks knew how to levitate, and that he would get there too. It was an obsession. Like a little child he really was convinced that he could do it. He even talked about a machine in which to train people to fly (McEvilley, 1982:62).

As "highest initiate" who had mastered the technique of flying, he would then be able to instruct others, thereby bringing in the new Age of Spirit. In 1954, Klein summarized Heindel's methodology as follows:

> To be transfigured is to think at each instant of the very essence of the purity of sanctity, and the breathing does the rest—that is, it spreads through the body a new life which enters into every separate atom and remakes each infinitesimal particle of the ordinary body into a body transfigured.

> What is necessary then is to breathe with joy an atmosphere and a climate intensely spiritual, which creates in the ego the power to purify the physical body and the astral body and the body of desire (quoted in McEvilley, 1982:33-34).

After ten years of practicing Heindel's techniques, he did not achieve the desired end of release from the body at will, so he abandoned the idea. It was through Judo that Klein had his only real experience of physical flying. In 1953, he attained mastery in this spiritual and physical discipline, reaching the level of 4th Dan, the highest degree of black belt for a Frenchman.

Flying is an essential and universally practiced activity

of shamans. In a trance state, induced by drumming, meditation or ritual practice, shamans are able to leave their body and ascend to the upperworld so that they can gain information or secure healing from spiritual allies. In his seminal study on shamanism, Mircea Eliade wrote,

> What concerns us in this instance is the fact that sorcerers and shamans are able, *here on earth* and *as often as they wish*, to accomplish "coming out of the body," that is, the death that alone has the power to transform the rest of mankind into "birds"; shamans and sorcerers can enjoy the condition of "souls," of "discarnate beings," which is accessible to the profane only when they die. Magical flight is the expression of both the soul's autonomy and ecstasy....The point of primary importance here is that the mythology and the rites of magical flight peculiar to shamans and sorcerers confirm and proclaim their transcendence in respect to the human condition; by flying into the air, in bird form or in their normal human shape, shamans as it were proclaim the degeneration of humanity. For as we have seen, a number of myths refer to the primordial time when *all human beings* could ascend to heaven, by climbing a mountain, a tree, or a ladder, or flying by their own power, or being carried by birds. The degeneration of humanity henceforth forbids the mass of mankind to fly to heaven; only death restores men (and not all of them!) to their primordial condition; only then can they ascend to heaven, fly like birds, and so forth (1964:479-480).

Eliade's description of shamanic flying shows important similarities to the ideas of Heindel and Klein. In fact, Heindel borrowed substantially from shamanic accounts and it is precisely the shamanic elements in Heindel's

"Cosmogenie" that Klein appropriated in his dream of flying. I believe that Klein's dream of flying was motivated by authentic spiritual concerns—in Eliade's words, "an expression of both the soul's desire for autonomy and ecstasy." But it was also motivated by Klein's desire to draw attention to himself as a superior human being who possessed magical powers. He even professed the desire to levitate several feet above the floor in front of spectators at the gallery where he exhibited his works.

Although, in exceptional cases, some yogis and shamans are said to have succeeded in levitating their physical body, the more advanced practitioners consider this practice to be a diversion from the spiritual goal of attaining knowledge. I am reminded of the famous anecdote about the Buddha meeting the yogi who, after many years of practice, had the ability to cross a river by walking on water. The Buddha told the yogi that it was hardly worth the effort given the fact that, for a small sum of money, he could take a ferry across the river. Also, true shamans do not want to draw attention to themselves. Showing off is considered an abuse of shamanic powers which will be followed by dire consequences. Both Heindel and Klein failed to understand that it is the astral not the physical body which leaves non-ordinary reality in a state of trance.

Klein's obsession with levitation and flight permeates his work, manifesting in his celebration of pure color and empty space as the expression of "immaterial sensibility" and, especially, in his famous performance entitled "The Painter of Space Hurls Himself into the Void" (1960). The famous photograph of this event (Illustration 20) shows Klein, dressed in a business suit and with tie, taking a swan dive off the second story of a building. He looks as though he is ascending to the sky, not falling to the ground.

There is some controversy as to whether the dive actually happened. Bernadette Alain, a former girlfriend of Klein, claimed that she had been present at the leap which took place on January 12, 1960, at the Gallery Collette Allendy. She gave the following account:

> For a *judoka* who knew how to fall it was not extraordinary....It would be expected of someone at his level of training to know how to recover and fall. He did it as a challenge or act of defiance, to prove that he was capable of leaping into the void—that is, not leaping out of a window, but leaping *toward the sky*. He wanted this known....He had nothing underneath him but the pavement—nothing. There was no faking....I was not amazed because I had seen him do far more interesting things on the judo mats...He knew that he could do it, too. It was only the public who were amazed....But as soon as he became a celebrity, everyone in the world claimed to have been there and told stories and more stories (quoted in McEvilley, 1982:64).

Pierre Restany, an important art critic who was supposed to officially document this event, arrived late at the scene. According to Restany,

> Yves was tremendously excited; he was in a kind of mystical ecstasy. He truly seemed to have just accomplished some prodigious physical feat. He said to me, "You have just missed one of the most important events of your life." He was limping slightly from a twisted ankle. I tell you, if I hadn't gone there and seen the state he was in, I would always have believed it was a photomontage (quoted in McEvilley, 1982:64).

Since Alain and Restany were the only people who believed that the event actually took place, Klein felt compelled to repeat it again and, after leaping only a short distance, broke his shoulder. Not wanting to injure himself again, he decided to stage a mock repeat of the leap in front of photographers on October 12, 1960. At this time he was caught by fellow judo practitioners in a net. The jump was repeated several times to get the facial expression exactly right. In the photograph, the net and the judo assistants were removed and we see a bicyclist peddling away. As McEvilley pointed out, this bicyclist recalls Breughel's ploughman in the "Fall of Icarus", who similarly goes about his business unaware of the momentous event transpiring near him (McEvilley, 1982:64).

Klein, like Icarus, failed as shaman. His attempt to fly was an act of hubris which resulted in a fall to earth. In fact, Klein's career suffered a decline from 1960 until his death in 1962. The 1961 exhibition of his works at Leo Castelli in New York, which Klein hoped would establish his career in America, was greeted with derision by American critics and avoided by American artists. He was also greatly distressed by the news that a Japanese artist, inspired by his 1960 leap, had died while leaping from a building onto a canvas in the street. Ironically, the canvas which this artist had willed to the Tokyo Museum of Modern Art was rejected by the Museum.

I believe that Klein's inability to fly led to a profound self-doubt as far as his true spiritual abilities were concerned, and the eventual result was his fatal heart failure on June 6, 1962.

In contrast to Yves Klein, Joseph Beuys was very much aware of his role as a shaman. During the Second World War, as a Stuka pilot, Beuys was shot down over Eastern Russia and rescued by a tribe of nomadic Tartars who wrapped the wounded Beuys in fat and felt to preserve his body heat and thereby saved his life. After the war he underwent a long recovery period that was both physical and mental. Having been seriously wounded four times as a Stuka pilot, he had to deal not only with his weakened body, but also suffered a mental breakdown between 1955-1957. Beuys said about this recovery period,

> Certainly incidents from the war produced an after-effect on me, but something had to die. I believe this phase was one of the most important for me in that I had to fully reorganize myself constitutionally; I had for too long a time dragged a body around with me. The initial stage was a totally exhausted state, which quickly turned into an orderly phase of renewal. The things inside me had to be totally transplanted; a physical change had to take place in me. Illnesses are almost always spiritual crises in life, in which old experiences and phases of thought are cast off in order to make positive changes (Adriani et al, 1979:56).

Talking about his death experiences, Beuys also said,

> death is quite a complicated thing. The purpose of Western thinking and the science that grew from it was to reach the material, but one only does that through death. If you take the brain as being the material basis of thought, as hard and blank as a mirror, then it becomes clear that thinking can only be fulfilled through death, and that a higher level exists for it through the liberation of death: a new life for thinking (1988:49).

From these statements, it appears that Beuys underwent a shamanic initiation of death and rebirth leading to a higher level of consciousness. This initiation eventually enabled him to realize

the part the artist can play in indicating the traumas

of time and initiating a healing process. That relates to medicine, or what people call alchemy or shamanism....

I take this form of ancient behaviour as the idea of transformation through concrete processes of life, nature and history. My intention is obviously not to return to such earlier cultures but to stress the idea of transformation and of substance. That is precisely what the shaman does in order to bring about change and development, his nature is therapeutic.

Of course the shaman can operate genuinely only in a society that is still intact because it lies in an earlier stage of development. Our society is far from intact, but this too is a necessary stage. It's the point of crisis that sets in at every stage of history and which we can observe in the past. Once the intactness has gone, a kind of metamorphosis begins. So while shamanism marks a point in the past, it also indicates a possibility for historical development. It could be described as the deepest root of the idea of spiritual life, deeper even than the mythological level of the later stages of Greek or Egyptian cultures for example. But even the Greeks and the Babylonians retained their link with shamanistic or magical behaviour. The mythological view of the world, the designation of particular places as sacred, and the building of temples like the Acropolis all belong to a later stage. They mark the beginning of the spiritual manipulation, in terms of visible and invisible substance, to which we are heirs.

When we consider our own stage of materialism and all the things we experience as negative in our current crisis, we have to admit too that this stage is also a historical necessity. I experienced it in the war and I feel it now every day; this state of decay that comes with a one-sided understanding of the idea of materialism. When people say that shamanistic practice is atavistic and irrational, one might answer that the attitude of contemporary scientists is equally old-fashioned and atavistic, because we should by now be at another state of development in our relationship to material.

So when I appear as a kind of shamanistic figure, or allude to it, I do it to stress my belief in other priorities and the need to come up with a completely different plan for working with substances. For instance, in places like universities, where everyone speaks too rationally, it is necessary for a kind of enchanter to appear (Tisdall, 1979:23).

Although Beuys began his career as a sculptor and graphic artist, working with substances in a more or less traditional way, he eventually realized that his main desire was to sculpt the consciousness of his students and spectators. "I want to become an energy center, like an atomic station," argued Beuys,

It's the same principal again: transmitter, and receiver....The spectator becomes the program....

...To be a teacher is my greatest work of art. The rest is the waste product, a demonstration. If you want to explain yourself you must present something tangible. But after a while this has only the function of a historic document. Objects aren't very important for me anymore. I want to get to the origin of matter, to the thought behind it (Sharp, 1969:44).

This attitude toward sculpture may have originated from Beuys' own professor of sculpture at the Düsseldorf Academy, Ewald Matare. While Matare's approach to sculpture was very conservative, towards the end of his life Matare was credited with saying, "sculpture must be like a footprint in the sand. I do not want any more aesthetic art work, I am making myself a fetish" (Adriani *et al*, 1979:28).

Although many of Beuys sculptures and drawings manifest his interest in shamanism,[1] he found that the best way to be a teacher-enchanter-energy center-shamanistic figure was through performance art.

Beuys always appeared for his performances wearing a fisherman's vest, heavy boots, and a businessman's hat. According to Beuys,

> This hat represents another kind of head and functions like another personality. Many people are strangely involved with it and it works like a permanent theatre, there in front of people's eyes but not immediately decipherable. When they describe it flatly as a trademark, this is because the meaning is not really clear to them. That's exactly what I meant when I talked of the shaman: it is impossible to decipher precisely the way it functions. A simple meaning would be that the hat alone can do the work and acts as a vehicle—and I personally am not so important anymore (quoted in Tisdall, 1979:25).

Following the Aachen meeting between Valery Giscard d'Estaing and Helmut Schmidt in September 1978, the German television newscasters spent more time discussing the hat of Beuys, who was present at their state lunch, than on reporting the political and economic agreements.

In tribal culture the hat is often considered the most important part of the costume. The anthropologist Kai Donner wrote,

According to these [Siberian] shamans, then, a great part of their power is hidden in these caps. This is why usually, when a shamanic exhibition is given at the request of Russians, the shaman performs without his cap (Eliade, 1964:154).

Also, as Mircea Eliade remarked,

By the mere fact of donning it—or by manipulating the objects that deputize for it—the shaman transcends profane space and prepares to enter into contact with the spirit world. Usually this preparation is almost a concrete introduction into that world; for the costume is donned after many preliminaries and just on the eve of shamanic trance (1964:147).

Usually Beuys' performances involved the use of repetitive gestures and/or sounds over a lengthy time period, putting both him and his audience in a trance state. For "The Chief," performed at the Rene Block Gallery in Berlin on December 1, 1964, Beuys spent nine hours completely wrapped in a felt roll near two dead hares. One of the hares was placed at his feet and the other above his head next to a copper rod. In addition he located fat strips parallel to his prone position and constructed two fat pieces in the corner of the room. Without moving, he uttered messages, at irregular intervals, that were greatly amplified by a microphone that was buried with him in the felt roll.

According to Beuys,

...The Chief was above all an important sound piece. The most recurrent sound was deep in the throat and hoarse like the cry of a stag: öö. This is a primary sound, reaching far back, and was later the main expression of a speech I gave on matriculation day as a Professor of Monumental Sculpture at the Düsseldorf Kunstakademie in 1967...Doubtless one of the things held against me years later when I was dismissed....

Such a performance always had a theory behind it, a partitur or score, which gives information without information. Acoustically it's like using just the carrier wave as a conveyor of energy without loading it with semantic information. The wave carries the kind of sound usually found in the animal kingdom. The wave is *unformed*; semantics would give it *form* (Theory of Sculpture). The sounds I make are taken consciously from animals. I see it as a way of coming into contact with other forms of existence, beyond the human one. It's a way of going beyond our restricted understanding to expand the scale of producers of energy among cooperators in other species, all of whom have different abilities—like the coyote for instance.

This means that my presence there in the felt was like that of a carrier wave, attempting to switch off my own species' range of semantics. It was a parallel to the old initiation of the coffin, a form of mock death. It takes a lot of discipline to avoid panicking in such a condition, floating empty and devoid of emotion and without specific feelings of claustrophobia or pain, for nine hours in the same position.

Such an action, and indeed every action changes me radically (1979:95).

Along with Ball, Beuys understood the magic ability of sounds to transport the singer to non-ordinary reality. By making the primordial sound of the stag, Beuys experienced a profound cessation of his ordinary consciousness, symbolized by his deathlike recumbent state that enabled him in part to go beyond "his own species range of semantics" and become a kind of interspecies transmitter to the hare, symbolized by the copper rod.

It is important, however, to recognize what Beuys himself explained in an interview with critic Caroline Tisdall, "My intention was not to create or depict symbols, but to express the [animal] powers that exist in the world" (1988:49). It is not surprising that, when Beuys uttered the sound of a stag at the matriculation speech, it created a shock that led to his eventual dismissal. Not only did he interject disorder into a fairly conventional academic environment but he challenged the primacy of human consciousness for those who have a heavy stake in maintaining it. Beuys has said, "the beginnings of the new [consciousness] always takes place in chaos" (Adriani *et al*, 1979:72-73).

For Beuys, the stag, the hare, and the swan were an important part of a "childhood close to German folklore" and I think they became Beuys' allies during his adult life. He was certainly aware of the special powers of these animals. "The stag," explained Beuys,

> appears in times of distress and danger. It brings a special element: the warm positive element of life. At the same time it is endowed with spiritual powers and insight and is the accompanier of the soul (1988:49).

In the cold atmosphere of the Düsseldorf Academy, calling on the stag was appropriate action for such a spiritually sensitive individual as Beuys, although it had serious conse quences. Indeed, it may have been the only choice Beuys had to preserve the integrity of his soul. Beuys has also discussed the powers of the hare:

> The hare has a direct relation to birth....For me the
> hare is a symbol of incarnation. The hare does in
> reality what man can only do mentally: he digs
> himself in, he digs a construction. He incarnates
> himself in the earth and that itself is important
> (Adriani et al, 1979:132).

The hare became for him a sign of alchemical transformation
and chemical change,

> the mobility of blood, the relationship between the
> hare and menstrual blood, birth and incarnation: the
> upper half for the soul, and the lower for fertility..."I
> am the hare" (1988:50).

In "How to Explain Pictures to a Dead Hare" (November
26, 1975), Beuys rhythmically tapped the iron sole attached to
his shoe on the hard stone floor as he walked around the gallery
showing and discussing the pictures. This tapping was especially effective in sonic trance inducing since his explanations
to the hare, lasting some three hours, were mute. Beuys
explained that "How to Explain Pictures to a Dead Hare"

> was a complex tableau about the problem of lan-
> guage, and about the problems of thought, of human
> consciousness and of the consciousness of
> animals....This is placed in an extreme position
> because this is not just an animal but a dead animal.
> Even this dead animal has a special power to pro-
> duce.
>
> ...even a dead animal preserves more powers of
> intuition than some human beings with their stub-
> born rationality (Tisdall, 1979:103, 105).

The hare was important in the context of this performance as a countervailing force to rationality because of its relationship to the earth and fertility. Moreover, Beuys applied a mask of honey and gold to his head which symbolized his transformation and moving out of the realm of reason—a necessary prerequisite to understanding the hare's language. "Using honey on my head," said Beuys,

> I am clearly naturally doing something that is concerned with thought. The human capacity is not to give honey, but to think—to produce ideas. In this way the deathlike character of thought is made living again. Honey is doubtlessly a living substance. Human thought can also be living. But it can also be deadly intellectually, and remain dead, externally deadly in the areas of politics and education (Adriani *et al*, 1979:132).

Shamans often converse in trance states with their power animals through elliptical body language, ambiguous images or even irrational human speech and the animal responds.

In another performance, "I like America and America Likes Me" (May 23-25, 1974, Illustration 21), at the Rene Block Gallery in New York, Beuys communicated for seven days with a live coyote that had just been taken from the wilderness. Beuys said about this work,

> I believe I made contact with the psychological trauma point of the United States' energy constellation: the whole American trauma with the Indian, the Red Man...
>
> ...You could say that a reckoning has to be made with the coyote, and only then can this trauma be lifted (1979:228).

Beuys knew that for the American Indian, especially the Pueblo Indians, the coyote is one of the most powerful animals—a trickster that symbolizes their own marginal status in American society. Beuys also believed that the tendency of white Americans to reduce native cultures to marginality extended beyond the boundaries of the United States to other cultures and that the Vietnam war was a direct result of this attitude. To emphasize the trauma of American relationships with the Indians, which is a kind of sickness, Beuys was taken directly from the airport to the gallery in an ambulance, completely wrapped in felt. Caroline Tisdall, who was present at this performance, described the interchange between Beuys and the coyote in the gallery space:

> The man had brought objects and elements from his world to place in this space, silent representatives of his ideas and beliefs. He introduced them to the coyote. The coyote responded coyote-style by claiming them with his gesture of possession. One by one as they were presented he pissed on them slowly and deliberately: felt, walking stick, gloves, flashlight and *Wall Street Journal*, but above all the *Wall Street Journal*....

> The man had also brought a repertoire of movements with him and a notion of time. These two were then subject to the coyote's responses, and were modulated and conditioned by them. The man never took his eyes off the animal. The line of sight between them became like the hands of a spiritual clockface measuring the timing of movements and setting the pace for the dialogue through time. The man carried out his sequence of movements, a choreography directed towards the coyote, the timing and the mood regulated by the animal. Generally the sequence lasted about an hour and a quarter,

sometimes much longer. In all it was repeated over thirty times, but the mood and the tone were never the same (1979:228, 230).

As part of this sequence, Beuys would leap up from a felt tent that completely covered him, "striking three clear resounding notes on the (metal) triangle from his waist," said Tisdall,

> The high sharp sound shattered the silence. Then the silence built up again over the next ten seconds to be blotted out again, this time by the reverberation of a twenty second-long blast of noise: the roar of turbine machines projected from a tape recorder beyond the barrier. The chaotic sound ended as abruptly as it had begun, and as it did so the man relaxed, took off his brown gloves, and threw them to the coyote to toss around. Then he walked across to rearrange the mauled and scattered *Wall Street Journals* into two neat piles again and came up front to chat with a friend through the barrier and to down a glass of...Punch.

> Then back to the far corner for a quiet smoke in the coyote's straw. Oddly enough, or surely enough, this was the only time the coyote took any notice of the straw. Usually he preferred the felt. But when the man was in the corner he joined him, and that interlude always had the atmosphere of a farmyard: long moments of far-away filtered sunlight. By and by the man got up, sorted out the piles of felt, drew the long grey length up over his head, and the sequence started again (1979:232).

Beuys' repeated cycle of identical gestures was a ritual, not of ordinary habitual behavior, but a ritual that led Beuys and the viewers into non-ordinary reality. The evidence Eugene d'Aquili and Charles Laughlin, Jr. brought up in their article "The Neurobiology of Myth and Ritual" shows that the rhythmic activity of ritual can be further assisted by sonic, photic and visual driving rhythms which lower blood pressure and heartbeat and synchronize E.E.G patterns, leading to a "positive, ineffable affect" akin to "oceanic experience" or "yogic ecstasy" (1979:151-182). [They demonstrated also that rituals produce effects similar to meditation but over a longer duration of time.]

From Tisdall's extended account (1976) of this performance in her book *Beuys/Coyote* we can deduct that Beuys' performance took on the quality of a sacred ritual. It is difficult to say, however, whether this ritual had a therapeutic influence on a white person's trauma concerning Indians. For Jimmy Boyle, a convict in a Glasgow prison who had become a well known British sculptor, seeing photographs of Beuys' dialogue with the coyote had a definite healing effect. Like American Indians, he identified with the marginal role of the coyote. Boyle exclaimed,

> There is much talk lately, of bringing art to all sectors of society, but I also experience tremendous confusion among artists on how to do this. The only worthwhile statement that had any effect on me and others in my environment is Joseph Beuys' dialogue with the Coyote (1976:5, author's translation from the original German).

Mary Beth Edelson is another shaman/performance artist who uses ritual to enter non-ordinary reality. After the legal kidnaping of one of her children, Edelson was given the following suggestion by her friend Lawra Gregory,

> Based on the way your work has changed in the past

in relation to major changes in your life, I want to project what you think would possibly be a change of similar magnitude, and how your work might change as a result. Do a piece that develops in that event—(1972; published, 1980:12).

"This was a painful suggestion," said Edelson.

While trying to avoid thinking about it I had the following dream:

I was cleaning my place, it was a mess—there was a large fireplace in the room with a roaring fire—I threw everything into the fireplace to get rid of the mess—the more I cleaned the messier the room got—I began to throw chairs and tables into the fire—a large bear came into the room—and I threw her into the fire. And then in horror, as I watched her burn, I realized what I had done—this beautiful wild beast was burning—she was holding a cub in her arms. Suddenly I realized that the bear was me and that the cub was my child, but I also knew in that moment that the love that the mother and child shared was so great that it transcended the flames— (1972; published, 1980:12).

This dream resulted in the "Fire Altar," a ring of fire sitting on a white baked-enamel kitchen table. According to Edelson, "The table served as both a familiar object and an altar. I thought of the fire as the instigator of transformation of sacred and profound change"—(1972; published, 1980:13).

Mircea Eliade maintained that "all the ecstatic experiences that determine the future shaman's vocation involve the traditional scheme of an initiation ceremony: suffering, death, resurrection" (1964:33). Edelson's dream is, indeed, a classic initiatory experience involving fire as a purifying medium.

Initiatory experiences often arise for the shamanic candidate following a profound trauma like the one suffered by Edelson over the kidnaping of her child.

After Edelson's initiatory dream, she completely changed her mode of work. After eighteen years of painting, she focused on creating ritual objects and rituals as a way of empowering herself and other women. In an unpublished manuscript of the critic Gary Schwindler, he mentioned that Edelson had written the following to him,

> I am not working with a set form or repetitious form; rather my work is often spontaneous and is an ever changing creative act. This was never true traditionally. So ritual has been profoundly changed in both its character and its form; it has been seized guerrilla-like and transformed not merely as a reflection of process and belief (as it is traditionally true) but has been provided with the possibility of changing even its own form. The ritual is taken into our own hands and body along with the power to create and define a sacred space as well as create solidarity with the group. For women especially, who have traditionally been denied participation in forming the culture that they live in, this is a radical revolutionary act of invention that stands as a model for symbolic, psychic and spiritual change (January, 1982).

Edelson identifies traditional ritual in Western culture with set forms or repetition of forms. Indeed, creation of new rituals by women is in itself a revolutionary act against the prevailing patriarchal culture. It is important to recognize here that new rituals can have an efficacy even though they do not follow set forms or use repetitious form.

The main function of religious ritual, according to anthropologist Felicitas Goodman, in *Ecstasy, Ritual and*

Alternate Reality, is to "propel the participants to an altogether different aspect of reality, or as other's see it, to an alternate one" (1988:34). And this transport can be accomplished, said Goodman, by just about any type of stimuli.

> The reason for this great variety lies in part in the fact that it is not so much the stimulus in and of itself that produces the switch from one state of consciousness to another, but rather the expectation that it will happen (1988:37).

According to Victor Turner, another anthropological expert on ritual,

> Modern views of ritual stress its rigid and obsessional character. But tribal rituals are anything but rigid. One should regard them as orchestrations of a wide range of performative genres....These may include dancing, gesturing, singing, chanting; the use of many musical instruments; mimetic displays; and the performance of drama during key episodes. All the senses are enlisted, and the symbolic actions and objects employed are in every sensory code. Since the rise of puritanism, we have inclined, in the West, to stress the pervasively solemn and strict character of ritual. But the majority of rituals still performed in the world contain festive, joyful, and playful episodes and incidents. What Huizinga has called the "ludic" interacts with the solemn in complex fashion. Again while there are fixed, stereotyped sequences of symbolic action, there are also episodes given over to verbal and non-verbal improvisation. Indeed, if we adapt the standpoint of culture history, it is clear that full scale rituals of this sort are the matrix from which later performative genres have sprung, both serious and entertaining (1977:35).

In Mary Beth Edelson's rituals there is a core of commonly shared symbols, or, in Turner's words, "symbolic actions" which serve as basis for the transformational process and fulfill the expectation of both her and her participants so that a transport to an alternate reality will occur. Edelson recounted:

> In my early performances, I tried to recreate the liturgy of the feminist movement as I perceived its evolution through the Seventies. Briefly, the liturgy presents our move from isolation to our earliest attempts at communication through our anger, rage, and protests, and then to our community, celebration and the grounding of our activism, basically the story of how we came together. When the liturgy is chanted, we seldom break into words—the communication is made through sounds. From releasing our anger, we gain control and find ourselves. As we define ourselves, we discover our commonality. Through these processes, we are able to reassure and enjoy each other; we unleash our sensuality and begin celebrating. The liturgy or ritual performance, mirroring this process, ends with celebration of our emergence and the beginning of a new culture. I believe some transformation on a small or large scale should be experienced during the performance. Unless that change happens, the performance is not successful (1982a:319-320).

Edelson classified her rituals as follows:

> As I developed my rituals over the years, I found that they fell into three distinct categories: private rituals created alone and usually outdoors, public rituals often performed with others and presented to an audience, and rituals conducted with a small

group of people in private for a particular person's need (1990:44).

Edelson's first private rituals emerged as ways of expressing deep feelings or, as she told me, an "undefined emotional urgency" that could not be realized in another medium. The early rituals were enacted after a long period of meditation and contemplation on the role of women in contemporary Western society. They culminated in a three part series of painted photographs, entitled "Women Rising/ Sexual Rites," "Women Rising/Earth," and "Women Rising/ Spirit" which documented the rituals Edelson enacted on a remote dune during the summer of 1974 at Outer Banks, North Carolina. "Having found a spot on an isolated part of the beach where I could not be stumbled upon," explained Edelson,

> it was my intention to communicate with the ancient goddesses. Using body paint to set me apart, as well as ritual body position, I hoped to move towards a psychological and physiological state of receptiveness. Once I did, I concentrated on communication. The circular signs that I painted on my body were to represent centroversion or the striving for wholeness: balancing the intellect (through forehead painting), sexual signification (breast painting), and the body itself (abdomen painting). The markings on the photographs enabled me to put down my feelings of spiritual energy, the forces that I felt rising from my body and mind, as extensions beyond myself. Putting markings on my body is both a playful and a serious act. I have the same ambivalence towards communicating with the great goddesses. I take it seriously and I can't possibly regard it with complete seriousness. Making photographs is joyously playful work, and yet elements of disapproval are there, of doing something which is forbidden (Burnham, 1975:78).

In "Women Rising/Earth," Edelson gradually took off the bandages that covered her naked supine body, opened her legs to reveal her vagina, and then stood up. According to Edelson, she "removes herself from being the wounded and covered of the earth, as she makes room to renegotiate the earth in her own terms"—(1973; published, 1980:17).

In "Women Rising/Sexual Rites," she cupped her breasts with her hands in one image, placed her hands behind her back in another photograph, and then lifted them above her head in a third photograph. In "Women Rising/Spirit," Edelson raised her outstretched arms above her head in a gesture that again affirmed her naked physical presence. The artist had painted concentric circular designs around her navel and nipples and superimposed spiral, half moon and inverted triangular shapes on the photographs. Snake-like rays issuing from her head and third eye region in "Women Rising/Spirit" also make this a particularly striking photograph. Circular, spiral, moon, and snake-like designs are the symbols of the ancient neolithic goddesses. Spirals and circles refer to the closeness of the goddess to the cycles of nature and the generating energies of the earth and womb. Snakes, which are held in the outstretched hands of Minoan goddesses, seem to refer to unfolding energies. The spiral and circular forms also refer to Edelson's artistic process. "Our common sources," argued Edelson in a 1973 lecture at the Corcoran Gallery of Art,

are the history and the experience of all who have gone before us—how we translate them has variations. I look at the complex and ever changing interrelationships and see a circular process. Rather than suppressing this movement of concerns in my art by selecting a singular area and steadfastly exploring that one line, I see my process as being circular/spiraling/encompassing. Circular because I go over the same ground of concerns, and spiraling because I go over the same ground on different levels, hoping to gain more insight on each passing....

The contents that my circular/spiral involvements encompass appear to fall into three parts. I break them down this way:
• Self (feminism and other inner searches)
• Others (responsibility to the community of our time and place)
• Cosmos (Symbol/Ritual/Myth interpreted on both psychological and philosophical levels)—(1973; published, 1975:55).[2]

Taking the pose of the goddess and assuming her symbols, albeit in a non-traditional way, enabled Edelson to tap into the power of this archetype. "These photographic images were defining images" maintained Edelson,

not who I am but who *we are*. The images were presented aggressively as sexuality, mind and spirit comfortable in one body. I was summoning the Goddess to make house calls, talking to Goddess with the body, and ending the dialogue with being. These rituals were photographic evidence of the manifestations and recognition of a powerful force: Everywoman—(1975; published, 1980:17).

Edelson informed me that she had a critical image of her body like many women, but the rituals of "Women Rising" transformed her identity with her body. Many feminists view the lack of a good body image as the product of the mind/body split that arose during the middle ages. During this period, the flesh was regarded as evil and, since women were considered to be more carnal and fleshy then men, they were held to be intrinsically evil. "Women Rising" was an attempt, in part, to end this mind/body dualism. "My rituals," said Edelson, referring to "Women Rising" and other rituals,

> also provided resistance to the mind/body split by acknowledging sexuality in spirituality [and challenging by theoretical discussion on these issues the notion that intuition, ritual, nature, etc. are reached at the expense of a cognitive mind; her brackets] (1989:35).

It should be pointed out that Edelson's poses draw attention to her sexuality but are not seductive or lascivious. The photographs intend to challenge how the female body has historically been viewed by both men and women. In fact, she is breaking the taboo of showing the naked female body for other than pornographic purposes. I agree with Edelson's statement that

> The female body in *Women Rising/Sexual Rites* is not a nude tantalizer, but is powerful and wild, with self generating energy. She takes a risk by not only exposing the body's naked form, but also by exposing the body's energy to potent energy forces in nature—(1973; published, 1980:17).

Edelson mentioned to me that the power she gained by fixing on the goddess was almost overwhelming, and it was only the "joyous and playful spirit" in which she carried out the work that kept her grounded.

In 1977, Edelson journeyed to a cave in Grapceva, Yugoslavia where worship of the Mother Goddess was enacted during the Neolithic period.

> For some years, I had been attempting to make a pilgrimage to a Goddess site. I had been doing private rituals in my art for some time, both out-

doors in nature and in the studio. I could feed off of them and hold them in my mind like totems, but I was actually hungry. I needed to do my rituals in an actual prehistoric cave; to experience a Neolithic site where I could smell the earth, poke around in the soil, breathe the air, and know that the cave air had circulated through my body and become a part of me. To go to a prehistoric site became an obsession, and represented the place to begin a new cycle. Numerous grants had not materialized and the trip was long overdue. I sold my car and bought the voyage (1978:96).

It is obvious from this passage that Edelson understood the potential energy to be gained by connecting with the Goddess at one of her power spots. And the effort it takes to get to the spot magnifies the experience of power as the pilgrim, on the journey, has already begun the transition from ordinary to non-ordinary reality.

Using the information from Marija Gimbutas's *The Goddesses and Gods of Old Europe...* (1974), Edelson located a village in proximity to an ancient cave on the island of Hvar, Yugoslavia, where Goddess worship had taken place during the neolithic period. She was able to get a guide in the village to lead her up to the remote mountain cave. Returning the next day, without the guide, she found an altar in the cave which held a stalagmite image of a full-figured Mother Goddess and performed a ritual of purification and meditation. She gave the following account of her experience:

Aware of the privilege of having the cave to myself, I felt like the center of the universe. My mouth was actually inhaling the cave, all of it and breathing it out again. The cave contracted and expanded with my rhythms, and shimmered on its way back and forth. I made a pact with the cave: it would tell me some of its secrets in exchange for my rituals, rituals that it had not seen for millennia. I in turn would learn some of its secrets now and some later—I had only to listen, to keep in touch (1978:98).

Edelson's account brings to mind the ancient Chinese proverb, "When a question is posed ceremoniously, the universe responds." Indeed, this is the essence of shamanic knowledge.

Edelson's public rituals emerge out of workshops she conducts with small groups where she guides the participants in an intensive program involving chanting, as well as development of interior vision, intuition, and the recollection of dreams and past experiences. Her own spiritual experiences as well as the subject matter that develops from these workshops become the basis for the public ritual and the workshop participants become the performers. It is important that the performers are not professional. "That is an essential aspect of ritual," said Edelson,

we are experiencing and not just acting. The audience can also identify with the performers because they can visualize themselves in their place. The more I perform the rituals, however, the more professional they become, even when I am starting with a new group each time (1982a:320).

One of the questions that "continued to haunt" Edelson when she was beginning her performance work was, "How was Goddess worship stamped out and when?" (1977:33). This led Edelson to study the witch hunts of the middle ages and to create a exhibition/performance entitled "Memorials to 9,000,000 Women Burned as Witches in the Christian Era" at the A.I.R. Gallery in New York on October 31, 1977 (Illustration 22). "To enter the space [of the gallery]," said Edelson,

one went through the portals of a passage, *Gate of*

Horns/Fig of Triumph, which set the exhibition apart as a sacred space. Both sides of the gate were lined with close-up photographs of hand gestures; on the front side *mano cornuta*: reclaimed as a sign of the horned bull and of female magic and power, and on the back side *mano infica* the fig, sacred fruit of the Goddess reclaimed as a symbol of Her body/ Our Body.

Through the gate one faced a fire ladder surrounded by a circular table. The table contained handmade books that further discussed witch hunts and sacred spaces. The ladder in the center of the table symbolized both positive and negative energy; during the Christian era when prosecutors were in a hurry to rid themselves of an accused witch they sometimes did not spend the time and money on a proper pyre, but grabbed a handy ladder and tied the poor woman to it, thrusting her into the bonfire.

The positive energy refers to the ladder as a universal mystical sign of leaving behind, of being able to transcend. On Halloween Eve nine women performed in a memorial ritual at the gallery around the fire ladder. As the audience entered each person was given a card with the name of an actual woman or man accused of witchcraft—most had been burned at the stake. The ritual began with a reading that documented some of the history surrounding witch hunts. The performers and the audience read aloud the names on their cards, and then chanted those names. The ritual ended with a procession through the streets of SoHo to Washington Square where 200 people from the park joined us, as we danced back and chanted "The Goddess is Here, The Goddess is Us," in the round fountain.

I hollowed out thirty small pumpkins placing candles inside and mounted them on five foot poles as women had done during the Middle Ages, to light their path while walking through the woods to secret meeting places. We carried these torches in our procession (1980:33-34).

Lucy Lippard wrote, in her introduction to *Seven Cycles: Public Rituals* (the catalogue in which Edelson describes the above mentioned ritual), that

There is a distinction between a ritual and a spectacle or festival. When a ritual doesn't work it is a self-conscious act that isolates the performer as an exclusive object of attention. When it does work, the form's importance diminishes to become only one element in a communal impulse connecting all the participants and all the times this action has been performed in the past or will be performed in the future (1980:8).

To go a step further than Lippard here, I would like to propose that in order for performance to become ritual the performers have to empty their egos, thereby enabling archetypal contents to emerge. Edelson herself said,

taking the spotlight off my individual ego also enables different process to take place during my ritual performances that help create an atmosphere in which I also become a participant with no greater or lesser role that the other participants, permitting me to meld in with the group geist. The process of relinquishing power encourages others in the group to fall back on themselves for responses rather than look to somebody else for clues for their behavior. It was the experience of the participants that gave meaning not only to the ritual itself, but ultimately to the work as art with substance.[3]

In "Memorials to 9,000 Witches," Mary Beth Edelson's main role was to establish a sacred space with sacred symbols that facilitated the manifestation of the Great Goddess in the activities of the participants. The situation itself engendered self-transcendence which, in the terminology of Felicitas Goodman, set off the "expectation" that "a shift from one state of consciousness to another would happen."

In 1980, at the University of Massachusetts, Edelson and her associates performed "Cycles I: Creation Begins with a Green Light/Ritual on the Earth," a new creation myth emphasizing the role of women. Edelson described "Cycles I" as follows:

> Green lights skimmed along the performers backs [three women] as they began jerky gyrating movements with their knees to the primordial sound that we had recorded earlier.
>
> ...The segment ends with exhaustion from the act of creation, and they sleep.
>
> The green lights turned to orange as they shifted from the sleepers to the backs of three women sitting in stylized positions. The front of a women's torso was painted on their nude backs, as if their torso had been reversed. They were both coming and going—they were three wise women, tricksters, all knowing and seeing.
>
> They began to move as if they were the images that the dreamers dreamed. Their movements were in two phases: the first was a series of formal poses that suggested the Goddess with upraised arms, and

the second, with their arms circling their bodies, suggested women as the center of the universe.

Slides of rituals performed in nature were projected on the wall as they prepared to make the passage and move mountains. The sleepers awoke and made their thundering sounds while the three wise women blew on children's party whistles. The whistles were the variety that have a long coiled tail that straightens out when you blow on it. Placing the whistles between their legs they looked like comic tongues or phalluses moving in and out from the women's buttocks. The whistles were signaling celebration and mountain moving day [the end of the male patriarchy]. The three wise women were covered with a cloth that became a mountain—a traveling mountain (1980:53).

The introduction of the trickster in "Cycles," especially evident in the "comic tongues or phalluses" between the naked women's legs, is an important part of the ritual process. "The trickster, here and in other ritual performances," said Edelson, "relaxes the participants and audience, breaking the tension of the event and allowing those present to enter into a sacred dimension."[4]

"In my work," Edelson further explained,

I have often used an archetypal character called the Trickster as a metaphor for chaos. Taking on the persona of the Trickster gives me permission to break taboos. The Trickster can also be a catalyst for profound change and the release of tensions in society. All these qualities can also be attributed to the role of the artist (1990:11).

Edelson's recent public rituals manifest her increasing

interest in ecology which is not surprising given her prior concerns with the Mother Goddess. "Black Spring," an installation at the Washington Project for the Arts in Washington, D.C. (1989), consisted of a spiral configuration, "oil slick" gloss on the inside and matte black on the outside, that led to an interior room containing a mirror surrounded by green lights which Edelson called "the room of New Beginnings." On the outside of the spiral Edelson painted hummingbirds, "the spirit guides for the journey to" the room of the New Beginnings. On the inside of the spiral was a row of twenty-four plaster skulls (modeled on actual skulls) with cherry blossom branches issuing from the their backs and inscriptions such as" raw," "cooked," "memory," "social code," and so forth written on their foreheads. These heads looked progressively more humanoid as the core of the spiral was reached, suggesting our distinct biological connection with the animal world and that their death is our death.

At the start of the exhibition the mirror was shattered. "The viewers saw themselves whole and shattered." related Edelson, "Breaking the mirror is breaking the mold. It is an act of anger, but it is also an act of courage-the catalyst needed to begin again."[5] "Black Spring" is both a commentary on the Exxon oil spill and a shamanic journey to connect the viewers with the animal world. This connection required a shattering of past mental constructs and "social codes." Indeed, in shamanic practice, as I have already indicated, the dismembering of the self is often an important prerequisite to spiritual growth and healing.

Edelson's private rituals are initiated by a desire to heal or empower her friends and associates. Yet she also considers these private rituals to be art work and documents some of them for exhibitions. "Just as there was no separation from art and life, there was no separation between my rituals, however private, and my artwork" (interview with the artist, June 1989).

After seven years of futile attempts to get pregnant,

Elaine Pagels requested a healing ritual from Edelson. Pagels's ritual took place at Edelson's Mercer Street Studio in New York. The whole loft was blackened out and Pagels was then led by Edelson and her collaborators to a special black box and asked to meditate on the exploding ovaries at the moment of conception. Then she was led to a womb-like sculpture where Edelson and collaborators thought of the most sensual things they could think of to say to her while a recording of ocean waves played in the background. "The idea," said Edelson, "was to get her body into another state of sensuality and receptiveness" (interview with the artist, June 1989). Next, Pagels was bound with a red ribbon to another sculpture that looked like a vagina, and was spun around while being told that her life would take a new direction. Finally, the ribbon was cut and Edelson and her collaborators placed their hands on Pagels womb, and felt heat rising from her body. This ritual was experienced deeply by everyone involved, especially Pagels who was ecstatic. In fact, Pagels became pregnant two weeks after the ritual.

Not all of Edelson's private rituals are successful on a therapeutic level. The healing ritual for Carolee Schneemann, which came to Edelson in a dream, was only partly effective because of Schneemann's resistance. Nevertheless, the visual aspects of the ritual were quite appealing and Edelson documented them in a series of photographs. As I mentioned earlier in the book, shamanic efficacy in traditional cultures does not depend on aesthetic qualities, so it is not surprising that an aesthetically appealing ritual may not bring about therapeutic results despite our expectations to the contrary.

Like Mary Beth Edelson, Karen Finley also turned to performance art as the result of a traumatic experience, in her case the suicide of her father in 1979. "I had difficulty being alone and doing static work when I was feeling such active emotion," she said. "Performing balances the pain she feels about his [her father's] death" (Carr:1986:17). "I was twenty one [at the time of her father's death], I was just starting to perform," Finley explained.

> I was home on Christmas break. I didn't expect him to do it. He went into the garage and shot himself....

> Nothing else matters. When something like that happens it doesn't make any difference if at that day I had a million dollars or if I had anything materially or careerwise, anything, it would not have made any difference in terms of that act happening. That really put me in such a reality state, of realizing that nothing really ever matters. In some ways it actually freed me: whatever you have won't matter. Somehow that energy I really put into and show in my work (quoted in Schechner, 1988:157-158).

As already said in the section on Frida Kahlo, being in the proximity of the duende enabled the artist to drop pettiness and ambition; it empowered her work. Finley performs in a state of trance. "That state of being is very natural," Finley maintains,

> so I'm surprised when people call it a trance state. It's something really lacking in our culture—any kind of religion, or any kind of spiritual mask, or any way of breaking the usual routine of day-to-day acting. When one is emotional, when an event takes someone by surprise, whether it's a death, a birth, or anything, it breaks that nine-to-five behavior. That's what I want to be showing (quoted in Schechner, 1988:154).

Finley's idea of the naturalness of the trance state is seconded by psychologist Charles Tart. People in non-western societies, said Tart, "believe that almost every normal adult has the ability to go into a trance state...the adult who can not do this is a psychological cripple" (1969:3).

Finley also made an important distinction between her performances and acting,

> I do go into somewhat of a trance because when I perform I want it to be different than acting. I hope that this doesn't sound too dorky or trite. I'm really interested in being a medium, and I have done a lot of psychic type of work. I put myself into a state, for some reason it's important, so that things come in and out of me, I'm almost like a vehicle. And so when I'm talking it's just coming through me, And its very exhausting. After I perform I have to vomit, my whole body shakes, I have to be picked up and sat down. It takes me about an hour before I stop shaking. When performing I pick up energies from the people, I got to completely psych into them because I want them to feel that I am really feeling it. Maybe not even my words, but just that energy. I am giving everything I have to make it an experience. You can't pick that up on film or disks. It's the live experience, and that's really important (quoted in Schechner, 1988:154).

Another persona takes over during Finley's performance, "a female id unfettered" (Howard, 1987:30), as one critic has remarked. In fact, in watching videotapes of her work, Finley maintained, "I have to close my eyes, I don't know who that person is" (quoted in Carr, 1986:20).

The ability to take on a different persona or personae while in an altered state of consciousness is typical of the trickster or sacred clown in tribal cultures, They "shift shape" and, at times, their antics become very extreme. According to

Elsie Crews Parsons, the sacred clowns of the Pueblos have been observed

> eating or drinking filth; drenching or being drenched with urine or water; simulating lust, fear, or anger; playing games together with the lookers-on; begging from house to house...burlesquing ceremonial;... acting or speaking in opposites (Parsons, 1939:130, quoted in Rothenberg & Rothenberg, 1983:270).

In one of Finley's most outrageous skits, she yanked her pants down, pushed yams up her anus, and talked, in a male voice, about sticking yams "up granny's butt but, I never touch her twat, baby" (Carr, 1986:17). In a 1981 performance in Cologne, Finley, dressed as Eva Braun, goosestepped while naked from the waist down, relieved herself on the side of the stage, attached toy sharks stuffed with hot dogs and sauerkraut to her body and, along with co-performer Harry Kipper, rubbed chocolate pudding on her backside.

In tribal societies, where a strict hierarchy of social conventions prevails, the trickster extends the boundaries of the permissible and interjects a much needed spirit of disorder into the rigid patterns of everyday existence. According to Karl Kerenyi,

> nothing demonstrates the meaning of the all-controlling social order more impressively than the religious recognition of that which evades this order, in a figure who is the exponent and personification of the life of the body: never wholly subdued, ruled by lust and hunger, for ever running into pain and injury, cunning and stupid in action. Disorder belongs to the totality of life, and the spirit of this disorder is the trickster. His function in an archaic society...is...to render possible, within the fixed

264 • Technicians of Ecstasy

bounds of what is permitted, an experience of what is not permitted (quoted in Radin, 1972:185).

In contemporary Western civilization there is no accepted role for the trickster. What is not permitted in Judeo-Christian morality is segregated and deprecated as evil. There is a refusal to understand that the purely good or evil individual is an abstraction. It is the sacred clown that mirrors the ambivalence of human conduct using taboo gestures. Our failure to recognize this ambivalence is highly dangerous. As Carl Jung has pointed out,

> The so-called civilized man has forgotten the trickster. He remembers him only figuratively and metaphorically, when irritated by his own ineptitude, he speaks of fate playing tricks on him or of things bewitched. He never suspects that his own hidden and apparently harmless shadow has qualities whose dangerousness exceeds his wildest dreams. As soon as people get together in masses and submerge the individual, the shadow is mobilized, and, as history shows, may even be personified and incarnated (quoted in Radin, 1972:206).

Comedians in contemporary Western society rarely touch upon the taboo areas that reflect the shadow side, so it is left to artists such as Karen Finley to present it. "I don't feel that my work is pornography at all," said Finley, "I'm just telling it like it is" (quoted in Carr, 1986:19). The fact that Finley got a bad response from her audience at the Cologne performance, indicates that some Germans still cannot face the shadow side of their own militaristic Nazi past. When she gets a bad response in her American performances, it is usually from men who cannot come to grips with their own sexual aggressiveness.

In fact, Finley's work has a strong feminist content

which was evident in the "Constant State of Desire," a mordant satire on the insatiable appetites of macho and yuppie men (first performed at the Kitchen in New York in December, 1986). The following is one of the less extreme sections, excerpted from a reprint of the script in *TDR (Tulane Drama Review)*:

Act II
(Easter baskets and stuffed animals sit on table. Take off clothes. Put colored unboiled eggs from basket and animals in one large clear-plastic bag. Smash contents till contents are yellow. Put mixture on body using soaked animals as applicators. Sprinkle glitter and confetti on body and wrap self in paper garlands as boas.

Scene 1

HATE YELLOW

I hate yellow. I hate yellow so much. And I see you walking down my neighborhood with your new teeth and solid pastel colored shirts. Yuk. Don't you know that I'm only happy when I'm depressed. Don't you know I'm only happy when I'm wearing black? That I'm only happy at night. Yes, I'm a creature at night.

NOTHING HAPPENED

So I took too many sleeping pills and nothing happened.
So I put a gun to my head and nothing happened.
So I put my head in the oven and nothing happened.
So I fucked you all night long and nothing happened.

So I went on a diet and nothing happened.
So I went macrobiotic and nothing happened.
So I went to the Palladium, the Tunnel, and nothing happened.
So I went down to Soho and checked out the art scene and nothing happened.
So I quit drugs and nothing happened.
So I worked for ERA, voted for Jesse Jackson and nothing happened.
So I put out a roach motel and nothing happened.

So I petitioned, rioted, terrorized, and organized and something is going to happen. Something is going to happen 'cause I'm not going to let you gang rape me anymore walking down my streets that I build with my own soul, my creativity, my spit. And you just look at all my art, Mr. Yuppie, as just another investment, another deal. My sweat, my music, my fashion is just another money-making scheme for you. You are the reason, Mr. Entrepreneur, why David's Cookie McDonald's is the symbol of my culture.

You are the reason why fast food is the only growth industry of this country (Schechner, 1988:140: 142).

Finley has brilliantly expressed the difficulties of being a young female artist in a patriarchal society that commodifies creativity. Finley's monologue is not a carefully constructed rational argument. As Finley related, about three days before a performance,

I go into a room and do associative writing. I just open up and start writing. Like I don't rewrite my performances, they're like trance writing, like lots of time I just wake up and it just comes to me. And sometimes I really believe that I have other voices coming to me. So I open up to the voices (quoted in Schechner, 1988:155).

Having seen the "Constant State of Desire" in San Francisco at the Intersection for the Arts, I can say that Finley's metamorphosis in her roles is totally convincing. She is actually in a mild state of possession and speaks with another voice. I think this explains the vomiting and shaking after the performance which is the result of letting these voices go. Taking off her clothes, rubbing her body with eggs and affixing glitter was part of the ritual that Finley enacted to assume another voice. This ritual also included fasting, seclusion and not taking baths the day of the performance. It is important to emphasize once again that Finley downplays the theatrical aspects of her work.

...I never see the audience, I never know if they're there. I won't perform for the audience—I mean, sometimes I do, sometimes I break it, sometimes it's too much so I break it—but usually I stay within this energy. I can have things happen to me up there, like pain. You see I never rehearse a performance, that the scariest thing—that I'm going to go out there and I don't know what I'm doing. That is to me the performance part (quoted in Schechner, 1988:155).

To be sure, "Constant State of Desire" had a written script and was repeated, but Finley believes that it changes every time. And "I still go into the trance," she says (quoted in Schechner, 1988:155). If repetition does limit "what can happen," it can, however, enhance the power of the performance ritual.

In traditional ritual performances, such as the *Wayang Kulit*, the Javanese shadow puppet play, the reenactment of the ritual more or less follows the original (there is a lot of improvisation in the *Wayang*) and the performers tap into the accumulated energy of all the prior reenactments. It is this accumulated energy that helps bring about the transformations in the lives of the participants.

For the most part, Finley performs in small spaces where, in her own words, the "whole idea of ritual is not destroyed" (Schechner, 1988:155). In these venues the audience is likely to be familiar with Finley's work and tends to be receptive to self-transformation. Richard Schechner called this kind of audience the "integral audience" and further characterized it as follows:

> Every "artistic community" develops an integral audience: people who know each other, are involved with each other, support each other. Audiences can be mixed—most public events focus on a show witnessed by an integral audience; but this audience is itself part of the spectacle for the general public. With film and TV even the "general public" becomes part of the performance for those watching it via media. In short, an accidental audience comes "to see the show" while an integral audience is "necessary to accomplish the work of the show." Or, to put it another way, the accidental audience attends from pleasure, the integral audience for ritual need. The presence of an integral audience is the surest evidence that the performance is a ritual drama (1977a:75).

Finley's work also fits Schechner's criteria for ritual which necessitates the suspension of time (Finley's performances seem either much shorter or longer than their actual duration), the "performer possessed, in trance," and the belief of the audience (Schechner, 1977b:75). "Whether one calls a specific performance ritual or theatre," Schechner has argued, "depends on the degree to which the performance tends toward efficacy or entertainment. No performance is pure efficacy or entertainment" (1977b:75). Indeed, Finley's performances do have their comic elements, although I would say that the exposure of the shadow side, the essence of Finley's performances, is neither fun nor pleasurable for her and the audience.

Rachel Rosenthal's performances are often similarly difficult to watch because, like Finley, she places enormous demands on herself and the audience. "In theatre you mostly work from or with a text," maintained Rosenthal,

> in performance you squeeze it out of yourself, you dredge it up from your unconscious. It is a process of giving it a form from the inner to the outer. The process cannot be frivolous, but must be a deep commitment to yourself. It can be really transformational (interview with the artist, April 1990).

Antonin Artaud's ideas about the Theatre of Cruelty had an important influence on Rosenthal's work. According to Antonin Artaud in *The Theatre and Its Double*, one of Rosenthal's favorite texts on the theatre,

> One can very well imagine a pure cruelty, without bodily laceration. And philosophically speaking what indeed is cruelty? From the point of the mind, cruelty signifies rigor, implacable intention and decision, irreversible and absolute determination.

> ...Cruelty is above all lucid, a kind of rigid control and submission to necessity. There is no cruelty without consciousness and without the application of consciousness (1958:101-102).

Artaud's description of "cruelty," which is the quintessential attitude of the warrior shaman, is a good description of what Rosenthal brings to her performances. Advocating the transformation of the actor and the audience through trance states and non-verbal forms of expression during the performance, Artaud, indeed, promoted a kind of shamanic theatre. In his own personal life, however, I believe, Artaud was too consumed by rage and too absorbed with drugs as a way of quelling his largely self-inflicted mental agonies to be considered a shaman or even a failed shaman.

After moving from New York, where she had worked in the visual arts and theatre, Rosenthal set up the Instant Theatre in Los Angeles in 1956 which, she said, was "based on the idea of Total Theater...[of] Barrault and Artaud" (Burnham, 1984:52). During the Instant Theater period, language, costumes, props, gestures and so forth were wholly improvised and unpremeditated. "We were risking our lives moment by moment in front of a paying audience," recalled Rosenthal (interview with the artist, April 1990). In fact, Rosenthal was one of the originators of the new genre of performance art during the period of the late Fifties and Sixties.

According to Rosenthal,

> Instant Theatre was mind altering. After relaxation exercises, and moving together with sound we entered another state of reality. People thought we were on drugs but we didn't need mind altering substances. We were completely sober and aware of the sacredness of our mission. We were the temple vestals, channels for an audience that was completely devoted to us. Miracles happened (interview with the artist, April 1990).

Indeed, Rosenthal believes that Instant Theatre was an important introduction into shamanic practice.

From 1975-1981, Rosenthal performance work involved "exorcising my own demons and obsessions" (interview with the artist, April 1990). In 1981 she lost all her life savings in an investment swindle. To cope with this crisis, she went on a kind of vision quest, for a few days in Death Valley with her pet rat Tattiwattles. It is "a very strong powerful place, which usually turns me around," maintained Rosenthal.

A month later she did a piece, "Leave her on Naxos." "This performance will be about allowing things to die in order for new things to grow," announced Rosenthal at the beginning. During the piece Rosenthal had her head shaved by a woman in scarlet while sitting in a heart-shaped field of votive candles and while listening to a tape recording of a Buddhist sutra. Two of the other performers in "Leave her on Naxos" then helped her to lie down in the heart and covered her with the white plastic pellets that are used for packing material. From under this white mountain of pellets, Rosenthal projected two red satin hearts on sticks.

"Soldier of Fortune," performed at the Tortue Gallery in Los Angeles (1981), marked another passage of initiation and transformation for Rosenthal. At the beginning of the performance, the director of the gallery announced that the performance had been canceled. As the audience started to file out of the gallery, Rosenthal, dressed in a beautiful flowing gown, wig and tiara, blocked their path. "I'm so sorry," she said, "I couldn't get my shit together." Then Rosenthal went into a long spiel about how performances are "so excruciating, like being flayed," etc.

Meanwhile, two elegantly dressed waiters set up a table for her and began to serve a seven course dinner, including a bottle of champagne. Since the performance was canceled, "I might as well eat," said Rosenthal. In the process of getting inebriated, Rosenthal told the audience about her rich and pampered childhood in Paris.

At the end of this talk, Rosenthal informed the audience that the man who took her money actually did her a favor. "Now I'm no longer the fat housewife from Tarzana who does art on the side, but I'm a hustler and soldier of fortune." Then Rosenthal took off her finery, revealing a camouflaged shirt and pants underneath (she could only afford army surplus clothing at this point). Finally, Rosenthal, in a state of extreme intoxication, climbed up a ladder and pelted the audience with pennies. In "Soldier of Fortune," said Rosenthal,

> I diffused a tremendous amount of guilt about my ineptitude with money, my relationship with my parents wealth, and so forth, without accepting blame. It was a real cleansing experience. The fog had lifted. The old Rachel had died and I was a new person" (interview with the artist, April 1990).

"Soldier of Fortune" accelerated Rosenthal's metamorphosis into an artist-warrior-shaman, a role she became aware of after studying shamanic techniques with Michael Harner in 1983.

From 1981 on, Rosenthal has become less introspective and increasingly concerned with healing and planetary issues in her performances, although the content of her work is filtered through her own experience and couched in her own artistic language. "My concern about broader issues," argued Rosenthal,

> the state of the world, starts of course from my very personal self. Who you are and what you make cannot be separated. There is a continuum between life and art. We make up artificial boundaries trying to imprison phenomena in certain categories (quoted in Lampe, 1988:173).

One of Rosenthal's most forceful performances as an artist-warrior-shaman was "KabbaLAmobile" (1984, Illustration 23), enacted as part of Carplays, a three-day festival in Los Angeles which celebrated the Southern Californian infatuation with automobile culture. Jacki Apple, a writer for

Artweek magazine gave the following account of "Kabba-LAmobile":

> In the intense late afternoon light, Rosenthal made an unforgettably dramatic entrance. She was dressed in a billowing white costume with red and black quilted sections and yellow sash, her head shaved, her face made up in white with black and yellow lines, brilliant blue across the eyes, her fingernails gleaming white. Arms wide open, palms up, kimonolike sleeves flapping in the wind, she walked the full length of the Department of Water and Power parking lot and climbed a scaffolding platform facing the audience, like a sorcerer who had suddenly and mysteriously materialized from the Tarot.

> ...Her voice thundered forth, "Remember the name YDVD, our God interpreted in my name...Porsche 962, Jaguar XJR5 Lola T616...Datsun 280Z SSA...Seven divided three against three, with one balancing the others...one has merit, one is defective and one balances the other two"

> ...two points—one under the other—serving the smallest golem-possessor of permutations, whose form is the shape of SAMEKH MEM...Bore and Stroke Turbocharger; Waste Gate; Valve Gear; Compression ratio; Maximum boost pressure; Redline Torque...and the point is the dwelling of the living God breathing through all of us."

> The cars appeared—six convertibles and one red Dodge Daytona—driven by three women and four men from Tom Anthony's Precision Driving Team. For the next twenty minutes, they performed elabo-

rately choreographed, synchronized maneuvers across the vast parking lot and around Rosenthal. They moved in blocks of three, circled in lines, about-faced; serpentine Ss turned into braids. Their "dance," which was directly related to the cabalistic aspects of the text, culminated with the red car approaching and circling Rosenthal on its side, on two wheels (1984:1).

During my perusal of the videotape of "Kabba-LAmobile," which captured only some of the aspects of this work, as described by Apple, I found that Rosenthal transformed herself from her normally sweet and benevolent self into a kind of old testament demiurge or shaman who actually seemed to be creating the cars which emerged suddenly from a garage underneath a building at the site. She also seemed to control their movements. Rosenthal's gestures, taken from both dance and martial arts, were extremely effective in combination with her vociferous chanting and Dark Bob's musical score. They brought forth a persona of inordinate strength. Apple said,

> Rosenthal wasn't "acting." She became the medium of expression for her material. She took us into her own reality, allowing us to experience it with her. And for that brief and precious moment, she altered our vision of the world (1984:1).

In *The Theatre and Its Double*, Artaud recommended a new use of language in performance. "To make metaphysics out of a spoken language," he said,

> is to make the language express what it does not ordinarily express: to make use of it in a new, exceptional and unaccustomed fashion; to reveal its possibilities for producing physical shock; to divide

and distribute it actively in space; to deal with intonations in an absolutely concrete manner, restoring their power to shatter as well as really to manifest something; to turn against language in its basicaly utilitarian, one could say alimentary, sources, against its trapped-beast origins; and finally, to consider language as a form of Incantation.

Everything in this active poetic mode of envisaging expression on the stage leads us to abandon the modern humanistic and psychological meaning of the theatre, in order to recover its religious and mystic preference of which our theatre has completely lost the sense (1958:102).

According to Artaud, it is through gesture and sound that one creates this metaphysics of language which can deeply affect the audience because communication occurs on a non-rational level. Like Artaud, Rosenthal, in "KabbaLAmobile" and her other works, consciously rejects a humanistic or psychological theatre, recovering the "religious and mystic preference" of the theatre through sound and gesture.

Of course, the Qabalists understood long before Artaud (who was influenced by the Qabalah) that the sound and shape of a word are more important than their meaning in magical practice. Thus, Rosenthal chanted a litany of automotive terms which signified essentially nothing as they were taken out of context from automotive magazines, yet had a holy resonance for devotees of the automobile culture. It was no accident that important elements of the text of "KabbaLAmobile" were also taken from Abraham Abulafia's *Book of Creation* (13th century). Abulafia, the most unorthodox of the Qabalists and the most inclined to shamanistic practices, developed a system of incantation involving a permutation of words and numbers that could affect ordinary reality and supposedly create beings (golem) if uttered in the correct pattern and intonation (Scholem, 1941:119-155). The true intention of Abulafia's system, however, was to affirm for its users that they were not powerless in the face of an apparently inflexible reality. Rosenthal's "KabbaLAmobile" similarly communicates the possibility of self-empowerment, probably the most important goal of shamanic practice.

In 1985, Rosenthal enacted the "Shamanic Ritual" as a benefit for the Women's Building in Los Angeles in conjunction with an exhibition entitled the "Artist as Shaman." Since there was not enough room for the performance at the Women's Building, Rosenthal used her own space, creating a complex labyrinth of black plastic corridors. One by one the audience had to go through this completely dark passageway and were told to see three scenes through small openings in the corridors. Each of these scenes were living tableaux of the three aspects of the goddess. The first scene was that of a beautiful naked young woman, the second was a mature naked woman embracing a naked man, and the third was a stern looking old lady with long gray hair. According to Rosenthal, "very few people actually saw these scenes, because they had freaked out trying to get into the labyrinth" (interview with the artist, April 1990). When the audience finally came to the end of the labyrinth, they had to crawl between the legs of a woman into a large space of the studio while they were flashed with a stroboscopic light. In going through the labyrinth, Rosenthal forced the audience to be reborn into a ritual. Once the participants had entered the larger room, they were seated by two assistants and listened to a tape of swamp sounds. Then Rosenthal began drumming, putting herself and her audience in a trance. In fact, drumming or shaking a rattle, accompanied by breathing and meditation is Rosenthal's standard preparation for all her performances.

During "Shamanic Ritual," she announced that the participants in the ritual would be involved in a mystery play for November, a time of going into darkness, as well as the time of endings, such as the conclusion of the millennium. The participants would witness the descent of Inanna, the Goddess of Love and Joy in Sumerian legend, into the underworld of Ereshkegal, the mother of destruction and death. First, Inanna, the young virgin of the first scene, had to pass through seven gates, which were lifted by the participants. At each of the gates, Inanna shed an article of clothing, because in the Sumerian legend Inanna has to strip away and sacrifice the old aspects of her self in order to begin the process of transformation. Then, in Rosenthal's ritual, the young virgin was hung on the back of a very lean assistant and slowly turned around in a circle for about fifteen minutes. This symbolized the sequence in Sumerian legend where Inanna is hung on a nail and left to rot, indicating her firm grounding in the underworld. Rosenthal placed a big cauldron near Inanna to catch the tears of her lament and invited the participants to fill the cauldron with their own tears. The participants began to mourn and, little by little, Inanna came back to life and led the participants in a spiral dance. At the end of this dance everyone exchanged presents and had a feast similar to a traditional community ritual.

Rosenthal took this adaptation of Inanna's descent into the realm of Ereshkegal from Sylvia Perera's account of the myth in *Descent to the Goddess*. According to Perera,

Inanna's path and its stages may thus present a paradigm for the life-enhancing descent into the abyss of the dark goddess and out again. Inanna shows us the way, and she is the first to sacrifice herself for a deep feminine wisdom and for atonement. She descends, submits, and dies. This openness to being acted upon is the essence of the experience of the human soul faced with the transpersonal. It is not based on passivity, but upon an active willingness to receive.

The process of initiation in the esoteric and mystical

traditions in the West involves exploring different
modes of consciousness and rediscovering the experience of unity with nature and the cosmos that is
inevitably lost through goal-directed development.
This necessity—for those destined to it—forces us
to go deep to reclaim modes of consciousness which
are different from the intellectual, "secondary process" levels the West has so well refined. It forces
us to the affect-laden magic dimension and archaic
depths that are embodied, ecstatic and transformative; these depths are pre-verbal, often pre-image,
capable of taking us over and shaking us to the core
(1981:13-14).

Instead of the Western concept of self-development,
based on material progress, Rosenthal offered the audience an
alternative of inner growth, founded on deep feminine receptivity and sacrifice of the ego. To realize this inner knowledge,
the audience had to be shaken to the core, so Rosenthal sent
them through a labyrinth. This forced the audience to confront
a side of themselves they would not ordinarily face and let
them participate in Inanna's mourning the loss of her self. It
is important to recognize that men also participated in the
"Shamanic Ritual" at the Women's Building and were deeply
moved. Several of the audience/participants told her months
and even years afterwards how much they were affected by it
because Inanna represents the "feminine" receptivity that is a
basic requirement prerequisite for inner growth in both men
and women. To be sure, many of the women had already
encountered the myth of Inanna and similar myths as part of
the feminist liturgy of the sixties and seventies, which made
Rosenthal's task much easier. "Nevertheless," said Rosenthal
"it still had to be set up as performance because not everyone
knew their part" (interview with the artist, April 1990).

In contemporary America, where rituals of growth and
transformation are usually devalued in standard religious

practice, performing artists such as Edelson, Finley and Rosenthal feel compelled to conduct them.

Rosenthal's "Shamanic Ritual" was the kind of performance that comes closest to "theatre like the plague," which Artaud explained as follows

> The theatre like the plague is a crisis which is resolved by death or cure. And the plague is a superior disease because it is a total crisis after which nothing remains except death or an extreme purification. Similarly the theatre is a disease because it is the supreme equilibrium which cannot be achieved without destruction. It invites the mind to share a delirium which exalts its energies; and we can see, to conclude, that from a human point of view, the action of the theatre, like that of the plague, is beneficial, for, impelling men to see themselves as they are, it causes the mask to fall, reveals the lie, the slackness, baseness, and hypocrisy of our world; it shakes off the asphyxiating inertia of matter which invades even the clearest testimony of the senses; and in revealing to collectivities of men their dark power, their hidden force, it invites them to take, in the face of destiny, a superior and heroic attitude they would never have assumed without it (1958:31-32).

Artaud's "theatre of the plague" is, in effect, an intense form of shamanic practice for both the audience and the performer.

It is not surprising that the underworld of Ereshkegal is also the realm of the plague and in "L.O.W. in Gaia" (1986), Rosenthal again brought the audience into the realm of Ereshkegal in a performance that once more, in its transformative elements, put demands on the audience and the performer and embodied some of Artaud's ideas on the theatre.

"L.O.W [Loner on Wheels] in Gaia" was a meditation

on the destruction of the earth and the aging of Rosenthal's sixty-year-old body in the context of a solitary journey the artist took to the Mohave desert in her Dodge van to commune with Gaia. Rosenthal first appeared as woman of the 40th century who has been deformed by nuclear waste which leaked into the desert soil. The text for "L.O.W. in Gaia" is elaborated in *Performing Artists Journal*. Typically, Rosenthal writes detailed scripts for publication only after her performance.

> ...She is wearing a black top, fatigue pants, her head is shaved bald. She is bent in half, walks stiffly, her hands retracted like a thalidomide baby's, no longer prehensile. Her jaw is fused open and cannot shut. She has no lips—a sign of degeneracy (Rosenthal folds her upper lip over her teeth).... She makes little sounds by sucking air in. This is our descendant, the irradiated monster. The creature looks around, unaware of the meaning of the monoliths [an early warning system for a nuclear dump site in the Mohave Desert planned by the Department of Energy] and looks for and catches flies (1987:77).

Whenever I watch the video tape of "L.O. W. in Gaia," this unsettling image of a victim who is remote from my everyday experience takes me directly to the underworld, preparing me for the later appearance of Ereshkegal in the performance. The live audience must have found this image even more difficult to watch. Rosenthal said,

> I'm getting less and less inclined to let people off easy....I would love to think that I could create a revolution with my work. I don't know if art can operate that way now that it is so commodified, but I do want my audiences to think, every time they breathe in an out, about how everything affects everything (quoted in Solomon, 1988:39).

Since Rosenthal realizes that she cannot always create the right circumstances to induce an audience to go through a death rebirth experience as in the "Shamanic Ritual", she uses difficulties to promote consciousness, if not transformation. In contrast to much of contemporary art, which is much easier to take and hence more readily sold, Rosenthal's performance pieces resist commodification, along with those of Finley and Edelson. Yet, Rosenthal is careful in her works to avoid the mood of despair, "which is paralyzing" (quoted in Solomon, 1988:39). In "Soldier of Fortune" she relied on humor to relieve the seriousness of her predicament for both herself and the audience. In "L.O.W in Gaia," she quickly shifted from a victim in the realm of the underworld to her more normal self in the middle realm, recounting her first experiences in the desert as a city person from Los Angeles.

"On the first day," related Rosenthal in "L.O.W in Gaia,"

> the Goddess sent me a gift....I am timid, reticent, I want to go slow. I coddle myself. Then I get lost in the San Gabriel Mountains. I climb up and down for nine hours! No food. No water. I have bad knees. I can't even feel my legs...I keep going. Numb. Out of breath. Heart pounding. Nauseous. Nearly passing out. I end up to my waist in snow, falling on my face every second step, racing the sun to the 5 p.m. setting. I must come down from 8000'. On my ass. Hands and feet cut and frozen. Exhausted. A miracle: I hit the highway at exactly 5 p.m. Its night. Pitch black. I thumb a ride back to the van, miles down the road, crash and figure "That's it. I've done it. Totalled. That's the end of the vacation!" But the next day, I'm not even sore! A true rite of passage (1987:79).

This rite of passage was greatly empowering for the artist. "I look, I drink in. I'm elated," said Rosenthal.

> I climb and hike for hours.
> I CAN DO ANYTHING!
> I am never afraid of Her...
> I am in love! I caress the dappled hills at a distance.
> I kiss the mauve sunsets filled with bees. I hug the
> Gambel Quail in her little 50's Dior hats, I am in
> love (1987:80).

But there is another side to the Mother Goddess. At Marble
Mountain, Rosenthal saw a portrait of the Death Crone in a
natural configuration of stones. "Absolutely real," exclaimed
Rosenthal.

> True portrait. Her left hand against her cheek. Her
> hollowed eyes. Her slit of a mouth. And the attend-
> ing boulders were all alive. Her court (1987:81).

After a slide show, in which Rosenthal showed photographs
of herself, from a child to a woman of sixty, the artist suddenly
changed into a angry crone in front of the audience.
"I am the Crone," Rosenthal shouted in loud gravelly
voice.

> The third aspect of the Triple Goddess. The one you
> most fear.
> You can accept the Virgin,
> barely stomach the Mother,
> but me, you have attempted to destroy.
> I am your Death.
> Not the glamorous death of battle, of heroism, of
> blood spilled for the cause.
> No. I am gout, ulcers, rheumatism, Alzheimer's and
> cancer.
> I am deterioration. I am helplessness and hopeless.
> You never wish to see me. For I remind you, in all
> my weakness, that I am stronger than you.

I am stronger than any god.
I am Nemesis of the Greeks.
Morgan Le Fay of the Celts.
Until I was suppressed, your patriarchal religions
could not exist.
Count not control your minds.
They feared me. The Divine Old woman...
In India I am Kali The Black.
In Scandinavia, Hel—Queen of Shades...
I am the Night Mare, the black mare-headed
Demeter, Demeter Chthonic, the Subterranean.
Your culture turned me into a Devil.
You reject me. You despise and fear older women.
You drove me mad with unendurable tortures dur-
ing the five hundred years of witch madness.
You tried to blot me out.
Yes, you've driven me underground.
But I am not the dead one.
You cannot kill Death!
Sooner or later, all of you. My Earth children, come
to me...
You are mine.
Come to me now.
Come...Come...Come...(1987:82-83)

Rosenthal mentioned in our conversation that some
members of the audience were literally quaking in the face of
such fierce anger and could barely look at her eyes. As Sylvia
Perera pointed out, Ereshkegal's eyes are those of death,
"pitiless, not personally caring" (1981:31). "These eyes,"
Perera continued,

see from and embody the starkness of the abyss that
takes all back, reduces the dancing, playing maya of
the goddess to inert matter and stops life on earth....

[Her] seeing is radical and dangerously innovative, but not necessarily evil unless unbalanced and therefore static and partial. It feels monstrous and ugly and even petrifying to the non-initiate. For it shears us of our defenses and entails a sacrifice of easy collective understandings and of the hopes and expectations of looking good and safely belonging. It is crude, chaotic, surprising, giving a view of the ground below ethics and aesthetics and the opposites themselves. It is the instinctual eye—an eye of the spirit in nature. This is the vision that Ereshkegal and Kali and the Gorgon bring to the initiate. It is the meaning of the meaning of the vision of the terrible guardian head at Shiva's temples. It is awful and yet bestows a refined perception of reality to those who can bear it (1981:32-33).

In Western culture, the ferocious Ereshkegal is replaced by an insignificant Father Time with an hour glass and scythe because the patriarchy cannot bear the loss of rational control represented by the Death Mother or Stone Mother. Yet, for those who can accept the Death Mother as a power ally, the end of rational consciousness means the beginnings of a different kind of consciousness which will not destroy the earth. In fact, if the Earth Mother is not treated properly, she will turn into the Death Mother. Near the end of "L.O.W in Gaia," Rosenthal became the Earth Mother and then suddenly metamorphosed into the Death Mother. "The desert is my second skin," affirmed Rosenthal,

I am a real bum now.
I feel at home. I stink!
I am a bum.
This is my true nature.
I'll go back to L.A., sell everything, and become a desert rat forever!

I'm an old cactus.

Gaia's a bum...(1987:88).

I'm an old cactus! And I am mean. I will defend my turf. I will protect the Earth. And I'll claw. Don't brush past me. My spikes will imbed themselves into your flesh. Just a hint. A reminder. "Attention must be paid."
At this point we want no affection, thank you. Just respect (1987:89).

Rosenthal fell to her knees and lamented her destruction as the Earth Mother. Then, slowly she stood up and became the Death Crone again, uttering in a rage, in the last long soliloquy of the performance, what she would do to the planet. The harsh tone of this soliloquy is evident in the following brief excerpts from the script:

...I shove the continents around.
Smash India into Tibet.
Crash Africa up Italy's boot.
Play scrabble with the North-American West.
Spin Europe around like a top.
Lift the seas up to the peaks.
With my fist I push deep buried rock up higher than the high plateaus, expose the sculpture within, polish and burnish with wind, water, and the fine abrasion of sanded rock.
I play and you die (1987:91).

Rosenthal's shape shifting throughout "L.O.W in Gaia," which occurred in a light trance, was not acting, although it had a dramatic content that Rosenthal consciously uses to manipulate the audience into an alternate state of consciousness.

Rosenthal is consciously aware of her role as a trickster, here and in other works such as "Soldier of Fortune." "The audience," said Rosenthal,

> goes to see a crazy avant-garde performance and experiences a surprise that goes beyond their readiness to receive based on their prior idea of this event. Suddenly, they feel very personally on an emotional level and hopefully on levels that they might not even realize. You have to be tremendously aware and responsible about how you use power on this level. When you are younger you are in the throes of the ego. I'm glad that I'm accepted as an artist but this is not an important component in my life. It is important to effect people, to reach them on levels that go beyond the intellect, and this is a gift that I'm grateful for and try to use wisely (interview with the artist, April 1990).

In addition to shape shifting, in "L.O.W. in Gaia", Rosenthal also worked with power objects to take the audience "beyond the intellect." She created an altar with a lighted candle and bleached white bones she had found in the desert. "My idea," explained Rosenthal,

> was to use these objects, which I invested with a great deal of power and life, to gradually bring the audience and myself into another reality while providing anecdotes about my sojourn in the desert (interview with the artist, April 1990).

During the sequence in which she became Gaia and fell to her knees, Rosenthal picked up two bones and used them in samurai gestures, eventually pointing the sharp bones at her scull in a menacing fashion. This greatly intensified the drama of her verbal lament, as Gaia scorned, for herself and for the animals. Then, while on her knees, Rosenthal poured the hot wax from the candle over her head and blew out the flame of the candle.

Rosenthal underwent a baptism and brought in the darkness, preparing the way for the reemergence of the Death Crone and the shadowy world she inhabits. The scorning of Gaia had its roots in the mind/body split, a dichotomy which Rosenthal began to explore after "L.O.W. in Gaia."

> I've been doing all these performances pieces about what is going wrong with the earth...and everything seemed to go back to the same source—the human brain." (quoted in Solomon, 1988:39).

An extended period of research and meditation on the topic of the human brain followed. Rosenthal said that material cooked "in a kind of semi-conscious state" for several months until a performance emerged (quoted in Lampe, 1988:178). She then created "Rachel's Brain" in which she presented the body/mind split as a product of the eighteenth century enlightenment.

Rosenthal made her first entrance in "Rachel's Brain" as Marie Antoinette, wearing an elaborate dress and beehive wig with a three-masted ship placed on top. "I am the flower of the enlightenment," said the Queen. "I am a higher animal, head severed from body...I am a thought machine. Je pense donc je suis...," and so forth. Rosenthal then took off the headdress and returned to her ordinary self, announcing, "I am ugly fat, nothing...500 years of brain evolution for this." It is fairly obvious that Rosenthal was questioning the reduction of consciousness to the realm of the rational or *tonal* and the results of this reduction, including morbid self-reflection.

In one of the later sequences of the performance, Rosenthal hacked away at a cauliflower (a pretty fair simulacrum of the human brain) in front of a large slide projection of a screaming monkey who had electrodes planted in its brain.

Did you know there are about 100 billion neurons in a single human brain, and that the number of possible connections exceed the number of atoms in the universe. The earth is overlaid with a layer in the image of the cortex: dry, smart, ingenious and deadly.

Following some further reflections about meat eating and greed in contemporary society which were accompanied by slides of the destruction of animals and the environment, she then exclaimed, "I eat when I'm not hungry to fill the empty spaces. I'm hungry but I'm so full I'm going to explode." For Rosenthal, the brain has an enormous capacity which can produce insatiable desires in conflict with authentic needs. In an interview with Alisa Solomon in the *Village Voice*, Rosenthal argued that

when the brain developed in the early evolution of the homo line, we almost immediately...created this fully completed large organ which went way beyond the necessities of the environment. We went way...ahead of ourselves and created an organ that had no use at the time, and which seems programmed to kill its own environment (quoted in Solomon, 1988:39).

Perhaps the most memorable sequence of the performance was when Rosenthal impersonated both Koko the gorilla and the trainer who attempted to teach Koko to talk. The trainer repeated to the Gorilla such phrases as, "To be or not to be," and "I think therefore I am", while Koko was thinking out loud about her connection with Mother Earth.

Animals have another type of consciousness from which we can learn. This has been apparent to Rosenthal for a long time and has been reinforced by her contact with animals in shamanic journeys. In fact, Rosenthal has actively campaigned for the rights of animals in several of her performances.

After having witnessed a performance of Balinese theatre in Paris in May or July of 1931, Artaud extolled its virtues in *The Theatre and Its Double*. "The situations [of the Balinese theatre]," Artaud wrote,

> are vague, abstract, extremely general. What brings them to life is the complex profusion of all the artifices of the stage, which impose on our minds, as it were, the idea of a metaphysics derived from a new utilization of gesture and voice.
>
> What is really curious about all these gestures, these angular and abruptly broken attitudes, these syncopated modulations formed at the back of the throat, these musical phrases that break off short, these flapping of insect wings, these rustlings of branches, these sounds of hollow drums, these creakings of robots, these dances of animated puppets, is this: that out of their labyrinth of gestures, attitudes and sudden cries, out of gyrations and turns that leave no portion of the space on the stage unused, there emerges a sense of a new physical language based on signs rather than words....No, these spiritual signs have a precise meaning which impresses us only intuitively, but with enough violence to render useless any translation into logical or discursive language (1976:215-216).

While Rachel Rosenthal's performances approach the language of signs, especially in "KabbaLAmobile," Sha Sha Higby's performances operate on a more abstract non-verbal or "pre-verbal" level of discourse (which was another of

Artaud's definitions for the Balinese theatre).

In fact, in 1972, Higby spent one year in Japan studying *Noh* and *Butoh* and five years (1977-1982) in Indonesia studying various forms of Javanese theatre and puppetry. The result of these studies is an ongoing corpus of performance work that communicates, in the words of one critic, metaphysical meanings with slow and complex gestures within an elaborate costume, a kind of "wearable environment" (Zimmer, E., 1988:6).

In the first stage of Higby's artistic process, she takes between six months to a year to create a costume (Illustration 24). The costumes are made of a wide variety of materials including shells, carved wood, sticks, twigs, feathers, rhinestones, paper, silk, gold leaf, ceramic pieces, fiber, leather, water buffalo hides, glass spines (a supporting mechanism), and so forth. The masks alone involve the application of fifty coats of a lacquer consisting of powdered eggshells and glue. (Higby studied mask making techniques with a master Noh drama mask maker in Kyoto). While the masks are highly refined, the equally well crafted costumes are much more earthy and organic. Mask and costume, however, mesh together into a funky latticework of abstract shapes that can include puppets which move as Higby moves. As Higby is almost completely enclosed by the mask and the costume, she is transformed into a primordial being or soul from the lower world, manipulating humans as if they were puppets. The performances also involve gradually entering or shedding the costume—a ritual metaphor for birth, death and metamorphosis that occurs in a non-ordinary realm (the lower world) in an altered state of consciousness.

This transportation of both Higby and the audience to another reality has been widely recognized by the commentators on her work. Kirsten Abboe wrote in *High Performance* about the "Bee on the Beach,"

Flickering in the foreground were merry little

houses, Higby's signature, twinkling from within in a row before the ponderous fantastic goddess form [a highly elaborate costume consisting of pieces of bone, buffalo hide, silk flags, wooden bangles, doll sections, rotating spinners, a wooden toy snake, and other folded toys]....Higby... moved up into the headdress, now encumbered and transformed by the costume, and wriggled and adjusted herself in place. It was as if the goddess or priestess were getting into her duds before a ceremony, and this process became sacred. The transformation was complete, the suspension lines were severed. The butterfly emerged by an inverse process, the assumption of the chrysalis. The audience was invited to begin playing instruments offered to them at the door. A quickening occurred–the excitement of participation in something magical.

...Neither her dance nor her costume was intellectually based, but the spirit involved was palpable at times. She seemed to have meditated on each aspect of the work and, in fact, appeared as if in a trance when performed (1988:110).

Judith Green, a critic for the *San Jose Mercury*, made similar remarks about "A Tin Duck in a Box of Wind."

The audience enters to find a fantastic sculpture suspended from an overhead beam. On the floor is a snowy pile of plastic scraps and half a dozen handmade high heeled shoes made for a doll's feet. Theses are lit from within by tiny lights. Outlined on another section of floor is a V of votive candles. As darkness settles over the water (the performance took place outdoors at the Baylands Center in Palo Alto, California) a black crouching shape vaguely

apelike tumbles along the outside roadway, past the
windows, barely discernible against the sky.
Slowly this creature works its way into the room, is
born through the V of candles, creeps across the
floor and dons the hanging sculpture. Made of
shells and bones, encrusted with pieces of wood and
pottery, woven together with cords and fiber, the
sculpture looks like a primitive fetish or totem...the
shamanistic figure of Higby scuffs through the pile
of scraps, explores the little shoes, plays with the
contents of a hand sewn pouch. Eventually she
doffs the sculpture, leaving it into a new shape on
the floor, and tumbles softly out, as she came
(1981:17).

For Higby, performances are opportunities of "dealing
with my own age, my own transitions in time for the short
period I have here" as well as surrendering aspects of the outer
self, "shedding layers of compressed auras to arrive at plain
energy or force" (quoted in Green 1981:17). And the audience
often identifies and is deeply moved by these transitions. I
think the emotional affect of Higby's works is in part the result
of the almost excruciatingly slow pace of the transitions
within the context of a performance which usually lasts about
an hour. My own response was feeling as though I was
undergoing a transition myself.

Shifting the normal time sequence, in combination with
the repetitive rhythms of the accompanying music (usually the
product of simple percussive instruments), also puts Higby
and the audience into a trance state in which Higby does not
feel the scratching of the costume against her naked body even
though the rubbing sometimes draws blood. The trance ensures that the content of the performance is communicated on
a level deeper than rational discourse. As a dance critic from
Singapore observed, "the entire performance is extremely
mystical. I think as long as we appreciate and enjoy it, we do

not need to understand it" (Lianhe Zaoboo, 1990).

For Higby, this slowing down process begins with the making of the costume. The great detail and intricacy of the work, which has to be seen close up and therefore cannot be appreciated by the audience during the performance, takes enormous time and patience to accomplish. Higby herself says, "I do it because it is difficult."[7] In meditation, which Higby continues to practice in the mornings, the difficulty of sitting quietly breaks down ordinary consciousness.

The pacing and movements of Higby's performances have been greatly influenced by her personal experience of *Butoh, Noh*, and Javanese dance. In the 1970s, Higby trained with *Butoh* dancers Eiko and Koma whose slow, rigorously controlled movements similarly allude to the basic acts of birth and death, creation and destruction. In the words of Eiko and Koma's mentor and the founder of *Butoh*, Tatsumi Hijikata,

> We must long for nothing but to return to the endlessness of the cosmos to be reborn. Min Tanaka tells us "Tatsumi Hijika longed for nothing." He longed for nothing that is, except to be born over and over. As he himself says, "I was born and transformed. It was no longer enough to be born only from the womb" (Holborn *et al*, 1987:129).

Hijikata created *Butoh* in part because of his distaste of Western dance. He wanted a medium that allowed profound truths to come out of the shape and movements of the body rather than a refined choreography of movements that were adapted to the body by the dancers. In Higby's work like Hijikata's, the costumes determine the performer's movements. Also, like Eiko and Koma, Higby often enters the performance space on all fours, rolling, gradually opening and spreading her limbs but not standing fully upright, while she maintains her connection with the ground. Higby has said,

There is a bond with nature....At high points [of the performance], sometimes I feel a powerful crush that the earth will take me, that I will melt and fade to become her, her hills (Weisang, 1987:67).

Eiko and Koma's "Moon Stories" (performed at the Brooklyn Academy of Music in November of 1986) began with Eiko and Koma portraying two luminous rocks in a dark lunar landscape. "We see landscape in human bodies and we see humanness in landscape" (Raven, 1987:86), the performers are saying about their work. In fact, this close relationship with the earth, which is evident in both Eiko and Koma's and Higby's performances, is a fundamental aspect of *Butoh*.

Mark Holborn in *Butoh: Dance of the Dark Soul* said,

Butoh has a primordial quality. It is dark. It is generated somewhere in the lower strata of the subconscious, in the murky areas of personal prehistory. Memory is its source. Its etymology refers specifically to dance through the character bu. Buyoh is the neutral world for dance, but it has a sense of jumping or leaping, whereas toh implies a stomping. Buyoh is in the ascendant like the vertical ascent of Vaslav Nijinsky or Isadora Duncan's leap toward the source of light. Butoh is a descent. Hijikata [the founder of Butoh] would always say, "I would never jump or leave the ground; it is on the ground in which I dance" (1987:8).

Holborn went on to say that "The origins of Butoh reside in a wild land inhabited by elemental spirits, which the rational mind cannot reach" (1987:8). In short, *Butoh*, as in the case of Higby's performances, is a descent to the underworld, and many of the *Butoh* performers become underworld spirits.

There are, however, some important differences between *Butoh* and Higby's performances. *Butoh* performers wear no costumes and almost no clothing and their movements are more representational and more dramatic than Higby's, partly because the bulky and heavy costumes restrict her movements. In fact, Higby's mostly minimal gestures are the product of her *Noh* studies. "Noh," she maintained, "demands little physical movement, but elaborate emotional goings-on" (Wheater, 1986:30).

According to Donald Keene, in his seminal monograph on the *Noh*, probably the foremost writer, theorist and actor of this art form, Zeami

> wrote that the movements without action were especially appreciated by the audience; the actor, unable to rely on movement or words to distract the audience, had somehow to communicate his underlying spiritual strength (1973:19).

Consequently each gesture in the *Noh* carries an enormous emotional weight. Generally, the more spiritual the theme, the fewer the gestures. Higby's slow and sparse gestures have a similar kind of emotional and spiritual gravitas. And her masks, which are based on the expressionless female masks of the *Noh*, cause the viewer's attention to shift to the gestures. Nevertheless, Higby's gestures do not follow a narrative plot and are less readily connected with specific emotions than the *Noh*.

Higby believes that her ornate costumes and fluid abstract movements were influenced by the *Bedaya* she witnessed in Java. This classical dance form tends to sublimate expressive impulses into a continuum of graceful movements that offer multiple associations to the viewer. Higby hopes that her gestures engender a similar multiplicity of interpretations. To my mind, Higby establishes a magical and indefinable emotional space, much like the numinous moods that shamans encounter on their journeys.

The performance artists in this section depart from traditional performance genres in their work. Although they may have been influenced by several traditions, their goal is to find a language of performance that is uniquely suited to personal statements and also appropriate to contemporary issues. They are searching for a form that has the capacity to transform themselves and their audience like sacred rituals did in the past.

Notes

1. Several of Beuys' drawings have the following titles: "Shaman," "Trance of the Shaman," "Dance of the Shaman," "The Shaman's Bag," "Stripes from the House of the Shaman." Although the imagery of these drawings is often rather elliptical, several of Beuys's figures have open mouths and pronounced third eyes, possibly indicating a state of ecstatic trance. Also, the "Shaman's Two Bags" (1977) clearly refers to the shaman's power bundle and "Stripes from the House of the Shaman" (1982) refers to a power bundle that Beuys actually made. It consisted of woven hare skins with quartz powder (see, Beuys, 1983).

2. Mary Beth Edelson, lecture at the Corcoran Gallery, Washington, D.C., 1973, published in Womansphere (May/June 1975):55-59.

3. Mary Beth Edelson, unpublished section of the interview with Mel Watkins, p.13. An abridged version of the interview appeared in *Shape Shifters* (1990).

4. Interview with the artist, June 1989. In 1981, at the A.I.R. Gallery, Edelson exhibited Trickster rabbit drawings and artifact entitled "Archaeology of the Trickster Rabbit in Recycled Time." The drawings and artifacts had accompanying written texts in which Edelson created new mythological variations for this powerful shamanic figure.

5. Artist's announcement for the "Black Spring" exhibition.

6. All subsequent quotations from this performance are taken from the publication of the script.

7. Interview with the artist in Bolinas, California, September 1990.

19. Hugo Ball reciting the sound poem "Karawane"
    at the Cabaret Voltaire, 1916
    Courtesy Harry N. Abrams, Inc., New York

20. Yves Klein
   "The Painter of Space Hurls Himself Into the Void,"
   Fontenay-aux-Roses near Paris, 1960
   Photograph by Harry Shunk

21. Joseph Beuys
From the performance "I Like America and America Likes Me,"
Rene Block Gallery, New York, 1974
Photo credit, Ute Klophaus, Wuppertal

22. Mary Beth Edelson
From the performance "Memorials to the 9,000,000 Women
Burned as Witches in the Christian Era, 1977,
A.I.R. Gallery, New York
Courtesy Mary Beth Edelson

23. Rachel Rosenthal
From the performance "KabbaLAmobile",
Department of Water and Light parking lot,
Los Angeles, 1985
Photo credit Basia

24. Sha Sha Higby
 Costume Made from Ikat Orissa, India
 Photograph by Albert Hollander

Conclusion

At the beginning, in prehistoric times, the roles of artist and shaman were not separated. Shamans were, in fact, the most gifted artists in their community. With the change in life patterns from nomadic to pastoral, agriculture, horticulture, and city dwelling, division of labor occurred and artists developed specialized skills. Over time, this specialization led to the emphasis of "art for art's sake."

Beyond their interest in aesthetic languages, the artists that I have discussed in *Technicians of Ecstasy* wish to invest their work with spiritual content. Currently, in post-modern art where, in the words of Nietzsche "nothing is true and everything is permitted," the task of re-valuing the world with spiritual meaning becomes especially urgent.

I believe the role of the artist as shaman will become increasingly attractive for artists who are seeking to go beyond the idiosyncratic selfishness, commodity fetishism, adherence to fashion, and sterile appropriation that informs much of contemporary art. Many contemporary artists simply borrow spiritual contents by appropriating images and styles from a wide range of cultures, including tribal art. The result is a simulacrum of meaning which lacks depth. Art that uncovers authentic truth requires difficult and sometimes dangerous journeys.

The artists in this book have journeyed into non-ordinary reality with support from only their close peers and small community, and sometimes even without knowing traditional shamanism at all. They have been looking instinctively for their shamanic roots. Their efforts are remarkable, even heroic.

Shamanic techniques, when used properly, offer essentially non-destructive means for artists to invite visions and gain knowledge about themselves. Works of art evolving from these visions continue to nourish their audiences. The opportunity for artists to make positive contributions to their communities also eliminates their own feelings of alienation and exclusion.

Shamanism does not rely on belief or adherence to any doctrine. In the hands of creative and technically capable artists, shamanism can become an effective tool in affirming other realities. In shifting attention from common sense or "consensus reality," artists as shamans succeed in expanding their consciousness and the consciousness of their communities and offer blueprints for spiritual development.

List of Illustrations

Seeing

1. Vincent Van Gogh
   A Pair of Boots, 1887
   Oil on canvas
   13 x 16⅛ inches
   Courtesy of The Baltimore Museum of Art,
   The Cone Collection, formed by Dr. Claribel Cone and
   Miss Etta Cone, Baltimore, MD

2. Paul Cézanne
   Chocquet Seated, 1877
   Oil on canvas
   18⅛ x 15 inches
   Courtesy of The Columbus Museum of Fine Arts, OH
   Howard Fund purchase

3. Giorgio Morandi
   Still Life, 1959
   Oil painting
   25 x 35 inches
   Private collection

4. Mu Chi
   Six Persimmons, late 13th century
   Ink on paper
   55 x 29 centimeters
   Ryuko-in, Daitokuji Monastery, Kyoto, Japan

5. Frida Kahlo
   The Broken Column, 1944
   Oil on masonite
   15¾ x 12¼ inches
   Collection of Dolores Olmedo, Mexico City

6. Max Ernst
   The Wheel of Light,
   from plate XXIX in the book, *Histoire Naturelle*, 1926
   Frottage, reproduced by photogravure
   9⅞ x 16½ inches

7. Gordon Onslow-Ford
   Round See, 1961
   Acrylic on mulberry paper
   67 x 102 inches
   Collection of Gordon Onslow-Ford
   With permission of the artist

8. Robert Irwin
   Market Street Studio, Venice, California, May 1980
   Installation with scrim
   Photo credit, Malinda Wyatt

9. Arthur Tress
   The Illumination, from the book *Shadow*, 1975
   Black and white photograph
   With permission of the artist

10. Alex Grey
    Journey of the Wounded Healer, 1984-1985
    Oil on linen
    90 x 224 inches
    Collection of Alex Grey
    With permission of the artist

Dreaming

11. Henri Rousseau
    The Dream, 1910
    Oil on canvas
    69½ x 99½ inches
    Courtesy of The Museum of Modern Art, New York
    Gift of Nelson A. Rockefeller

12. Giorgio de Chirico
    The Southsayer's Recompense, 1913
    Oil on canvas
    53½ x 71 inches
    Courtesy of The Philadelphia Museum of Art,
    The Louise and Walter Arensberg Collection

13. Salvador Dali
    The Persistence of Memory, 1931
    Oil on canvas
    9½ x 13 inches
    Courtesy of The Museum of Modern Art, New York
    Given anonymously

14. Luis Buñuel
    Still photo from *"Un Chien Andalou,"* 1928
    Courtesy of The Museum of Modern Art, New York

15. Man Ray
    Le Tournant (The Turning Point)
    from the book *Les Main Libres*, 1936
    India ink
    25 x 19¾ inches

16. Carolee Schneemann
    Meat Joy, May 29, 1964
    performance at the Festival de la Libre Expression, Paris
    With permission of the artist

17. Ann McCoy
    Temple of Isis, Pompeii, 1987
    Pencil, paper on canvas
    9 x 15 feet 8 inches
    Photo credit, Ivan Dalla Tana

18. Jonathan Borofsky
    Shinto Priest, 1977
    Ink, day-glow paint on wall
    5 x 3½ feet
    installation at the Men's Shelter in the Bowery,
    New York
    Courtesy of the Paula Cooper Gallery

Performing

19. Hugo Ball, reciting the sound poem "Karawane"
    at the Cabaret Voltaire, winter 1916
    Courtesy of Harry N. Abrams Inc., New York

20. Yves Klein
    The Painter of Space Hurls Himself Into the Void
    Paris, January 12, 1960
    Photo credit, Harry Shunk

21. Joseph Beuys
    performing "I Like America and America Likes Me"
    Rene Block Gallery, New York, 1974
    Photo credit, Ute Klophaus, Wuppertal

22. Mary Beth Edelson
    performing "Memorials to the 9,000,000 Women
    Burned as Witches in the Christian Era, 1977
    A.I.R. Gallery, New York
    With permission of the artist

23. Rachel Rosenthal
    performing "KabbaLAmobile"
    Department of Water and Power parking lot,
    Los Angeles, 1985
    Photo credit, Basia

24. Sha Sha Higby
    Costume made from Ikat, Orissa, India
    Photo credit, Albert Hollander

Appendix

Shamanic Techniques To Stimulate Creativity

1. Isolation

The most fertile period of creativity in my life occurred during the month I spent in a small cabin near the ocean in an isolated area of California. Withdrawal from my usually comfortable pattern of existence created a sensory deprivation effect which produced very strong results in combination with meditation and occasional fasting.

The Native American vision quest consisting of a three-day solitary retreat in nature with minimal shelter and fasting is a very powerful shamanic seeing technique. I do not recommend this kind of vision quest without preparation and proper support.

2. Not-Doing

Robert Irwin achieved an important artistic breakthrough by going to Ibiza for eight months and doing practically nothing. Steady production is important for industrialists but not for those who produce works of art or anything involving a high level of creativity. Not-doing is as important for the creative process as doing, but the materialists in our culture refuse to recognize this fact.

Not-doing may be combined with erasing personal history (quitting one's studio, job, etc.) to break a particularly strong creative impasse.

3. Drugs

Ayahuasca and peyote are used by shamans in some tribal cultures. However, most shamans employ drumming or rattling to get into trance states. Drugs are very toxic to the body and can cause mental and emotional trauma under the best of circumstances. Moreover, the reliance on drugs as trance-inducing technique precludes the development of the ability to shift back and forth at will from ordinary to non-ordinary reality.

My own carefully planned experience with hallucinatory drugs had the aftereffect of numbing my nervous system for weeks. During this period, I was unable to enter a trance state through rattling, drumming or meditation.

Don Juan had Carlos Castaneda use peyote in a controlled situation because Carlos was so dense and mentally preoccupied that no other means of entering non-ordinary reality would work. It has been my experience that sensitive individuals such as artists do not need strong substances to induce trance; drumming and rattling produce the same results.

4. Prolonged Looking

Over a period of six months, look at the same object for ten minutes each day. At some point there should be a shift from looking to seeing. (One can also achieve a shift from listening to hearing by listening to the sounds in the environment for ten minutes a day for several months.)

During the process of looking, breathe as slowly as possible through the *chakra* two inches below the navel. This breathing calms the mind and the emotions, preventing the superimposition of personal projections on the object of attention.

Being on the same physical level with the object is an act of humility and openness that also facilitates seeing.

Try beginning with an "inanimate" object, then progress to a plant, an animal, and a human being. I have found that the more complex the object of attention the more difficult it is to "see," but the knowledge it reveals will be more interesting and subtle.

After several months of seeing practice, objects may begin to dissolve before your eyes and merge with an overall pattern of energy lines that include your own. When I reached this level of seeing, I noticed that when something inside or outside of my field of vision moved, the whole web of lines would jiggle. At this point, I was not aware of doing the seeing. I had moved from an I-it relationship with the object to a state of fundamental unity with the object and everything around me. The experience of this unity through the activity of seeing continues to be an emotional one for me. It gives me a profound sense of well-being that goes beyond the realm of knowledge.

5. The Strong Eye

The "strong eye" refers to Australian Aboriginal shamans who look inside a patient for abnormalities, but it is also a technique in which the practitioner narrows the eyes in non-focused attention on a 180 degree field.

The purpose of this technique is to locate the light lines of a particular landscape including concentrations of light at power spots, and any disruption in the lines that would indicate the presence of a hidden animal or a human in motion.

The "strong eye" technique can be used to heighten the awareness of any environment. It is an effective tool for artists wishing to install a work to good advantage in a particular environment. It is also helpful for locating power objects.

6. Setting Up Dreaming

Non-focused attention, such as breathing from the lower

chakra, is also an easy way of calming the mind and emotions before dream incubation. When asking for a particular message or image to appear in your dreams, it is necessary to "stop the internal dialogue."

While sitting on the edge of the bed in a state of non-focused attention, verbalize the question or request. You may even put it in writing and place it under your pillow. Make it brief, definite and positive. Keep trying.

You may not get the answer during one night or the material you get may not seem to relate to the question. On waking, try to remember the dream before thinking of anything else. If you only remember a fragment, you still may be able to use it to unravel the entire dream. Also, if you have difficulty in remembering a dream, try shifting your position in bed; recall is sometimes helped when you assume the same position in which you had the dream.

For lucid dreaming, I have found that in addition to continued autosuggestion (telling yourself that you will be conscious while dreaming), the best technique is to place a power object near the bed. When the power object appears in the dream, it is a clue to become aware that one is dreaming. The next step is to continue the dream according to your conscious intentions without waking up—a delicate procedure that requires practice.

Dream interpretation may be enhanced by picking out the symbols of the dream and relating them to other symbols in art, literature, mythological stories, and spiritual texts. This technique of dream amplification has been suggested by Jung. You might also dialogue with figures or objects in your dreams.

Perhaps the most important method of dream interpretation is asking the following questions: "Why am I having this dream now?" or "What is being brought to my attention in this dream?" "What am I ignoring in waking life?"

Bibliography

Abboe, Kirsten. "Sha Sha Higby, A Bee on the Beach," *High Performance*, (Spring/Summer 1988):41-42.

A.C.A. *Ann McCoy: Contemporary Exhibition Catalogue.* New York: A.C.A., 1988.

Ades, Dawn. *Dali and Surrealism.* New York: Harper and Row, 1982.

Adriani, Gotz, Winfried Konnertz, Karin Thomas. *Joseph Beuys: Life and Work*, trans. Patricia Lech. Woodbury: Barron's Educational Series, 1979.

Apollinaire, Guillaume. "Le Dounaier," *Les Soirées de Paris* (January 15, 1913).

Apple, Jacki. "The Romance of Automobiles," *Artweek*, 15:32 (September 29, 1984):1.

d'Aquili, Eugene and Charles Laughlin. "The Neurobiology of Myth and Ritual," *The Spectrum of Ritual*, eds Eugene d'Aquili, Charles Laughlin, and John McManus. New York: Columbia University Press, 1979.

Aranda, Franceso. *Luis Buñuel: A Critical Autobiography*, trans. and ed. David Robinson. London, England: Seker and Warburg, 1976.

Armstrong, Richard. "Jonathan Borofsky," *Artforum*, 22 (February 1984):75.

Arp, Jean. *Arp on Arp: Poems, Essays, Memories*, trans. Joachim Neugroschel. New York: Viking Press, 1972.

Artaud, Antonin. *Antonin Artaud, Selected Writings*, ed. and intro. Susan Sonntag. New York: Farrar, Straus, and Giroux, 1976.

_____ *The Theatre and its Double*, trans. Mary Caroline Richards. New York: Grove Press, 1958.

Ball, Hugo. *Flight out of Time: A Dada Diary*, ed. John Elderfield, trans. Ann Raimes. New York: Viking Press, 1974.

Barthes, Roland. *Critical Essays*, trans. Richard Howard. Evanston, IL: Northwestern University Press, 1972.

Bergson, Henri. *Creative Evolution*, trans. Arthur Mitchel. New York: H. Holt & Co., 1911.

Beuys, Joseph. *Drawings*. London, England: Victoria and Albert Museum, 1983.

Borofsky, Jonathan. *Dreams*. London/Basel, England/Switzerland: Institute of Contemporary Art, 1981.

Bourdon, David. "Discerning the Shaman from the Showman," *The Village Voice* (July 4, 1977):83.

Bourgeade, Pierre. *Bon Soir Man Ray*. Paris, France: Pierre Belfond, 1972.

Breton, André. "Introduction to the Discourse on the Paucity of Reality," *What is Surrealism and other Writings*, ed. Franklin Rosemont. New York: Monad Books, 1978.

____. *Surrealism and Painting*, trans. Simon Watson Taylor. New York: Harper and Row, 1972a.

____. *Manifestoes of Surrealism*, trans. Richard Seaver and Helen Lane. Ann Arbor, MI: University of Michigan Press, 1972b.

____. *Les Vases Communicants*. Paris, France: Gallimard, 1932.

Brody, Patricia. "A Conversation with Alex Grey, Performance Artist," *Boston Visual Artists Union News*, 12:5 (January 1984):1.

Buddhaghosa. *Visuddhimagga: The Path of Purity*, trans. Pe Maung Ting. London, England: Routledge and Kegan Paul, 1975.

Buñuel, Luis. *My last Sigh*, trans. Abagail Israel. New York: Alfred A. Knopf, 1983.

____. *L'Age d'Or* and *Un Chien Andalou*, trans. Marianne Alexander. New York: Simon and Schuster, 1963.

Burnham, Jack. "Mary Beth Edelson's Great Goddess," *Arts Magazine* (November 1975):75-78.

____. *Great Western Salt Works*. New York: George Braziller, 1974.

Burnham, Linda. "Rachel Rosenthal's Mind/Body Spa: A Bath for the Soul," *High Performance*, 7:2 (1984):48-53, 90-91.

Cage, John. *Silence*. Middletown, CN: Wesleyan University Press, 1961.

Carr, C. "Unspeakable Practices, Unnatural Acts," *The Village Voice* (June 24, 1986):19.

Carra, Massimo, ed. *Metaphysical Art*, trans. Caroline Tisdall. New York: Praeger, 1971.

Carrouges, Michel. *André Breton and the Basic Concepts of Surrealism*, trans. Maura Prendergast. Tuscaloosa, AL: University of Alabama Press, 1974.

Castaneda, Carlos. *Tales of Power*. New York: Simon and Schuster, 1974.

_____. *Journey to Ixtlan*. New York: Simon and Schuster, Inc., 1972.

Cézanne, Paul. *Letters*, ed. and trans. John Rewald. New York: Hacker Art Books, 1976.

Chirico, Giorgio de. *Memoirs*, trans. Margaret Crosland. London, England: Peter Owen, 1971.

Cleary, Thomas, transl. *The Flower Ornament Scripture: A Translation of the Avatamsaka Sutra*. Boulder, CO: Shambhala, 1984.

Dali, Salvador. "The Conquest of the Irrational," trans. Joachim Neugroschel, *Conversations with Dali*, by Alain Bosquert. New York: Dutton, 1969.

_____. *The Secret Life of Salvador Dali*, trans. Haakon Chevalier. New York: Dial Press, 1942.

Deitch, Jeffrey. "The New Work of Jonathan Borofsky," *Arts Magazine*, 52 (October 1976):98-99.

Des Moines Art Center. *Giorgio Morandi*. Des Moines, IA: Exhibition Catalogue, 1981. [contains essays by Kenneth Baker, James T. Demetrion, Joan M. Lukach, Luigi Magnani, and Amy Namowitz Worthen].

Dodds, E.R. *The Greeks and the Irrational*. Berkeley, CA: University of California Press, 1951.

Dogen. *Moon in a Dewdrop*, trans. Kazuaki Tanahashi. San Francisco, CA: North Point Press, 1985.

Duerr, Hans Peter. *Dreamtime, Concerning the Boundary Between Wilderness and Civilization*, trans. Felicitas Goodman. Oxford, England: Basil Blackwell, 1985.

Dumoulin, Heinrich. *A History of Zen Buddhism*. Boston, MA: Beacon Press, 1963.

Durham, Linda. "The D.B.D. Experience: Rachel Rosenthal's Mind Body Spa," *High Performance*, 7:2 (1984):48-51, 90.

Edelson, Mary Beth. *Shape Shifter: Seven Mediums*. New York: Self-published, to accompany an exhibition, 1990.

_____. "An Open Letter to Thomas McEvilley," *New Art Examiner* (April 1989):34-38.

_____."See For Yourself: Women's Spirituality in Holistic Art," *The Politics of Women's Spirituality*, ed. Charlene Spretnak. New York: Doubleday, 1982.

_____. *Seven Cycles: Public Rituals*. New York: Self-published, 1980.

_____. "Pilgrimage/See For Yourself: A Journey to a Neolithic Goddess Cave, 1977," *Heresies*, 2:1 (1978):96-99.

_____. "Speaking for Myself," *Womansphere* (May/June 1975):55-59.

Edwards, Gwynne. *Luis Buñuel*. London, England: Marion Boyars, 1982.

Eliade, Mircea. *Shamanism, Archaic Techniques of Ecstasy*, trans. Willard Trask. Princeton, NJ: Princeton University Press, 1964.

Elkin, A.P. *Aboriginal Men of High Degree*. New York: St.Martin's Press, 1977.

Ernst, Max. *Ecritures*. Paris, France: Gallimard, 1970.

_____. *Beyond Painting*, trans. Dorothea Tanning. New York: Wittenborn and Co., 1948.

Feldman, Edmond B. *The Artist*. Englewood Cliffs, NY: Prentice Hall, 1982.

Finley, Karen. "A Constant State of Desire," *TDR* (Tulane Drama Review), 32:1 (Spring 1988):139-151.

Fowlie, Wallace. *Rimbaud: A Critical Study*. Chicago, IL: University of Chicago Press, 1967.

Freud, Sigmund. *The Interpretation of Dreams*, trans. James Strachey. New York: Avon Books, 4th printing, 1969.

_____. *The Psychopathology of Everyday Life*, trans. Alan Tyson. New York: N.J. Norton, 1966.

Garfield, Patricia. *Creative Dreaming*. New York: Ballantine Books, 1974.

Gimbutas, Marija. *The Goddesses and Gods of Old Europe, 6,500 to 3,500 B.C., Myths and Cult Images*. London, England: Thames and Hughes, 1982 (1974).

Globus, Gordon. *Dream Life Wake Life*. Albany, NY: State University of New York, 1987.

Goodman, Felicitas. *Ritual and Alternate Reality: Religion in a Pluralistic World*. Bloomington, IN: Indiana University Press, 1988.

Gould, Claudia. "Mythologies of the Feminine: A Conversation with Ann McCoy," *Arts Magazine* (February 1989):68.

Green, Judith. "Potent Dance/Sculpture Redeems Performance Art," *San Jose Mercury News* (June 18, 1981):17.

Grey, Alex. *Sacred Mirrors, The Visionary Art of Alex Grey*, with essays by Ken Wilber, Carlo McCoron, and Alex Grey. Rochester, VT: Inner Traditions International, 1990.

_____. "Polar Unity," *The CoEvolutionary Quarterly*, (Winter 1978/79):21-24.

Halifax, Joan. *Shaman: The Wounded Healer*. New York: Thames and Hudson, 1982.

_____. *Shamanic Voices: A Survey of Visionary Narratives*. New York: E.P. Dutton, 1979.

Hamilton, George Heard. "Cézanne, Bergson and the Image of Time," *College Art Journal*, xvi:1 (Fall 1956):2-12.

Harner, Michael. *The Way of the Shaman: A Guide to Power and Healing*. New York: Harper and Row, 1980.

Heidegger, Martin. *Existence and Being*. Chicago, IL: Henry Regnery Company, 1968.

_____. "The Origin of the Work of Art," *Philosophies of Art and Beauty, Selected Readings in Aesthetics from Plato to Heidegger*, eds Richard Hofstater and Richard Kuhns. Chicago, IL: University of Chicago Press, 1964.

Heinze, Ruth-Inge. *Shamans of the 20th Century*. New York: Irvington Publishers, Inc., 1991.

Henes, Donna. "Spider Woman," *High Performance*, 2:2 (June 1979):24-79.

Herrera, Hayden. *Frida: A Biography of Frida Kahlo*. New York: Harper and Row, 1983.

Hiller, Susan and David Coxhead. *Dreams*. London, England: Thames and Hudson, 1976.

Hillman, James. *The Dream and the Underworld*. New York: Harper and Row, 1979.

Hofstater, Richard and Richard Kuhns, eds. *Philosophies of Art and Beauty, Selected Readings in Aesthetics from Plato to Heidegger*. Chicago, IL: University of Chicago Press, 1964.

Holborn, Mark, Yukio Mishima and Hijikata Tatsumi. *Butoh: The Dance of the Dark Soul*. New York: Aperture, 1987.

Howard, John. "Karen Finley," *Artforum* (March, 1987):130-131.

Hughes, Robert. "Morandi," *House and Garden*, 158:6 (June 1986): 158-162, 184.

Huxley, Aldous. *The Doors of Perception* and *Heaven and Hell*. New York: Harper and Rox, 1963.

Irwin, Robert. *Being and Circumstance: Notes Toward a Conditional Art*. San Francisco, CA: Lapis Press, 1985.

Jamal, Michele. *Shape Shifters, Shaman Women in Contemporary Society*. New York/London: Arcana, 1987.

Jarrell, Joseph. "The Disquieting Mind of Jonathan Borofsky," *Sculpture*, 9 (September 1990):48-52.

Jung, Carl G. *Psychological Reflections, A New Anthology of His Writings*, eds. Jolande Jacobi and R.F.C. Hull. New York: Pantheon Books, 1953.

Kaku, Michio and Jennifer Trainer. *Beyond Einstein: The Cosmic Quest for the Theory of the Universe*. New York: Bantam Books, 1987.

Kaufman, Arenberg, Lynn Countryman, Lawrence Bernstein and George Shambaugh Jr. "Van Gogh Had Meniere's Disease and Not Epilepsy," *Journal of the American Medical Association*, 264:4 (July, 1990):493.

Keene, Donald. *Noh*. Tokyo, Japan: Kodansha, Ltd., 1973.

Kerenyi, Carl. *Asklepios*, trans. Ralph Mannheim. New York: Bollingen Foundation, 1959.

Kilton, Stewart. "Dream Theory in Malaysia," *Altered States of Consciousness*, ed. Charles Tart. New York: John Wiley and Sons, Inc., 1969.

Lampe, Eilke. "Rachel Rosenthal Creating Her Selves," *TDR* (Tulane Drama Review), 32:1 (Spring 1988):170-190.

Le Pichon, Yam. *The World of Henri Rousseau*, trans. Joachim Neugroschel. New York: Viking Press, 1982.

Levi, Eliphas. *Transcendental Magic, Its Doctrine and Ritual*, trans. Arthur Edward Waite. Philadelphia, PA: David M'Kaay Co., 1923.

Levy, Mark. "Seeing the Light Lines," *Proceedings of the Eighth International Conference on the Study of Shamanism and Alternate Modes of Healing, 1991*, ed. Ruth-Inge Heinze. Berkeley, CA: Independent Scholars of Asia, 1991, pp. 308-317.

_____."Wayang Kulit: Indonesia's Shadow Puppet Plays as a Model for Performance," *High Performance*, 46 (Summer 1989):38-52.

Lewis, I.M. *Ecstatic Religion*. Hammondworth, England: Penguin, 1971.

Lianhe, Zaobao. "Review of Sha Sha Higby," *Lianhe Bao Limited* (Singapore, June 14, 1990).

Lommel, Andreas. *Shamanism: The Beginnnings of Art.* New York: McGraw Hill, 1967.

Lorca, Federico Garcia. "Play and Theory of the Duende," *Deep Song and Other Prose*, ed. and trans. Christopher Maurer. New York: New Directions, 1975.

Macadams, Lewis. "It Started Out With Death," *High Performance* (Spring/Summer, 1982):43-44.

Machado, Antoniol. *Times Alone: Selected Poetry of Antonio Machado*, ed. and trans. Robert Bly. Middleton, GA: Wesleyan University Press, 1983.

Malinowsky, Bronislaw. "The Meaning of Meaningless Words and the Coefficient of Wierdness," *Symposium of the Whole*, ed. Jerome Rothenberg. Berkeley, CA: University of California Press, 1983.

Malraux, André. *Man's Fate*, trans. Haakon M. Chevalier. New York: Vintage Books, 1968.

_____. *Voices of Silence*, trans. Stuart Gilbert. New York: Doubleday and Co., 1953.

Maurer, Evan M. "Images of Dream and Desire: The Prints and Collage Novels of Max Ernst," *Max Ernst: Beyond Surrealism*, ed. Robert Rainwater. New York: New York Public Library and Oxford University Press, 1986.

McCoy, Ann. "Reason and Emotion in Contemporary Art," *Edinborough International Exhibition Catalogue*, Royal Scottish Academy (December 1987):108.

McEvilley, Thomas. "Art in the Dark," *Artforum*, 21:10 (Summer 1983):62-71.

_____. "Yves Klein, Conquistador of the Void," *Yves Klein: A Retrospective*. New York: The Arts Publisher, 1982.

Meier, C.A. *Healing Dream and Ritual*. Einsiedeln, Switzerland: Daimon Verlag, 1989.

Mellen, Joan, ed. *The World of Louis Buñuel*. New York: Oxford University Press, 1978.

Meyerhoff, Barbara. *Peyote Hunt: The Sacred Journey of the Huichol Indians*. Ithaca, NY: Cornell University Press, 1974.

Museum of Modern Art. *Henri Rousseau*. New York: Museum of Modern Art, 1985.

Nietzsche, Friedrich. *The Gay Science*, trans. Walter Kaufman. New York: Random House, 1974.

_____. *Basic Writings*, trans. and ed. Walter Kaufman. New York: The Modern Library, 1968.

O'Flaherty, Wendy Doniger. *Dreams, Illusion and Other Realities*. Chicago, IL: University of Chicago Press, 1984.

Onslow-Ford, Gordon. *Creation*. Basel, Switzerland: Galerie Schreiner, 1978.

_____. *Painting in the Instant*. New York: Harry Abrams, 1964.

_____. *Towards a New Subject in Painting*. San Francisco, CA: San Francisco Museum of Modern Art, 1948.

Padmasambhava, *Self-Liberation Through Seeing With Naked Awareness*, trans. and notes John Reynolds, foreword Namkhai Norbu. Barytown, NY: Station Hills Press, 1989.

Parsons, Elsie Crews and Ralph L. Beals. "The Sacred Clowns of the Pueblo and Mayo Yaqui Indians," *American Anthropologist*, 36:4 (October-December, 1934).

Perera, Sylvia Brinton. *Descent to the Goddess: A Way of Initiation for Women.* Toronto, Canada: Inner City Books, 1981.

Peterson, William. "Of Cats, Dreams and Interior Knowledge: An Interview with Carolee Schneemann," *Performance* (Winter 1990):11-23.

Petitfils, Pierre. *Rimbaud.* Charlottesville, VA: University of Virginia Press, 1987.

Rackaw, Ken and Maureen Martin. "Interview with Sha Sha Highby," *Vox Art Magazine*, 1:1 (Fall 1989):6.

Radin, Paul. *The Trickster.* New York: Schocken Books, 1972.

Raven, Arlene. "Eiko and Koma," *High Performance*, Issue 37, 1:10 (1987):6.

Ray, Man. *Self-Portrait.* Boston, MA: Little Brown and Co., 1988.

Rexroth, Kenneth. *Classics Revisited.* New York: New Directions, 1986.

Rilke, Rainer Maria. *Sonnets to Orpheus*, trans. Stephen Mitchell. New York: Simon and Schuster, 1986.

328 • Technichians of Ecstasy

_____. *Letters on Cézanne*, ed. Clara Rilke, trans. Joel Agee. New York: Fromm International Publishing Corp., 1985.

_____. *Selected Poetry*, ed. and trans. Stephen Mitchell. New York: Vintage Books, 1984.

_____. *Letters to a Young Poet*, trans. M.D. Herbert Norton. New York: Norton and Co., Inc., 1962.

_____. *Letters of Rainer Maria Rilke: 1910-1926*, trans. and eds Jane Bannad Greene and M.D. Herter Norton. New York: W.W. Norton and Co., Inc., 1948.

Rimbaud, Arthur. *Complete Works, Selected Poems*, trans., intro. and notes Wallace Fowlie. Chicago, IL: University of Chicago Press, 1967.

Roditi, Edouard. *Dialogues in Art*. New York: Horizon Press, 1961.

Rosemont, Franklin, ed. *What is Surrealism and Other Writings*. New York: Monad Books, 1978.

Rosenthal, Mark and Richard Marshall. *Jonathan Borofsky*. Philadelphia, PA: Philadelphia Museum of Art, 1984.

Rosenthal, Rachel. "'L.O.W.' in Gaia," *Performing Arts Journal*, 3:3 (1988):76-93.

Rubin, William. *Giorgio di Chirico*. New York: Museum of Modern Art, 1982.

_____. *Dada and Surrealist Art*. New York: Harry Abrams, 1969.

Schapiro, Meyer. *Paul Cézanne*. New York: Harry Abrams, Inc., 1952.

Schechner, Richard. "Karen Finley: A Constant State of Becoming," *TDR* (Tulane Drama Review), 32:1 (Spring 1988):152-155.

_____. "Selective Inattention," *Essays on Performance Theory*. New York: Drama Book Specialists, 1977a.

_____. "From Ritual to Theatre and Back," *Essays on Performance Theory*. New York: Drama Book Specialists, 1977b.

Schmied, Wieland. "Max Ernst and Giorgio de Chirico," *Inside the Sight*. Houston, TX: Rice University, Institute for the Arts, 1973.

Schneede, Uwe M. *Max Ernst*, trans. R.W. Last. New York: Praeger Publishers, 1973.

Schneemann, Carolee. *Fresh Blood*. Unpublished, 1988.

_____. *More than Meat* Joy. New Paltz, NY: Documentext, 1979.

_____. *Cézanne She Was a Great Painter*. New Paltz, NY: Tresspuss Press, 1975.

Scholem, Gershom G. "Abraham Abulafia and the Doctrine of Prophetic Kabbalah," *On Major Trends in Jewish Mysticism*. New York: Schocken Books, 1941.

Schrade, Herbert. *German Romantic Landscape Painting*, trans. Maria Pelikan. New York: Abrams, 1977.

Schwarz, Arturo. *Man Ray*. New York: Rizzoli, 1977.

Sharp, Willoughby. "An Interview with Joseph Beuys," *Artforum* (December 1969):40-45.

Shattuck, Roger. *The Banquet Years*. New York: Vintage Books, 1968.

Simon, Joan. "An Interview with Jonathan Borofsky," *Art in America*, 69 (November 1981):157-167.

Snyder, Gary. "Poetry and the Primitive, Notes on Poetry as an Ecological Survival Technique," *Symposium of the Whole*, ed. Jerome Rothenberg. Berkeley, CA: University of California Press, 1983.

Soby, James Thrall. *Giorgio de Chirico*. New York: Museum of Modern Art, 1966.

Solomon, Alisa. "Signaling Through the Dioxin," *Village Voice*, XXXIII:4 (October 4, 1988.):39.

Spies, Werner. *Max Ernst's Loplop: The Artist is the Third Person*. New York: George Braziller, 1983.

Starkie, Enid. *Rimbaud*. New York: New Directions, 1961.

Stein, Howard, Cornell Capra, and Elaine King. *Artists Observed*. New York: Harry Abrams, 1986.

Stone, Irving. *Dear Theo*. New York: New American Library, 1969.

Tart, Charles. *Altered States of Consciousness*. New York: Doubleday, 1969.

Tisdall, Caroline. "Interview with Joseph Beuys," *The Secret Block for a Secret Person in Ireland*. Munich, Germany: Shimer Mosel, 1988.

____. *Joseph Beuys*. New York: Simon R. Guggenheim Museum, 1979.

____. *Beuys/Coyote*. Munich, Germany: Shirmer Mosel, 1976.

Tress, Arthur. *The Teapot Opera*. New York: Abbeyville Press, 1988.

____. *Talisman*. New York: Thames and Hudson, 1986.

____. *Theatre of the Mind*. New York: Morgan and Morgan, 1976.

Truffaut, Francois. *Hitchcock*, with the collaboration of Helen G. Scott. New York: Simon and Schuster, 1966.

Tucker, Marcia. *Choices: Making an Art of Everyday Life*. New York: New Museum of Contemporary Art, 1986.

Turner, Victor. "Frame Flow and Reflection: Ritual and Dream as Public Liminality," *Performance in Post Modern Culture*, eds. Michel Benamou and Charles Caramello. Milwaukee, WS: University of Wisconsin Press, 1977.

Tylor, Sir Edward B. "The Soul Goes Hunting and Dancing," *The New World of Dreams*, eds. Ralph Woods and Herbert Greenhouse. New York: Macmillan Press, 1974.

Van Gogh, Vincent. *Complete Letters of Vincent Van Gogh*, preface and memoir V.W. Van Gogh, 3. New York: New York Graphic Society, 1958.

_____. *Dear Theo, The Autobiography of Vincent Van Gogh*. New York: New American Library, 1937.

Van Hattingberg, Magda, ed. *Rilke and Benvenuta: An Intimate Correspondence*, trans. Joel Agee. New York: From International Publishing Corp., 1987.

Varnadoe, Kirk. "Contemporary Explorations," *Primitivism in Twentieth Century Art*, ed. William Rubin. New York: Museum of Modern Art, 1984, pp.661-685.

Waldberg, Diane. *Introduction to Chinese Painting*. New York: Grove Press, 1958.

Waldberg, Patrick. *Max Ernst*. Paris, France: Jean-Jaques Pauvert, 1958.

Waldman, Diane. *Max Ernst, A Retrospective*. New York: Simon R. Guggenheim Foundation, 1975.

Waley, Arthur. *Introduction to Chinese Painting*. New York: Grove Press, 1958.

Wechsler. *Seeing is Forgetting the Name of the Thing One Sees*. Berkeley, CA: University of California Press, 1982a.

_____. "Lines of Inquiry," *Art in America* (March 1982b):102-109.

Weisang, Myrian. "Aiming for the Mind's Eye," *Theatre Arts*, 4 (April 1987):47-67.

Wheater, Kathin. "Clothed Mind, the Elusive Art of Sha Sha Higby," *Image, San Francisco Examiner* (October 12, 1986):29-31.

Wilber, Ken. *The Holographic Paradigm and Other Paradoxes.* Boulder, CO: Shambhala, 1982.

Wortz, Melinda. "Surrendering to Presence: Robert Irwin's Esthetic Imagination," *Artforum*, 20 (November 1981):63-69.

Zimmer, Elizabeth. "Highby Dances Out of This World," *Los Angeles Herald Examiner* (October 24, 1988):6.

Zimmer, Heinrich. *Myths and Symbols in Indian Art and Civilization.* Princeton, NJ: Bollingen Series/Princeton University Press, 1974.

Index